DO YOU EAT THE RED ONES LAST?

CANADA'S NOT-SO-CLANDESTINE
WAR TO EXPROPRIATE INDIGENOUS
LANDS AND RESOURCES

An Anthropologist's Curious Journey through the Mind-fields of Indigenous Knowledge, Rights, and Culture

MARC G. STEVENSON, PhD

FriesenPress

Suite 300 - 990 Fort St
Victoria, BC, V8V 3K2
Canada

www.friesenpress.com

Copyright © 2021 by Marc G. Stevenson
First Edition — 2021

All rights reserved.

No part of this publication may be reproduced in any form, or by any means, electronic or mechanical, including photocopying, recording, or any information browsing, storage, or retrieval system, without permission in writing from FriesenPress.

ISBN
978-1-5255-8584-5 (Hardcover)
978-1-5255-8583-8 (Paperback)
978-1-5255-8585-2 (eBook)

1. SOCIAL SCIENCE, INDIGENOUS STUDIES

Distributed to the trade by The Ingram Book Company

Praise for *Do You Eat the Red Ones Last?*...

Dr. Stevenson articulates the complexities of land rights, resources, and Indigenous knowledge, and I would certainly see this book as a major part of student curricula. As someone who was born on the land and fought for Inuit land rights, the recognition of Indigenous knowledge, and Inuit fundamental human rights, I feel that this book in part captures this story and is profound, compelling, and much needed in greater Canadian society to tell the whole story of Canada and for Inuit to be folded into the human family.

—Rosemarie Kuptana, former president of the Inuit Tapirisat of Canada (now Inuit Tapiriit Kanatami)

By identifying some of the institutional barriers that prevent Indigenous peoples from accessing, retaining management responsibility over, and developing their lands and resources, Dr. Marc Stevenson hits a home run with Do You Eat the Red Ones Last? As a seasoned observer of those contentious spaces where Indigenous peoples fight for rights to their lands, resources, and futures Stevenson's unique insights, and those handed down to him from Indigenous elders, should give all Canadians pause to reflect on the future of this country.

—Jean-Paul Gladu, former president and CEO, Canadian Council for Aboriginal Business

The book, which blends reportage, memoir, and analysis, explores... issues of land management, Indigenous contributions to ecological knowledge, continued marginalization of Indigenous governing bodies, and the fight for Indigenous rights across many facets of Canadian society. Stevenson's prose is always technical, often fiery, and usually rooted in that most intricate and foundational of topics, the land... Most intriguing are the sections in which Indigenous traditional ecological knowledge challenges the claims of environmental scientists—a dispute many readers may not know much about. The author('s)... enthusiasm for addressing the injustices still perpetrated against Indigenous people is contagious... A wide-ranging and well-researched work. A dense but captivating window into Canada's modern land wars.

—Kirkus Reviews

BIOGRAPHY

MARC STEVENSON HAS WORKED WITH INUIT, FIRST NATIONS, AND MÉTIS COMMUNITIES FOR over three decades on matters directly impacting their rights and interests in lands and resources that have sustained them for generations. He has also held positions with Parks Canada, the government of the Northwest Territories, and the University of Alberta, in addition to advising multi-stakeholder wildlife co-management, environmental monitoring, and land-use planning boards. Marc has written extensively on Indigenous ecological knowledge, Indigenous research protocols, wildlife co-management, traditional economies, Inuit socio-political organization, and archaeological method and theory. He is the author and editor of numerous academic books and articles, and holds a PhD in anthropology from the University of Alberta as well as a masters and a bachelor of honours degree in archaeology from Simon Fraser University. This book represents Dr. Stevenson's most recent and candid attempt to share his experiences and perspectives on Indigenous-non-Indigenous relations in Canada with a wider audience. He is currently enjoying semi-retirement in Halfmoon Bay (*xwilkway*), *Shíshálh Swiya* (Sechelt traditional territory), BC, with his wife Kathryn, Alaskan malamutes Naya and Suliq, and Himalayan cat Tynaq.

Dedicated to the memory of my twin
Ian A. Stevenson, my *attatasaq* Etuangat Aksayuk,
and my brothers from another mother, Tony
Mercredi and Baptiste Metchooyeah

INTRODUCTION

Canada's Clandestine War

CANADA IS AT WAR. NOT WITH ANY HOSTILE FOREIGN POWER OR DOMESTIC TERRORIST organization, but its Indigenous peoples. Having spent most of my career working with and for the descendants of our country's original inhabitants, I cannot come to a different conclusion. I am not talking about the kind of war involving armed conflict with weapons of murder and mass destruction. I am talking about the more furtive agenda of Canada's governing and corporate elites to dispossess Indigenous Canadians of their lands and resources while pursuing, in the words of Canada's Truth and Reconciliation Commission, *"a policy of cultural genocide, in order to divest themselves of any legal and financial obligations to Aboriginal peoples."*[1]

Sure, Canada no longer hangs Indigenous leaders for resisting the colonial takeover of their lands, starves First Nations peoples into submission, confines Indigenous peoples to reserves under threat of imprisonment, sterilizes Indigenous women against their will (apparently), or forcibly removes Indigenous children from their families to be herded into overcrowded residential schools and subjected to unspeakable forms of abuse and cruelty. And, sure, Canada no longer overtly administers a policy of outright assimilation in order to deprive its Indigenous peoples of their cultures, lands, and resources. Rather, consumed by avarice and cowardice and emboldened by an ill-informed populace that supports them, Canada's elites continue to implement a form of ethnic warfare designed to achieve their goals of expropriating Indigenous lands, of cultural cleansing, and of total subjugation of its Indigenous peoples by more subtle—and to many, almost imperceptible—means.

I am referring to the covert, craven, disingenuous form of perpetual warfare perpetrated by a colonial oppressor that ultimately results in the cultural genocide of the displaced and oppressed, and just as many fatalities. It is more than a war of attrition and has far-reaching consequences—intended or not—that few care to redress let alone acknowledge. Its

---

[1] The Truth and Reconciliation Commission (2015). *Honouring the Truth, Reconciling for the Future: Summary of the Final Report of the Truth and Reconciliation Commission.*

weapons are false promises, chicanery, obfuscation, buck-passing, slow-walking, stonewalling, coercion, double-dealing, divide and conquer strategies, bait and switch tactics, and other machinations intended to wear down the resolve of an impediment and adversary. A death by a thousand cuts is still a death and arguably just as inhumane, and certainly more mendacious and cowardly than outright warfare.

Yet Canadians have grown so accustomed, so blind, to how unscrupulously this country deals with its founding peoples, even as we try to convince ourselves otherwise, pulling off one of the greatest parlour tricks of all time. We—and by this I mean *all of us*, not just our governments and their corporate masters—are complicit in this act, even those among us who work on behalf of Indigenous peoples. Sure, few Canadians are actively waging war on our First Peoples. But the willful ignorance, fake empathy, and surreptitious racism that dogs our relationship with Indigenous Canadians, combined with our ongoing complacency with the status quo and unshakeable intransigence to do anything meaningful about it, amount to the same thing.

The war is unfolding on multiple fronts—social, economic, political, cultural, spiritual, and psychological—and is being fought in arenas where the rights and interests of the two cultures clash. But first and foremost, the war is being waged in the minds of Canadians. Fear of the other, of risk, of uncertainty, of change, of rocking the boat, of confrontation, of rejection, of failure, of giving up (and back) too much ground, and other quintessential Canadian quirks has led us to paralysis and keeps us from finding any real justice for our Indigenous peoples.

We were not always like this. Somewhere along the way—principally in the decades after Confederation—we changed. As John Ralston Saul reminds us in a *Fair Country, Telling Truths About Canada. . .* , we once aspired to *"peace, justice, and good governance."* We have since become staunch defenders of *"peace, order, and good governance,"* no matter the cost. Because order is easy and justice is hard, the best we can do in our paralysis is toss crumbs and apologies to our Indigenous peoples in their enervated condition while regurgitating that tired old cliché: *why can't we just all get along?*

Some of the battlefields where the war is being fought may be familiar to many Canadians. Others may not. No battles between colonial agents and Indigenous peoples, regardless of time or location, have been harder fought than those over land. Territorial sovereignty—the ability to govern access to, and use of, land—is foundational to all Indigenous Canadians. Exposés of several battlefields that play predominant roles in divesting our Indigenous peoples of their lands and resources form much of the following narrative. I do not provide historical or thorough analyses of wildlife co-management, environment impact assessment, comprehensive land claim settlements, provincial land-use planning, or cultural resource management. The reader will have to find those elsewhere. Rather, drawing from my familiarity with these spaces, I examine how the traditional knowledge, rights, and cultures of Indigenous Canadians continue to be crushed by witting and unwitting agents of the colonial order. In turn, the constitutionally protected rights of Indigenous peoples to their lands and resources are directly sabotaged, leaving initiatives and claims that assert otherwise little more than a charade.

The first three parts of this book—*Knowledge Wars, Land Rights and Title Wars, and Cultural Wars*—rely indirectly on my experiences and the wisdom of Indigenous elders and scholars. In many ways, these sections find their origins in the same root causes— namely, the erroneous belief in the superiority of settler ways and institutions (particularly industrial capitalism), our lack of empathy for the *other*, and our inability to confront the real challenges before us or see any way out of this dilemma. The last part, *Agents of the Colonial Order or Post-Colonial Allies?*, offers some suggestions on how we may yet honour and embrace our Indigenous hosts and welcome them as true and equal partners in Confederation and the future of this country.

Some may view this book as an admonishment of this country's unforgivable treatment of its Indigenous peoples in arenas about which they may know little. Others may see it as more of a memoir than anything else. Neither would be wrong. In some ways, what follows tells the story of my journey toward becoming an anthropologist and a defender of cultural values, perspectives, and traditions different from those with which I was raised. I have been truly fortunate to befriend and to work with Indigenous elders, hunters, and leaders who became my mentors, shared their experiences, and trusted me to assist them in their efforts to protect their cultures and ways of life. Having experienced an unusual succession of learning opportunities, having seen first-hand how agents of the colonial order act to keep the balance of power and privilege squarely in their hands, I would hope that this book justifies the faith my mentors placed in me and, maybe, in some small measure, honours their lives and memory.

Part One: Knowledge Wars

A peculiar anecdote involving a bag of Smarties introduces Chapter 1 (*Do You Eat the Red Ones Last?*),[2] and sets the tone for the book. Highlighting the conceptual gulf between Inuit and non-Inuit, and how each views and relates to nature, this chapter traces the history of an antagonistic Arctic wildlife management controversy in which I was personally involved. Inuit hunters, relying on centuries-old knowledge of beluga whales, steadfastly challenged and ultimately overcame the Department of Fisheries and Oceans' efforts to extinguish the southeast Baffin Inuit beluga hunt. While the chapter exposes some of the duplicitous tactics employed by DFO to impose its knowledge and regulations on Inuit hunters, it

---

2 This phrase is the refrain from the popular 1970s Smarties jingle.

concludes on a more sanguine note. The two parties found a patch of common ground (and calm water) where Inuit could sustain their relationship with a non-endangered species essential to their cultural survival.

If memory serves, an individual with only a modicum of native ancestry writing with authority about Indigenous knowledge, culture, history, and rights—subjects that might test the mettle of many Canadians, if they consider them at all—will likely engender misgivings and a sense of déjà vu among Indigenous scholars, leaders, and their supporters. Chapter 2 (*Maakusi Inuminniq*) dispels much of the criticism that might arise in this regard. I claim no great currency or expertise with respect to Indigenous cultures. And I certainly cannot speak for them. Rather, my decades-long involvement with Indigenous elders and hunters has allowed me to become a skilled observer of the society and culture in which I was raised. Specifically, I have spent much of my career observing how settler institutions and their beneficiaries interact with Canada's Indigenous peoples, particularly at the acrimonious interface of competing claims to knowledge, lands, and resources. I want to know how the respective rights and interests of the two cultures are negotiated and reconciled (or not) in contexts where rights to lands and natural resources are rigorously contested. This chapter traces this writer's evolution from student athlete to archaeologist to anthropologist, highlighting various experiences and anecdotes that have sharpened my perspective and provide the social license to own what follows.

The incorporation of Indigenous ecological knowledge into wildlife co-management—long held to be the flagship of this incipient institution—has been a dismal failure, despite the occasional claim to the contrary, from both sides. Almost without exception, only those decontextualized morsels of Indigenous knowledge that fit neatly into the dominant scientific paradigm of environmental resource management are given any consideration. The rest is dismissed as anecdotal, hearsay, and/or irrelevant. Chapter 3 (*Where Have all the Whales and Polar Bears Gone?*) recounts two Arctic wildlife conservation crises in which the knowledge claims of wildlife scientists and Inuit hunters were diametrically opposed. The plights of Canada's polar bears and bowhead whales have attracted international condemnation. Even so, little recognition and even less room have been afforded Inuit ecological knowledge in efforts by scientists to construct narratives and measures intended to conserve these charismatic Arctic species. Yet ironically, what passes as scientific knowledge of these enigmatic creatures rarely holds up under close scrutiny. In the end, *Science* (with a capital "S") becomes little more than a blunt instrument of subjugation and cultural assimilation for the dominant culture.

Canada's governing and corporate elites' resistance to Indigenous peoples' efforts to bring their knowledge to bear on environmental management came to a head with the federal environmental impact assessment of Canada's first diamond mine. As the anthropologist hired by BHP Diamonds Inc. to comply with the federal review panel's guidelines to *"give equal consideration to traditional knowledge in assessing the impacts of the project,"* I soon found myself in a lions' den of hostile combatants. There is no better illustration of this country's growing rancor toward Indigenous efforts to assert their rights and to preserve their cultures in the face of unbridled resource development than Frances Widdowson and Albert Howard's *Disrobing the Aboriginal Industry* . . . born during BHP's public review hearing on traditional knowledge. Highlighted by Mohawk scholar Taiaiake Alfred's crushing critique, Chapter 4 (*Listening to the Silence*) exposes the sophistry of these authors' malicious diatribe—currently a cult classic among this country's elites.

In the final analysis, the silence we hear emanating from the contested spaces in which Indigenous knowledge fights for its voice does not come from its creators and supporters championing an obstructionist, fallaciously hollow agenda as Widdowson and Howard claim. Rather, the silence comes from the hubris, complacency, and intransigence of the privileged and disproportionately empowered guardians and colonial institutions of settler society. So far, the space for Indigenous ecological knowledge in environmental decision-making has yet to be found.

Canada's ongoing failure to protect the rights of Indigenous Canadians and meaningfully engage them and their knowledge in environmental decisions resulted in one of Canada's most reprehensible wildlife management decisions to date. Indeed, it would be difficult to find a more egregious treatment of its Indigenous peoples than the Sayisi Dene abduction and relocation fiasco. The forced removal of this formerly self-sufficient and proud people from their homelands—and its aftereffects—is retold in Chapter 5 (*Where Have All the Caribou and Caribou Eater Chipewyan Gone?*) through the author's experiences with the Beverly-Qamanirjuaq Caribou Management Board and eyewitness accounts. Unknown to most Canadians, the tragic story of the Sayisi Dene had its genesis in a federal wildlife management decision that concluded that they had decimated the barren ground caribou to such an extent that in order to save the herds the entire band needed to be relocated to Churchill, Manitoba. Unprepared for life in the slums of Churchill, nearly half of the Sayisi Dene died violent, horrific deaths over the next two decades as a dispassionate and uncaring bureaucracy stood idly by. In the end, the scientific basis for the relocation was erroneous, resulting in what Sayisi Dene chief Ila Bussidor described as *"nothing less than genocide."*

What is Indigenous knowledge (aka traditional ecological knowledge, Native science, etc.)? How does it differ from knowledge sought and constructed by Western scientists? Why is there so little room within existing institutional and sociopolitical arrangements to accommodate Indigenous peoples and their knowledge into environmental decisions that directly impact their rights, lands, and resources? These are the kinds of questions that this chapter examines. While the content and fabric of Indigenous knowledge systems vary from culture to culture, I have learned from Inuit, Cree, Dene, and Métis elders that most have nothing to do with numbers, but everything to do with relationships. In fact, *numbers* may be the antithesis of *relationships*. How can complex, non-linear relationships within vastly intricate ecological networks be described in simple numerical terms without doing them violence? Yet in their quest to be *scientific*, to be accountable in the only way they know, wildlife biologists, conservation bureaucrats, and the like depend almost exclusively on numbers to construct their narratives, frame their conclusions, and set their regulations. But try as they might, they never come close to understanding the true nature and interdependencies connecting the components of ecological systems. In effect, in their effort to fit square pegs into round holes, they are propelled further and further from a more complete and nuanced comprehension of nature and humankind's place in it.

The realization that relationships between things are as, if not more, essential than that which is connected is not new. Drawing on the work of Indigenous and non-Indigenous scholars and philosophers such as Richard Atleo (Umeek) and Gregory Bateson, we see how Western science's materialistic preoccupation with separating things from other things without reference to their interconnections, and then taking them apart, prevents us "*from seeing the delicate interdependencies in ecological systems that give them their integrity.*" Such perspectives steer us toward a more enlightened appreciation of the relationships among the parts comprising ecological systems, and our place in them. However, not only are we not there yet, society continues to dismiss the potency and vitality of the ecological knowledge and management systems of those peoples who have come closest to this understanding. Chapter 6 (*Breathing Authenticity into the Unseparated: Knowledge that Connects*) lays it all out.

Part Two: Land Rights and Title Wars

Knowledge about local environments and ecological systems, and how to maintain sustainable relationships with them, ground many Indigenous peoples to their traditional territories and the natural world. However, colonial forces have overwhelmed their efforts to access and use their lands, and to preserve, protect, and pass on their cultural knowledge and values. I am not a lawyer, but I have seen how the application of Canada's laws and institutions cripples the rights of our First Peoples to their lands, cultural practices, and futures.

In Chapters 7 and 8 (*The Existing Aboriginal and Treaty Rights of the Aboriginal Peoples of Canada are Hereby Recognized and Affirmed: Parts 1 and 2*)[3] I examine the roles that historic treaties, comprehensive land claims, existing Aboriginal jurisprudence, and lawyers

---

3   *Canadian Constitution Act, 1982 Section 35:1.*

play in this process. One thing I learned early on from Indigenous elders is that our focus on rights is misplaced. Rather, we must shift our emphasis from one of *rights* to one of *responsibilities*. For many Indigenous societies, there are no rights without responsibilities. But instead of recognizing and enshrining these responsibilities in legislation and reconfiguring/building institutions to accommodate them, the discourse has been hijacked by lawyers on both sides. Invariably, the debate degenerates into a battle of *my rights versus your rights*, relying on an epistemology and lexicon that exact grave injustices on Indigenous cultures. A new—actually old and Indigenous—perspective on Aboriginal title concludes (for the time being) my polemic on current Aboriginal jurisprudence.

Part Three: Cultural Wars

Indigenous cultures continue to be crushed by government agents of the colonial order despite sustained resistance and efforts to protect their lands and resources. Several examples continue to resonate with me. The first involves regional land-use planning in the province of Alberta. The remaining cases illustrate how our governments continue to marginalize Indigenous cultures by obliterating centuries-old knowledge and evidence of their presence on their traditional lands.

Overhauling outdated provincial land-use policies is no easy feat. The menagerie of existing land-use footprints and variety of stakeholders in most jurisdictions present a formidable challenge for provincial regulators. The task is made far easier, however, by skipping principled and ethical consultation efforts with Indigenous constituents altogether. While some provincial land-use frameworks might arguably be an improvement over previous regimes—insofar as watersheds are the focus of management—they have failed to accommodate the rights and responsibilities of our Indigenous hosts. This readily became apparent to me during my fifteen-month tenure as the Treaty 6 representative on a Province of Alberta committee charged with developing a fifty-year land-use management framework for Canada's largest and most controversial industrial gamble, the Alberta's tar sands. Chapter 9 (*Trust Us Again, Just One More Time: Adventures in Land-Use Planning*) describes my experiences on the Lower Athabasca Regional Advisory Council, and my thoughts about Indigenous land-use planning generally. In the end, Alberta's process was a sham. Not only was the advice presented to the province by our multi-stakeholder committee rejected outright, it was replaced with what Alberta's governing and corporate elites wanted all along—a land-use framework that put revenues and profits ahead of Indigenous peoples and the environment.

Indigenous Canadians were in no mood to celebrate. In the months leading up to Canada's 150th anniversary as a country, there was a growing resistance in *Indian country* toward the proposed commemorations. After all, what was there to celebrate after a century and a half of subjugation and cultural genocide? However, a few of Canada's Indigenous leaders—in particular, Chief Steve Courtoreille of the Mikisew Cree First Nation and Chief Allan Adam of the Athabasca Chipewyan First Nation—saw July 1st, 2017, as an opportunity to recognize and honour the integrity of this country's Indigenous peoples in the face colonial oppression, and maybe even educate fellow Canadians about their history. Chapter 10 (*Divided No More: Adventures in Indigenous Cultural Preservation and Resurgence*) describes the collaborative effort by these chiefs to celebrate the great peace forged between Canada's Cree and Dene peoples at Peace Point in northern Alberta a century before Confederation. Located in Wood Buffalo National Park, Peace Point is one of Canada's most significant archaeological sites and the point of land after which the great river is named. The fact that two battle-scarred and sovereign Indigenous peoples concluded a peace treaty here between themselves decades before any colonial agent entered the region was something that both chiefs agreed should be recognized and celebrated widely, especially in 2017. The prime minister's office, other senior public officials, and Parks Canada thought otherwise.

Chapter 10 concludes with some examples of how Indigenous peoples are challenging provincial and territorial government practices that continue to eviscerate thousands of years of Indigenous occupation of, and knowledge about, their lands. For decades, the Alberta government has allowed industry in northern Alberta to bulldoze into oblivion past evidence of First Nations' use and occupation of their lands. A humble Dene Tha' First Nation elder and a resolute archaeologist are putting an end to this practice. Further north in Nunavut, one would have thought that the preservation and resurgence of Inuit culture would have been a high priority for the Nunavut government. Yet protecting the territory's colonial governing apparatus continues to trump efforts by Inuit to reclaim their culture and affect change in the status quo. The natives are getting restless.

Part Four: Agents of the Colonial Order or Post-Colonial Allies?

Indigenous Canadians fight for their rights on many fronts, none more critical or consequential than those involving their traditional lands and resources. Some battlegrounds, like wildlife co-management, environmental impact assessment, and land-use planning are perhaps less familiar to the general public than others. Yet Indigenous peoples participate in these institutions at great cost to themselves and, arguably, the lands, waters, and resources that sustain them. How do we dismantle the systemic barriers that marginalize Indigenous participation in these colonial institutions? How do we erase our colonial mindsets and attitudes? Where will change most profitably be pursued? Will Canada's not-so-clandestine war with our First Peoples ever end? Will we ever find peace, not only with our Indigenous hosts, but ourselves? These are the questions that this book's penultimate chapter (*Capacity for What? Capacity for Whom?*) ponders.

Many Indigenous Canadians will have formulated their own approaches and solutions to this quandary, and these, in no small measure, need to be heard and accommodated. Two things remain certain, however: change will not be easy, and we can no longer look to our governing elites and their corporate masters for the sea-change we all know must come. Nonetheless, there are some things we can do right now to facilitate the transformation. Chapter 12 (*Stumbling Toward Reconciliation*), highlighted by a recap of the recent Wet'sewet'en conflict, concludes with some suggestions that may bring us closer to true reconciliation, co-existence, and our potential as a country where fairness, justice, and restitution prevail over avarice, animus, and paralysis.

PART ONE

Knowledge Wars

CHAPTER 1

Do You Eat the Red Ones Last?

The greatest danger lies in the fact [that] *... human beings have to depend entirely on the souls of other beings for food.*
(Aua, Inuit shaman, 1922)

No Ordinary Bag of Smarties!

THIS WAS NO ORDINARY BAG OF SMARTIES. THAT MUCH WAS EVIDENT TO LEVI (EVIC) AND his Inuit companions as the Department of Fisheries and Oceans co-chair emptied it onto the meeting room table. Clearly out of his element, but finding the fortitude to carefully organize the Smarties into four differently coloured rows, the biologist began with a halting and curious mix of apprehension and hubris: *"Let's pretend these candies are the beluga you hunt."* Unimpressed, and with a collective and nagging feeling that they had seen this all before, Levi, Joannie (Ikkidluaq), Adamee (Veevee), and Meeka (Kilabuk) waited the biologist out as Becky (Mike) translated. One row, by far the largest, represented juvenile males. Two others were proxies for juvenile females and adult males. The last, by far the smallest, substituted for mature females.

You see, over the previous few years, in order to placate mounting DFO concerns about the decimation of beluga by Inuit in Cumberland Sound, Baffin Island, hunters from Pangnirtung had been providing DFO with information about their annual beluga hunts. The claims that the biologist was trying to make was that there were very few beluga, particularly breeding females, left in the Cumberland Sound beluga stock. If Pang's hunters did not stop hunting beluga, especially adult females—which apparently give birth every three years according to DFO, one year more than Inuit knowledge avows—there would be no beluga left for their children and grandchildren.

At the conclusion of the lecture, Levi, being the closest to the biologist, glanced towards his fellow Inuit for tacit approval for what they had all been thinking would be the most appropriate response. With a nod of their heads, Levi, in one deft movement, scooped up as many Smarties as he could in his bony, weathered hands and jammed them into his mouth. Almost simultaneously, I am told, the biologist's lower jaw damn near hit the table and the Inuit burst into fits of laughter.[4]

We Cooperate, You Manage?

It was my friend and *Kalaallit Nunaat's* (Greenland's) well known Inuit rights advocate, Ingmar Egede, who first coined this now iconic (in some circles) phrase to describe wildlife co-management with Indigenous Canadians and other northern regions. Perhaps more than any other, the Smarties incident provides a snapshot of what wildlife co-management with Indigenous Canadians looked like in the 1980s. Most comprehensive land claims agreements in northern Canada were in the process of being negotiated, or were just about to be. Those in progress relied exclusively on federal government statutes, regulations, and procedures to get the job done. Discussions were conducted in one of Canada's two official languages, and the concepts, knowledge, and language systems of wildlife managers, conservation bureaucrats, and lawyers set the agenda and dominated the discourse. This was the context in which wildlife co-management arrangements within comprehensive land claims agreements were and still are, negotiated, apparently.

Another context in which wildlife co-management arrangements with Indigenous Canadians arises emerge from perceived conservation crises manufactured by territorial, provincial, and/or federal government agencies. Rarely do these crises originate out of concerns raised by Indigenous and local users. Again, many of the features that govern the design and implementation of co-management provisions within comprehensive land claims agreements are in play. Among the first wildlife management crises to result in a co-management agreement with Canada's Indigenous peoples was the Southeast Baffin Beluga controversy.

Fighting Over Beluga

By 1990, some ten years after the Smarties incident, the rift between DFO biologists and Inuit hunters had grown exponentially wider. With anger and resentment still festering over the conviction of several community members for contravening DFO's narwhal regulations,

---

4   *Qujanamiq* (thanks) to Rebecca Mike and Meeka Kilabuk for clarifying details surrounding this charade.

Pangnirtung's whale hunters in 1980 reluctantly agreed to an interim annual quota of forty beluga (*qillalugaq*). Inuit opposition to this measure was immediate, widespread, and not unfounded. Quotas were anticipated to increase competition among hunters, hunting pressure on whales, and struck-and-loss rates as Inuit leaders knew that more whales would be hunted in weather conditions and seasons not conducive to their recovery.

Pang's hunters were further aggrieved as they felt singled out. Never before had they been subjected to such a quota. As Clearwater Fiord in Cumberland Sound was the only beluga summering grounds in the southeast Baffin area known to DFO at that time, Iqaluit and Kimmirut (Lake Harbour) hunters were dragged into the fray. By the late 1980s, the issue had grown into a regional wildlife management crisis, and no one was happy about it.

Even though quotas were regarded as yet another assault on Inuit culture and hunting traditions, Pang's hunters by the mid-1980s were undertaking survey counts with biologists—a technique they hoped would bring Inuit hunters over to their way of thinking. Meanwhile, DFO continued to collect and analyze samples from the hunts. Yet according to the surveys there were now 200 fewer whales in the stock than a decade earlier, and a far cry from DFO's original estimate of 5,000+. Again, hunters were forced to make concessions including refraining to hunt in Clearwater Fiord, not hunting pregnant females or females accompanied by calves, abandoning a cursory foray into the inter-settlement trade of *maqtaaq* (the most valued and desired part of the beluga), and participating in an ad hoc management committee.

Meetings of the so-called Beluga Management Committee throughout the 1980s were often characterized by colourful and heated exchanges, frequently concluding with Inuit hunters storming out of the room behind their spokesperson, Meeka Kilabuk. A human dynamo, political activist, and as uncompromising a champion of Inuit culture as there ever was, Meeka would often exclaim, pointing her meaty finger at DFO personnel, "*You don't know shit*" before exiting the room with her entourage in tow. You see, Inuit on the BMC had long realized that they had no real influence on planning or decision-making, and that their knowledge was considered irrelevant by biologists. DFO personnel had not only underestimated the nutritional, economic, social, and cultural significance of beluga to Inuit, but the latter's resolve to defend their rights. In later meetings of the Southeast Baffin Beluga Committee, I often felt sympathy—admittedly only just a little—for the DFO co-chair as he struggled, often without success, to find the opening words to meetings that would not incur Meeka's wrath.

Ultimately, the conflict came to a head in 1990 after two national scientific advisory boards declared the southeast Baffin beluga stock to be *endangered*, while recommending a ten-year moratorium be placed on the hunt. Over the previous five years hunters from Pangnirtung, Iqaluit, and Kimmirut had landed about 100 beluga annually from a regional stock that DFO now considered to be fewer than 500 animals. Simple math (500 - [100 x 5] = 0) dictated that Inuit could not continue to hunt beluga. Something had to be done. Subsequently, with the blessing of the fledgling Nunavut Wildlife Management Advisory Board of the yet-to-be created Nunavut Territorial Government, the minister of DFO amended the *Fisheries Act*, setting a new total allowable harvest of five beluga for each of the three communities. Ignored in this process were Inuit hunters who, over the last few years, had been conscientiously implementing additional traditional conservation measures, including reducing the loss of wounded beluga, taking only one animal at a time, and striking no more than two whales in each pod encountered.

In the aftermath of the economic, social, and cultural devastation of the anti-sealing campaigns of the previous decades, a 700 percent reduction in community beluga quotas poured gasoline on the wounds of the three Inuit communities, and set them ablaze. The hunting and sharing of beluga was (and is) so integral to maintaining south Baffin Inuit nutritional health, psychological well-being, cultural traditions, and social relationships that the severely reduced quota was described as having the same effect as *"the death of a loved one."*

No food is more highly prized by south Baffin Inuit (Okomiut) than *maqtaaq*, and for good reason. It is a delicacy shared near and far that reaffirms social relationships and cultural values. During the 1990s, I often participated with Inuit elder Minnie Aodla Freeman in healing ceremonies/feasts at the Bowden Penitentiary south of Edmonton, where beluga *maqtaaq* was not only the most highly sought-after item on the menu, but served to nurture a sense of cultural identity, solidarity among Inuit inmates, and social obligation to folks back home.

For years Inuit hunters in the south Baffin region had felt deep regret over their battle for beluga. Few things are more distasteful and dangerous to Inuit survival than fighting over animals. And the anger, frustration, and betrayal that Inuit hunters felt over the quota could not be contained. Emboldened by the resistance of Mohawk warriors during the 1990 Oka crisis, small groups of dissident Inuit hunters directly challenged DFO authority, deliberately exceeding quotas, occupying DFO offices in Iqaluit, and even accosting local DFO officials. Prior to 1990, Inuit participants on the BMC felt that their knowledge and observations had no currency whatsoever. Moreover, they had not had the opportunity to review thoroughly the plethora of scientific studies and claims thrown at them, or publicly debate the new quotas in their respective communities. In addition, Inuit participation on the BMC was at the behest of DFO, arbitrary at best, and perpetually in a state of flux. With no community-sanctioned representation of Inuit members, hunters refused to recognize the authority of the BMC or any other ad hoc wildlife management committee.

At the same time, various Inuit organizations and leaders across the Nunavut Settlement Area came out in support of the hunters, denouncing federal government actions. National and international media attention, however, sided with DFO officials as Inuit hunters came under increasing pressure from southern politicians and animal rights groups to cease the hunt. Later in the year, the government leader of the Northwest Territories intervened, securing funds from the feds to establish yet another ad hoc committee to resolve the issue. Though short-lived, this interim committee did manage to provide recommendations to DFO and the soon-to-be-created Nunavut Wildlife Management Board. A report for the DFO minister recommended the establishment of a formal co-management structure compatible with the Nunavut Final Agreement, and an interim quota of thirty-five beluga for each of the three communities.

Cracks, however, soon began to emerge in DFO's narrative. Aerial surveys were now counting even more beluga than they had in the mid-1980s, despite the removal of 100 or so animals each year. In addition, a thorough review of existing Inuit and scientific knowledge was beginning to reveal a very different picture of southeast Baffin beluga than that painted by Fisheries biologists. Specifically, the interim committee considered it most likely that beluga wintering in southeast Baffin waters divide into at least two summering groups, with one entering Cumberland Sound after break-up and the other migrating west through Hudson Strait into Hudson Bay. It was also determined that there was no mixing of summer beluga populations between Frobisher Bay and Cumberland Sound. Perhaps most importantly, it concluded that that the number of beluga utilizing Cumberland Sound and Clearwater Fiord must be substantially larger than that determined by DFO.

Consequently, the DFO minister in the summer of 1991 accepted the new interim measures for two years, and the Southeast Baffin Beluga Committee was established on the condition that a co-management plan be developed at the end of this time. But despite an initial and renewed spirit of cooperation between DFO personnel and Inuit hunters, meetings soon devolved into heated exchanges over endless minutiae. After eighteen months of wrangling, the gulf between Inuit and DFO personnel seemed as vast as ever. With the pending deadline hanging over their heads like the sword of Damocles, SEBBC members agreed to hire additional outside help. This was to be my first, but not last, exposure to and involvement in wildlife co-management.

But my hiring, though unanimously supported by Inuit committee members, was rigorously opposed by DFO personnel. In their view, only a whale biologist could resolve the impasse and convince Inuit of the validity of DFO's position. Besides, what could an anthropologist possibly know about whales? In retrospect, it is difficult to conceive how anyone other than a social scientist familiar with and respectful of Inuit ways could have assisted committee members to find common ground. After a decade of working and conducting research with Inuit from Pangnirtung, including countless embarrassing gaffes and the odd *faux pas*, I had gotten to know the Pangnirtarmiut, and Pang's elders and hunters had gotten to know me. I even picked up some of the language. But more than that, Inuit members of the SEBBC trusted that I would work tirelessly on their behalf and the beluga upon which they depended, even as they teased me that I was a *Qallunamarialuq* (a real white man).

Clearly, DFO personnel did not understand that the Southeast Baffin Beluga controversy was not a political or legal conflict where neither the facts of each party nor the meanings and values assigned to them agreed. Rather, it was a cultural conflict where no amount of *scientific facts* and strong-arming could convince Inuit hunters to abandon their ways of thinking. The case of the southeast Baffin Inuit and beluga was one of the first co-management initiatives in Canada's North, and as it turned out, one of the most successful.

But progress toward the development of an acceptable co-management plan was hard won. Translation of written materials was tedious and time-consuming. Logistical problems and linguistic barriers were formidable. Inuit members needed adequate opportunity to collectively digest the scientific information and materials provided. And they needed time to formulate their positions on a variety of issues in consultation with community members. Subsequently, a request for a year's extension to the deadline was accepted by the minister.

Who Talks Like That?

English (*Qallunnatitut*), like *Inuktitut* and all human languages, reflects the assumptions, biases, values, concepts, and worldviews of its speakers. In this respect language does not so much *"describe the world we see, but sees the world we describe!"*[5] The terms and concepts of wildlife management derive from a cultural tradition fundamentally different from that of the Inuit. The former reflects man's separation from and dominance over nature. The latter embraces man's reciprocal relationship or partnership with nature, which involves certain duties, responsibilities, and obligations. As much as any factor, the conceptual underpinnings of *wildlife management* were a major stumbling block preventing consensus among SEBBC members.

DFO's continuing effort to frame its narrative around the concept of stock was particularly problematic for Inuit hunters. There is no word in Inuktitut for such a concept. Inuit have words for groups of animals that are within their field of vision, *katimayut*. But they have never found a reason to assign other, unseen members of the same species to a hypothetical larger *stock* or population. Conversely, for marine biologists, whale *stocks*

---

5   This quote and its variants have been attributed to several authors, most notably Descartes.

are designated on the basis of perceived geographic, morphological, behavioural, genetic, and/or other differences in an effort to develop discrete management units that provide a focus for research, knowledge construction, management, and conservation. Inuit consider such concepts nonsensical when applied to animals (*umaijuit*) such as *qillalugaq* and other whales that travel great distances in multi-generational extended family units that vary through time and space. And while Inuit know that beluga pods may intermingle at certain times and locations, to assign these to a discreet *stock* implies a sense of unvarying permanence that is at odds with their experience.

The concept of *wildlife* was almost as problematic. There is no bifurcation of the animal world into *wild* and *domestic* in traditional Inuit thinking. There is only *umaijuit* and dogs (*qimmit*), which occupy a special status in relation to Inuit. In other words, there was no reason to assign separate labels for *wild* and domesticated animals. They weren't needed, they weren't relevant.

Other words and concepts commonly employed in *wildlife* management—e.g., *harvest, sustainable yield, total allowable catch*, etc.—continued to challenge Inuit committee members as they imply a relationship with *umaijuit* where humans are in charge. To think that Inuit could control or *manage* animals—sentient and self-determining life forms in their own right—was ludicrous and offensive to Inuit committee members. As Joannie continually reminded me, "*only God can do that*." I soon learned that in the Inuit worldview and knowledge system (aka *Inuit qaujimajatuqungit*), *umaijuit* give or present themselves to hunters if they are properly respected and treated before, during, and after the hunt. Not surprisingly, Inuit embrace a variety of cultural norms that ensure that the hunt is sustainable, including not hunting whales again for five days after a kill and sharing all parts of the whale—failing to do so being a gross violation of the animal's sacrifice. To reject an animal's offering once it has given itself to the hunter is unthinkable and an invitation for disaster. Joavee Alivaktuk once told me that Inuit hunters are revulsed by the disrespect shown to fish by televised catch-and-release fishing shows. Inuit ideas of *conservation* are clearly at odds with mainstream society.

Inuit qaujimajatuqungit is the cumulative knowledge and blueprint for Inuit economic, social, and cultural survival. The product of generations of direct observation and experience handed down through oral tradition, it provides an evolving baseline of knowledge and information of a quality and time-depth rarely available to southern scientists. While primarily qualitative, holistic, and practical in nature, *Inuit qaujimajatuqungit* also tends to be local or regional in scope, as opposed to scientific knowledge, which seeks to construct universal knowledge or *truths* from limited data sets systematically—supposedly—acquired over brief periods of time.

So, what do Inuit manage, if anything? This is a question we explored in depth as we attempted to deconstruct DFO claims. After many discussions, I learned that, to the extent that Inuit manage or control anything, it is themselves, the hunt, and their relationship with beluga. For me, this was a profound revelation. The kinds of information and knowledge needed to *manage* and *conserve* sustainable relationships with *umaijuit*, as opposed to animals themselves, were different from that which scientists considered important. When pressed, committee biologists were forced to admit that their use of the word *stock* when applied to highly transient and social mammals such beluga was more or less "*an educated guess,*" an "*arbitrary management unit*" that may have little basis in reality, especially the reality of Inuit hunters. Still, Inuit committee members said they would reasonably consider any scientific information that might support use of this word, including genetic analyses, as long as it was based on "*good Science.*" As Meeka often reminded me, "*Inuit qaujimajatuqungit is not static!*"

Turds and Berries

Right from the start of the controversy, DFO researchers claimed that the original size of the southeast Baffin beluga *stock* was 5,000+ animals. This estimate appears to have been based on the total number of whales taken by the Hudson's Bay Company in Cumberland Sound from the early 1920s to the mid-1940s—about the average lifespan of beluga—as well as models of beluga behaviour and population dynamics developed elsewhere. Yet aerial and cliff-top surveys in Clearwater Fiord during the 1970s and 1980s counted no more than about 500 whales at any one time. With about 100 whales removed from the southeast Baffin beluga *stock* each of the previous several years, the Arctic Fisheries Scientific Advisory Committee and the Committee on the Status of Endangered Wildlife in Canada had seen enough, and alarm bells went off at DFO offices in Ottawa and Winnipeg.

But something was amiss with DFO's model. Aerial and cliff top surveys in the early 1990s were still counting about 500 beluga in Clearwater Fiord at the head of Cumberland Sound. Moreover, DFO's *stock* size estimates did not consider newborns added each year, or the replacement of hunted whales by others through in-migration. Inuit knowledge indicated that beluga summering in Cumberland Sound were not, and never have been, an unchanging seasonal aggregate of estuary-bound whales that can be conceptualized as a single *stock*.

Inuit members on the SEBBC pointed out to DFO personnel that it had been comparing apples to oranges, though I think the words used were *pauna* (berries) and *tuktu anuq* (caribou turds). Never before had they observed thousands of beluga at any one time or place. Subsequently, a close review of HBC archival records supported Inuit observations.

To wit, the single largest commercial whale drive ever recorded in Cumberland Sound occurred in 1930 when 500 animals were driven into the shallows, with 300 being released the following tide. Moreover, in subsequent years, small drives of less than 200 whales one year were often followed the next year by drives twice the size. The scientific model advanced by DFO biologists, especially its original and current *stock* size estimates, was clearly in error, a fact they finally had to acknowledge:

> *A stock of 500 animals cannot sustain removal of more than 12 animals per year, yet this stock had been subjected to much greater removals since 1967, without a decline in stock size being detected by aerial surveys. This suggests that the stock is larger than 500 animals and may be declining more slowly than expected.*[6]

No Adult Females, No Adult Males, No Problem!

The original size of the Southeast Baffin Beluga *stock* had become a non-issue. Nevertheless, something else began to gnaw away at DFO personnel; there were very few adult females left in the *stock*. For years, Inuit had been providing the department with tissue and organ samples from the beluga they hunted. All indications were that hunting pressure on adult females was and had been so great that if Inuit did not stop hunting altogether, the *stock* would soon become extinct. Inuit on the SEBBC, however, were quick to disabuse biologists of this notion. Specifically, they reminded them that not only had they not hunted pregnant females and females with newborns or older calves for years, they had done so at Fisheries and Oceans' request.

Undaunted, DFO personnel turned their attention to adult males as there were comparatively few large males in the samples provided. Clearly, Inuit had killed far too many adult males, and needed to cease and desist. Once again, Inuit committee members had to remind the biologists that their claims were spurious. There were hardly any large males in the samples provided simply because, compared to younger beluga, adult males are very difficult to hunt. Through repeated exposure to hunting, older beluga had learned to avoid the sound of boat motors and gunfire. Rarely could hunters get within rifle shot of a large male to make a kill. Besides, Inuit have a preference for the *maqtaaq* of younger whales, and older males are not the first item of choice on the menu. For years, the annual Cumberland Sound beluga hunt had returned predominantly younger males. Compared to the more balanced age and sex distributions of beluga hunts elsewhere, Pangnirtung's hunt was skewed towards this cohort.

---

6   S. Cosens et al (1993). Report of the Arctic Fisheries Scientific Advisory Committee for 1991/91 and 1992/93. *Canadian Manuscript Report of Fisheries and Aquatic Sciences* 2224.

By the early 1990s, the Fisheries department had invested too much time and too much money to back down. It needed something, anything, it could hang on to in order to justify the years of effort, expense, and confrontation. Treating the unquestionably biased samples provided by Inuit hunters as representative of the population under study—a major *faux pas* in scientific procedure—was a last ditch effort to save face. It didn't work. Ultimately, the department was forced to admit its transgressions, more or less:

> *By simplifying the information we brought them* [Inuit hunters], *de-emphasizing the imprecision of our methods and over-emphasizing the certainty of our conclusions, we did ourselves a disservice* [never mind the Inuit]. *Had we shown the detail of the results and acknowledged the imprecision and uncertainty, we could have explained that our alarm at the status of the stock is an educated guess based on various sources of data, not on certainty, and that the precision of the methods may not allow certainty until it's too late. This failure at openness about the detail of our results and the thought processes behind our conclusions and the dire predictions had a very negative consequence.*[7]

A Co-management Plan for Southeast Baffin Inuit and Beluga

With the slate cleared, the deadline looming, and a greater understanding and appreciation of the veracity of Inuit knowledge and their relationship with beluga, the SEBBC set about to develop a co-management plan acceptable to the minister. Perhaps more than anything else, Inuit and DFO committee members agreed to disagree about the *facts*, while recognizing the cultural values that inform each other's knowledge. In the end, SEBBC members recommended that no management action be taken until *Inuit qaujimajatuqungit* and Western science agreed that beluga in Cumberland Sound were increasing, decreasing, or remaining stable. Agreement was also reached on the types of management actions required in each scenario. For example, should beluga numbers remain stable under current hunting pressure, the size of *no-hunting zones* would be increased and the length of hunting seasons reduced. Should beluga found to be declining, quotas, hunting zones, and hunting seasons would be set to limits agreed to by both parties. The plan also called for a five-year extension on existing annual quotas. After nearly a decade and a half of protracted confrontation, progress had been achieved. In 1994, a co-management plan was submitted to and approved by the minister of DFO.

---

7   P. Richard and D. Pike (1993). Small Whale Co-management in the Eastern Canadian Arctic: A Case History and Analysis. *Arctic* 46(2):138-143.

Like DFO members, Inuit on the SEBBC didn't get all that they wanted. For example, Inuit hunters were not happy about how their geographic knowledge was graphically portrayed in the plan. In contrast to most of the developed world, South Baffin Inuit orient their maps with north at the bottom as most Inuit settlements are located in productive winter habitats at the heads of south-facing inlets where tidal forces create open water areas (*sarbut*, aka polynyas) attractive to marine mammals. Likewise, a request that the title of the plan highlight the relationship between Inuit and beluga—not beluga per se—as the focus of management was dismissed outright. In fact, DFO committee members vehemently opposed this suggestion. Ultimately, the plan was given the misleading title of *Co-management Plan for Southeast Baffin Beluga*, and a teachable moment and rare opportunity to create ethical space for *Inuit qaujimajatuqungit* in *wildlife co-management* were lost.

By 2003 Inuit knowledge and further scientific studies had determined that beluga reside year-round in Cumberland Sound and are distinct from those hunted near Iqaluit and Kimmirut, with perhaps two or three morphologically distinguishable sub-groupings. With new population estimates of around 1,500 for Cumberland Sound beluga, Pangnirtung's quota was increased to forty-one. Today, the plan continues to evolve and is being implemented under the Nunavut Wildlife Management Board with no significant management actions taken in recent years. Although the concept of *stock* still forms the basis of management decisions, the animosity that formerly characterized DFO and Inuit relations is becoming a distant memory, and the ethical space for Inuit to *manage their relationship* with beluga may yet be found.

Postscript: Look What Happened to Luuq!

Fisheries and Oceans began to conduct research on Cumberland Sound beluga around 1970 when biologists became concerned about the presumed decimation of the *stock* by Inuit hunters during the 1950s and 60s. What the department did not consider was the possibility that this *wildlife conservation crisis* was caused by one of their own implementing a poorly designed government sponsored beluga test fishery.

In the summers of 1966 and 1967 over 100 beluga, including several large males, were indiscriminately netted and drowned in Clearwater Fiord. While local Inuit hunters salvaged some of the *maqtaaq*, much of what was generally known about beluga reproductive biology back then came from this study. When interviewing Jamasie Mike (Becky's father) in the early 1990s as part of my PhD research into Cumberland Sound Inuit social organization, our conversation turned to the current beluga controversy. I asked Jamasie when he first began to notice a decline in *qillalugaq* in Cumberland Sound. His response floored me.

During the late 1960s beluga in the upper part of Cumberland Sound became far more dispersed and difficult to hunt in open water than previously. An astute observer of *umaijuit*, but mediocre manager of personal financial records, Jamasie further added that had he saved his gas receipts he could show me just how much more it cost him to hunt beluga after this time. Prior to the test fishery, beluga pods summering in Cumberland Sound were led by large adult males referred to as *Luuq*, or *Luumaijuq* (the one who goes "*luuq*")—a reference to the deep guttural vocalizations that these whales made in contrast to the higher-pitched sounds of other beluga. *Luumajuit* were the *malittaq* (the one others follow) of their extended family groups and were often seen scouting out various inlets and fiords before retrieving the rest of their pods, sometimes numbering in the hundreds.

Jamasie continued with one of his youngest daughters and my long-time friend and mentor Meeka Mike translating. For generations, Inuit living in camps at the head of the Sound were instructed never to hunt the "*ones who go luuq*" as they knew from experience that without their *malittaq* beluga would become more dispersed and much harder to hunt. Inuit, like other Indigenous northerners, know that aggregations of large mammalian species, whether on land (e.g., caribou, *tuktuit*) or in water, have leaders (primarily adult males) that are responsible for the movements, safety, and survival of their groups. For this reason they must never be disturbed or hunted. When I asked Jamasie about the last time he saw a *luuq*, he responded, "*around the time qillalugaq became very difficult to hunt.*"

It was then that I realized that the southeast Baffin beluga crisis was most likely caused not by Inuit, but by a poorly designed and executed test fishery led by biologists. Jamasie did not appear to be amused when I told him that the testes of one or more *luuq* may be found in pickle jars at DFO's Freshwater Institute in Winnipeg.

Many years had passed since I had thought about my conversation with Jamasie. But it all came rushing back to me on a 2015 floatplane flight from Vancouver airport to my new home in Halfmoon Bay in *Shíshálh* traditional territory north of Sechelt. Flying low between Point Grey and Bowen Island we spotted a group of perhaps 120 or more Pacific white-sided dolphins. There, some 300 metres or so in front of the larger pod, was a tightly packed cohort of about five or six larger dolphins leading the way.

CHAPTER 2
Maakusi Inuminniq

HAVE I SOMETHING TO CONTRIBUTE TO THE EVOLVING NARRATIVE OF INDIGENOUS-NON-Indigenous relations in Canada? Are my experiences with Canada's First Peoples worth sharing? Will anything I have to say move the pendulum towards decolonization, reconciliation, and coexistence? Is it politically correct—or, more importantly, ethically appropriate—for a person with only a modicum of Indigenous ancestry to write about Indigenous reality and experience? Does an anthropologist, especially one whose ancestors come mostly from the ranks of the colonizers rather than the colonized, have any rights in these spaces or to write with certitude on such matters? These are the kinds of questions I asked myself in the years leading up to this book.

I do not claim to be an Indigenous person. Sure, I have Aboriginal blood flowing through my veins, as do/did my siblings, my mother, her parents, her siblings, and most anyone in Canada who can trace their roots in this country back several generations or more. Of the six biologically related children my mother and father raised, three possess typically Amerindian features (brown eyes, black hair, dark complexions), while three exhibit more typical Caucasian features (blue eyes and fairer hair and complexions). But unlike some of my aunts, cousins, and nieces, I do not feel that I am entitled to Métis status. Rather, I was brought up in a predominantly Catholic family of white privilege where French was rarely spoken, and only by my mom, especially when she got mad. When I was a kid, a few Musqueam First Nation (Halkomelem) families attended our church in south Vancouver, but I really never got to know them. And though I grew up in the summers on the banks of the Winnipeg River near Lac du Bonnet, Manitoba, listening to my Auntie Bert tell stories of her paternal uncle, Louie Fournier, a French-Mi'gmaq trapper from Gapsé, that was about as close as I got to growing up Indigenous. But finding stone projectile points on the shores of the Winnipeg River and in my family's garden in Marpole when I was a lad peaked my curiosity in the Indigenous part of my heritage and eventually archaeology.

Some authors writing about the cultures of our founding peoples have recently been chastised by Canada's Indigenous community for feigning an Aboriginal identity. Other non-Aboriginals have claimed to be experts on Indigenous peoples because of their long association with them. Some even feel entitled to speak on their behalf. If I have gained any knowledge from my engagement with Indigenous Canadians it is that I cannot speak for them. I have not lived nor shared their life experiences, good, bad, or indifferent. Rather, I am a student of the culture and society in which I was raised. And my particular interests lie at the gritty interface, and overlapping and turbulent waters, of mainstream and Indigenous societies, polities, and cultures. As an anthropologist, I want to know how Indigenous and non-Indigenous peoples and institutions interact, and how their respective rights and interests are negotiated and reconciled (or not), particularly in contexts where rights to lands and natural resources are vigorously contested.

Having grown up in a middle-class family with the resources and support network to obtain a masters in archaeology and a doctorate in anthropology, I am aware of my good fortune. But I also realize that with my privileged position comes a duty and responsibility to the peoples I have chosen to work with and for. I must also admit that I come by my interest in social justice honestly. My uncle, Ray Stevenson, was for many years a trade union activist, executive member of the World Peace Congress, and editor for the United Steel Workers of America publication, *Information*. I further believe that it is the duty of every Canadian to confront the systemic racism—and how it manifests itself in our attitudes, institutions, and complacence with the status quo—that has marginalized our Indigenous peoples and keeps us from realizing our true potential as a country and as Canadians.

That said, I must say that the crude tools I acquired during my upbringing and formal education did little to prepare me for my first meaningful experience with Indigenous peoples.

Life Before Archaeology

I did not always want to be an archaeologist, or even an anthropologist. In high school I was a straight C+ student, and did just enough to get by. Rugby and baseball were my primary, but not only, interests. I was a fairly decent athlete and was playing first-division men's rugby in Vancouver by my senior year. But I had no idea what I was going to do after high school. An acquaintance of mine had just accepted a football scholarship at a NCAA Division 1 school in California, so I thought that might be something I could do. But never having played organized football in my life my chances were slim. Undeterred, I contacted the BC Lions football club through my rugby coach to request a try-out at its upcoming *All-Comers* camp—an annual event held by the Canadian Football League team to recruit fodder for its main training camp, and who knows, maybe discover a diamond in the rough. Surprisingly, I received an invitation, along with about eighty other local and regional university, semi-pro, ex-college, and junior football players.

But I had little idea how the game was played, a fact that became readily apparent to the Lions coaching staff when, on the first morning of camp, head coach and CFL legend Jackie Parker damn near pulled me off my feet as I jogged onto the field at Empire Stadium for a *no-pads* practice.

"*Where you going, son?*" he quipped in his thick Alabama accent.

"*Ah, ah, going to try out for the team, sir,*" I stammered.

"*Not like that you're not. You go back up* [to the locker room] *and put your pants on properly.*"

You see, I had put my pants on backwards, the laces in the back. Once in a while I would run into Jackie In Edmonton where I lived with my family for twenty-six years, and we'd share a good laugh about our first meeting.

I must have impressed somebody over the next two days as I was one of four players invited back to the main camp. But common sense soon prevailed and Bobby Ackles, the director of player personnel for the Lions (and later the Dallas Cowboys), phoned to tell me "*no eighteen-year-old kid with no football experience was going to make a CFL team.*" Instead, he floated the idea of getting me a football scholarship in the States, and said I had better start studying for my SATs. My plan was coming together.

Two months later, however, he called to say that none of his American contacts was interested in a Canadian kid with no football experience, but Simon Fraser University—the only Canadian university at that time offering football scholarships—might be. I subsequently accepted a half scholarship at SFU, enrolled in classes, and turned up for training camp. (I did not tell them that I had failed the SAT exam). I *red-shirted* my first year, started the next four, and earned a few American small college honours along the way. I even set two US college football records that may yet still stand, the most infamous being a sixty-yard penalty and subsequent ejection from a University of California (Riverside) homecoming game. As a *marked man*, I am sure the yardage would have been greater had there been more flag-throwing officials on the field.

The first two years of juggling classes and football were gruelling, and with academic probation looming, I decided to take some archaeology classes. Hell, I needed to get my 1.3 GPA up in a hurry. So I decided to switch from sciences to arts. Within a year or so, I was fortunate to find some great professors and qualify for full academic and athletic scholarships. Three years later, I graduated with a 3.75 GPA and a honours degree in archaeology. Even though I was drafted by the Lions in my junior year, more and more frequently football was taking a backseat to archaeology. Getting injured during the Lions training camp was just the spark I needed to go back to school and obtain a master's degree in archaeology.

Digging up Shit and Making up Stories about It!

Over the next three years, with the assistance of my advisor Herb Alexander—an acerbic, vertically challenged Texan with a love of Mexican food, women, and football—I was fortunate to cut my teeth as an archaeologist digging 1,500-year-old Interior Salish villages in south-central British Columbia, 12,000-year-old Paleo-Indian rock shelters in central Texas, and 16,000-year-old Upper Palaeolithic cave sites in southwest Germany. But times were tough financially and jobs in archaeology were, well, non-existent. So, in 1978, I decided to give football one more try. You see, I had several CFL teams phone me after I quit in 1975 to say that if I ever changed my mind about professional football to give them a call. A step slower and twenty pounds lighter, I was getting the crap kicked out of me at the Toronto Argonauts training camp. My bruised and battered body was screaming at me to reconsider my decision. Although Argonaut head coach Leo Cahill questioned my intention to leave camp to, as he put it, "*dig up pyramids in Egypt,*" I knew I had made the right decision as I boarded the flight home. Soon after, I got wind from Dr. David Burley of my first real paying job in archaeology—a six-month contract documenting historic gold-mining sites in the pristine mountainous terrain of Kluane National Park, southwest Yukon.

The job as it turned out was with Parks Canada, and I soon found myself in Haines Junction at the foot of the ruggedly beautiful St. Elias mountains. Not infrequently in the wilds of Kluane I would come across a smouldering patch of ground above a creek bed where an old gold miner's camp once stood. Apparently, two to three weeks earlier, park wardens had beaten me to these sites implementing a project called *mining clean-up* and burning to the ground any structure that didn't fit Parks Canada's aesthetic for national parks. This was my first insight into how Parks Canada managed Canada's archaeological heritage in national parks.

My six-month contract turned into a four-year position with Parks Canada in Winnipeg with the impressive-in-name-only job title of national parks archaeologist, prairie region. In actual fact, I could not have been any lower on the totem pole. You see, historic and prehistoric archaeological sites in Canada's national parks are an inconvenience—at best, an afterthought. Indeed, Kluane is not the only national park whose boundaries purposely avoid culturally significant archaeological and historic sites. Assisted by First Nation park wardens Chuck Hume and Ronny Chambers, and fellow graduate student Jeff Hunston, I spent two more summers in Kluane, recording prehistoric sites of the Southern Tutchone peoples and excavating post-Klondike gold-rush sites on Bullion Creek. My job also took me to Wood Buffalo National Park, Alberta/Northwest Territories, where I was charged with undertaking an archaeological survey of an area larger than some countries. Over the course of my last two summers with Parks Canada my assistant (Doug Proch) and I recorded scores of prehistoric sites, none more impressive than Peace Point after which the Peace River is named.

Shortly before the first European ever set eyes on the Peace River members of Canada's two great founding First Nations peoples—the Algonquin-speaking Ojibway-Cree and the Athabascan-speaking Dene—concluded a peace treaty at Peace Point. For centuries the relationship between Cree and Dene peoples in Western Canada was one of begrudging co-existence, bordering at times on mutual animosity and hostility. Warring between the two great nations intensified after the early 1700s when the Cree, being the first to acquire firearms from fur traders, began to displace the Dene further to the north and west. Decades of enmity eventually came to a head sometime around 1760 when a collective of Dene bands made their stand on the Peace River. Here, 1,200 Dene and Cree warriors engaged in an epic battle, after which a lasting peace was forged downriver at Peace Point. This fact alone warrants Peace Point's place among Canada's most significant historic sites. But for some reason Parks Canada and the Historic Sites and Monuments Board of Canada remain silent about the national significance of Peace Point. Yet Peace Point had more surprises in store when I arrived there to assess its archaeological significance in 1980.

It did not take a genius to realize how rare and unique Peace Point's archaeological deposits were. A deeply stratified series of discrete ancient living floors spanning two-and-a-half millennia, with excellent preservation and virtually no post-occupational disturbance, is about as good as it gets in Canadian archaeology. In two-metre-thick river deposits that span two kilometres atop an ancient limestone escarpment that includes both national park and Mikisew Cree reserve lands, I recorded as many as eighteen ancient and distinct occupation layers in some areas, each separated by a sterile layer of river sand/silt, and each documenting a unique chapter of First Nations' use and occupation. Living floors in some areas even appeared to capture the outlines of people where they kneeled to make stone tools 2,300 years ago (feature "a" in living floor plan).

Excavations at Bullion City in Kluane National Park presented a very different, but almost as unique, set of circumstances. An early-1900s post-Klondike gold-rush site virtually untouched after it was rapidly abandoned in 1904 allowed me to explore how various abandonment behaviours leave contrasting archaeological signatures, and what social contexts facilitate the formation of ethnic group identity. The former led me to conclude that much of the spatial distribution of artifacts in archaeological sites may not be the result of everyday behaviours and activities, but abandonment processes, which may have little to do with what went on during major periods of occupation.

Stratigraphic profile photo of 18 ancient living surfaces at Peace Point, spanning 2,400 years

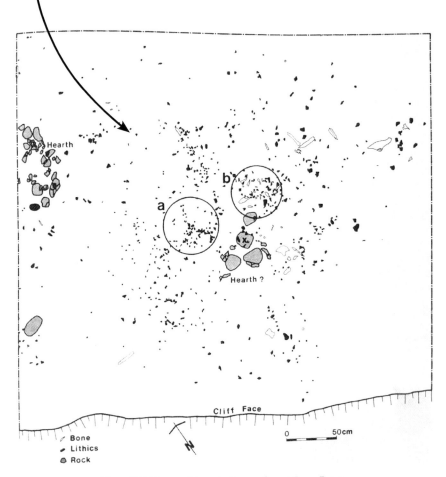

Plan of 2300 year-old occupation surface at Peace Point.

Bullion Creek in 1903-04 was inundated with hundreds of would-be gold miners (aka *Cheechakos* in the local dialect), some newer than others. The latest arrivals and those who came up with the Klondike gold rush eight years prior, however, were not that much different socially or culturally. Nevertheless, the archaeological signatures of the latter—most saliently the packed arrangement and stylistic similarities of their dwellings compared to those of the former—indicated that they quickly adopted the cultural mystic and niche vacated by a few hundred pre-Klondike Yukon prospectors (aka *Sourdoughs*) who had been overwhelmed and displaced by thousands of Cheechakos a few years earlier. These investigations helped me to better understand how ethnic groups form and in what contexts. Specifically, ethnic group identity and stereotyping do not develop in isolation, but in situations of intergroup interaction where stylistic aspects of material culture are often enlisted to create and accentuate cultural differences. This, in turn, led me to advance alternative explanations for the emergence of new stylistic traits in archaeological contexts as diverse as the famous Upper Palaeolithic cave site of Altamira in Spain and recently abandoned !Kung bushmen sites in the central Kalahari.

My time with Parks Canada also allowed me to complete a master's thesis, and to publish a number of academic articles as well as my first book.[8] It even attracted the attention of the Canadian Broadcasting Corporation, where, for a few brief years, I was the resident archaeologist for CBC's popular Saturday morning program, *Basic Black*. Among other topics, Arthur Black interviewed me about my excavation of a three-hole privy associated with Bullion City's saloon. What could an archaeologist conceivably learn from the contents of an early twentieth-century Yukon gold rush three-holer? While the possibilities might seem elusive or endless, depending on one's perspective, part of me wanted to know how much local, as opposed to imported, food Bullion City's inhabitants were consuming. I must also confess that I also secretly wanted to know how Parks staff in Ottawa would react to my request to analyze the contents of an eighty-year-old privy. Perhaps not surprisingly, the package I had carefully wrapped and sent off was returned to me a month or so later unopened with a rather terse covering letter.

My employment with Parks was never going to be long-term. I was not a lifer. Under new management, archaeology division staff at the regional office in Winnipeg soon grew tired of my act. I had learned how to get things done within a bureaucracy of stifling ineptitude. The enmity was mutual, so in early in 1983 I accepted the only job available. By spring, my wife (Kathryn), two toddlers (Saara and Benjamin), and I had settled in Yellowknife, where I assumed the position of historic archaeologist for the Northwest Territories at the Prince of Wales Northern Heritage Centre. The two-year position was created to develop a

---

8   M. Stevenson (1986). *Window on the Past: Archaeological Assessment of the Peace Point Site, Wood Buffalo National Park, Alberta.* Studies in Archaeology, Architecture and History, Parks Canada.

management plan for historic archaeological sites in the NWT, which at that time included Nunavut—an area the size of some continents. But *Job One* was to work with Inuit from Pangnirtung to record and assess historic Inuit settlements in Cumberland Sound where local hunters joined with British and American whalers during the nineteenth century to hunt bowhead whales. You see, Pang's traditional sealing economy had just collapsed owing to the impacts of the anti-sealing lobby. Unable to feed their families, Pang's hunters were desperately looking for alternative ways—including developing their former settlements as tourist attractions—to generate income to keep up the hunt.

This was to be my first meaningful experience working with, and for, an Indigenous people. Sure, I had worked with First Nation peoples on archaeological digs in Kluane, Wood Buffalo, and southcentral BC. But this was the first time where the investigations I was about to undertake had the potential to make a real difference in Indigenous lives. It was also the first time where Indigenous peoples called the shots and everything I was charged with doing—indeed, my very survival—was dependent on Inuit guides, hunters, elders, and assistants.

It was a cold, blustery day in August of 1983 when July (Papatsie), Joavee (Alivaktuk), his younger brother Koni, and I first arrived at Kekerten (aka Qikirtan or Qikirtat) in Cumberland Sound. Fortuitously, my arrival coincided almost to the day with the centenary of Franz Boas' arrival here to conduct his pioneering fieldwork in anthropology. You see, Boas is known as the father of American anthropology, and it was honour just to walk on the same ground and to work with the descendants of the people he lived with one hundred years later. Kekerten was one of two major shore-based whaling stations in Canada's eastern Arctic during the nineteenth century, and thus a magnet for foreign interlopers. More Inuit settlements than industrial whale-processing sites, Kekerten and Blacklead Island (Umanaqjuaq) across the Sound were the birthplaces of Pangnirtung's most senior elders at the time. While all *Pangnirtarmiut* have a deep connection to either or both historic settlements, Kekerten was much closer to Pang, and thus determined by local and territorial officials—over objections by some Parks Canada historians—to be the better candidate for historic park development. But first, it needed to be assessed by an archaeologist.

Kekerten was at once breathtaking and overwhelmingly intimidating. The remains of scores of late-nineteenth and early twentieth-century Inuit sod/whalebone/rock houses, the foundations of Scottish and American whaling station buildings, a whalers' graveyard, blubber rendering pots and vats, and countless whaling era Inuit artifacts lay stretched out before our eyes. Most intriguing of all were dozens of Inuit cask and rifle box burials surrounding the settlement—many broken apart, with their skeletal contents migrating slowly downhill toward the shoreline. Surely, a physical anthropologist would be needed to repatriate these remains back to their original locations—the latter eventually becoming the subject of Dr. Ann Keenlyside's doctoral dissertation. Some of these burials spoke to us from the grave even after a century or so. One in particular told the story of a prominent Inuit hunter/shaman who had survived a polar bear attack only to be keel-hauled to death sometime later by a whaling captain.

Mapping and documenting the history of Kekerten's features were high priorities. In subsequent seasons, excavating the remains of Inuit houses (*qammat*), exposing the foundations of Kekerten's British and American station buildings, and developing interpretive products for historic park development consumed my days and invaded my sleep as I began to dream in *Inuktitut*. Clearly, I was going through some sort of existential catharsis. However, the highlight—indeed the pinnacle—of my career as an archaeologist was working with Inuit elders to document their history and that of Kekerten, Umanaqjuaq, and other Inuit settlements across Cumberland Sound. As an archaeologist, I was incredibly fortunate to interview the very people who once occupied the houses I was documenting and excavating. How many archaeologists ever get that opportunity? In particular, I spent countless hours with Meeka Mike, interviewing Etuangat Aksayuk and Qatsuq Evic.

In the years to follow, every time I returned to Pang, Etuangat and I were inseparable. I think he initially took me under his wing because he felt sorry for me. Years later, Etuangat confided in me that when he thinks of *Qallunaat* (Caucasian people), he thinks of me. I took this as a compliment. Born at Kekerten at the turn of the century, Etuangat was one of the last Inuit whalers to have participated in the eastern Arctic bowhead whale fishery. Yet he was *Inumaarit* (a real Inuk) all the way and a treasure trove of Inuit knowledge and culture. Having been raised at Kekerten, Etuangat also knew everything about the settlement, its history, who lived where, how they were related, and what activities consumed their days in each of the six Inuit seasons. During the latter stages of interpretive development at Kekerten Historic Park and the Angmarlik Cultural Centre in Pangnirtung, Etuangat and I reconstructed Inuit whalebone houses and created signage and artifact displays that would best describe Inuit life during last decades of the whaling era.

Etuangat was doubly fortunate at an early age when Kekerten's leader, Angmarlik, took him under his wing, teaching him to be a harpooner aboard one of Kekerten's whaleboats and giving him a female puppy from the lead of his dog team. You see, Angmarlik's dogs were no ordinary dogs. After years of careful breeding the half-dozen or so dogs that comprised Angmarlik's dog team—far fewer than most hunters—were the biggest, fastest, and *baddest* anywhere. They were the *Ferraris* of the dog world, a fact I learned when I asked Etuangat and Qatsuq why there was a bewilderingly large empty space between Angmarlik's *qammaq* at the back of the settlement and Kekerten's shoreline. Apparently, every time Angmarlik hitched his dog team up to his sled to go hunting, his dogs would bolt uncontrollably, trampling everything in their path including tents, houses, other dogs, and small children. Angmarlik was unequivocally the best hunter in Cumberland Sound and his dogs knew that they were soon going to eat, and eat well. Etuangat singled out Angmarlik's gift as the reason for his decades-long career as the dog team driver for the only hospital on Baffin Island—a key consideration in Etuangat being awarded one of Canada's highest civilian honours, the *Order of Canada*, months before his passing in 1995.

Etuangat Aksayuk, Pangnirtung, Nunavut, 1989 (original photo by J. Riley)

Time spent with Qatsuq, Angmarlik's daughter, provided a more nuanced perspective on Inuit domestic life during the late whaling period. Women were the rulers of the household and essential to the survival of its members. If a woman was the partner of a productive hunter, she would often bring in a younger woman to help with chores—a custom that fuelled the ire of later missionaries. Born in 1896 to Ashivak and Angmarlik, Qatsuq witnessed Etuangat's birth several years later.

As the new century approached life had become increasingly difficult for the Cumberland Sound Inuit. Decades of commercial whaling had decimated the bowhead population. Meanwhile, baleen (aka whalebone) and whale oil were being replaced worldwide by petroleum-based products. The days when hundreds of British and American whalers overwintered in the Sound were over. Only rarely would a supply ship reach the whaling stations in consecutive years. As Inuit elders raised during the height of the bowhead fishery passed away, the Cumberland Sound Inuit gradually lost their fluency in *Qallunnatitut*.

Against this backdrop a new type of foreign interloper set up shop at Umanaqjuaq. Almost immediately, Inuit women across the Sound began to embrace the new religion brought by Anglican missionaries in 1894. Men, however, rejected it, creating a palpable rift in Inuit gender relations and domestic life. When asked what the significance was of an additional room in Angmarlik's and Ashivak's *qammaq* (house), Etuangat was adamant that it was because Angmarlik was *cut-off* for refusing to accept Christianity. Qatsuq, however, ventured that it was because of all the skins that needed to be processed and made into clothing. The cause of this calamitous fissure in Inuit households was apparently the feast of *Sedna* (the mother to all sea mammals), where the chief shaman (*qailertitung*) presided over the ritual exchange of spouses. Seizing the moment, Ashivak and the women of Kekerten, in a particularly symbolic gesture, made the ceremonial costume of the *qailertitung* and cast it and the old religious order into the sea:

> *My mother got some women together to make caribou clothes that . . . were at least two times as big as the ones Eskimos wore . . . maybe bigger than anybody could use on earth. They made everything, the parkas, the kamiks [boots], the mittens, the pants, in fact, the whole works. After they finished, everything was thrown into the water. . . so that they could . . . no longer be followers of this god.*[9]

It was an act of sacrilege—in traditional Inuit religious ideology the remains of land and sea mammals must never come into contact for fear of offending Sedna—akin to evangelicals abandoning Christian values to follow a deranged malevolent demagogue. Even so, most *Qikirtarmiut* and *Umanaqjuarmiut* men in the years to follow came to adopt a syncretic religion that fused elements of the old and new belief systems. It is a matter of conjecture whether Christianity improved the lives of the Cumberland Sound Inuit. Nonetheless, things surely would have been different had the good reverend (E. J. Peck) and his companions packed their bags and sailed for home after their church—the first built in Canada's eastern Arctic—being made of seal skins, was eaten by a pack of ravenous sled dogs. The *Umanaqjuarmiut* could have only sat back and scratched their heads in wonder.

My two years as the historic archaeologist for the NWT came to an abrupt end in 1985, without my contract being renewed. Clearly, a pattern was emerging and I was forced to face the hard truth: I was not government material! Of course, I knew this from the start, but figured that no one would notice or care. After all, this was the Northwest Territories. For the next two years, I continued to work under contract with Etuangat, Pang's elders, the Pangnirtung Tourism Committee, and GNWT personnel (Dave Monteith and Gary Magee) developing Kekerten Historic Park and the Angmarlik Cultural Centre in

---

[9] K. Evic (1976). Things That We Used to do in the Old Days that no Longer Exist. In *Stories from Pangnirtung. pp. 78-89*, Hurtig Pub.

Pangnirtung as tourist attractions. These projects, however, had less to do with archaeology than interpreting the historic and contemporary realities of the *Pangnirtarmiut* for local and visitor consumption, education, and edification.

Becoming an Anthropologist

As my education by Inuit continued, I became more fascinated with their culture and society and how they had changed and persevered under the juggernaut of acculturative forces and agents that descended upon them. After working with and for an Indigenous community as welcoming and warm as the *Pangnirtarmiut*, *digging up shit* and making up stories about it was beginning to wear thin.

I was earning my stripes as an anthropologist. I had always felt something was amiss when excavating archaeological sites produced by the ancestors of present-day Indigenous Canadians. There seemed to be little or no accountability to the contemporary descendants of the people who produced the sites and lived the history I was investigating. Working with Indigenous peoples was definitely more challenging, but eminently more rewarding and meaningful. In subsequent years, I still kept my hand in archaeology, occasionally lamenting—but then only briefly—my decision not to commit fully my career to that discipline. Artifacts, unlike people, don't talk back. Think Meeka Kilabuk!

It was around this time that I discovered that the *Pangnirtarmiut* had been referring to me as *qammarminiqtiatit* (someone who researches or plays around with old houses). This was not really a term of endearment—that would come later—but Inuit ethos. Why would anybody want to dig around old houses? Aren't there better things that a man could be doing, like hunting? In the following years, my Inuktitut name went through additional iterations. Within a year or two, I became known as Maakusi (Inuktitut for Marc).[10] An old Inuit whaler, Maakusi Pitsulak, had just passed and it was common for newborns and sometimes even new arrivals to the community to be given the name of the recently deceased. As I spent more time with Inuit elders and began to pick up more of the language my name morphed into Maakusi Inuqsaq, lit. "*Marc, who has the potential to become an Inuk*" (i.e., a person). Inuit hunters, elders, and translators had been trying to teach me adult speak, and even though I was a slow learner, I think they appreciated my effort. The name didn't stick, however, and my final moniker became, Maakusi Inuminniq, lit. "*Marc, who used to be a person.*" You see, despite their best efforts to convert me, the *Pangnirtarmiut* eventually resigned themselves to the fact that I was never going to become one of them. Yet, because I apparently exhibited some quirks of a crusty, old Inuit hunter, I must have

---

10   Inuit eventually adopted biblical names such as Mark, Matthew, Luke, and John, which became Maakusi, Maatusie, Lukasie and Joanasie, and so on.

been one in a former life. You see, traditional Inuit (*Inumarrit*) believe in reincarnation of the soul. The suffix, *minniq,* translates roughly as *used to be* as in *tuqturminniq* (i.e., caribou meat, or food that used to be a caribou). My naming process, of course, evolved in typically Inuit fashion with a great deal of good-natured ribbing and laughter.

In 1987 I decided to leave Yellowknife for Edmonton to pursue a PhD in anthropology at the University of Alberta, a move I had been contemplating for several years. It was either now or never. With Cliff Hickey as my supervisor, and Milton Freeman, Gurston Dacks, Nelson Graburn, and Michael Asch—the son of Folkways Records founder, Moses Asch—riding shotgun, I could not have found a better advisory committee, anywhere, period. Cliff, in particular, went far beyond the normal duties of a thesis advisor. Each time I submitted a chapter of my dissertation, he handed it back to me the next day, heavily edited with marginal notations, with but one exception. A particularly thick and dense chapter loaded with kinship diagrams delayed Cliff for several months as he painstakingly traced for consistency and accuracy several hundred named individuals in these charts as they moved through time and space across Cumberland Sound.

There was no doubt in my mind as to what my dissertation research would be about: Cumberland Sound Inuit social and cultural change as a consequence of their contact with British and American whalers. I was especially intrigued by the hierarchical social organization of the *Qikirtarmiut* during and after the commercial whaling period. I found this remarkable for a society where social, political, and economic relationships were supposed to be egalitarian, or at least so I thought. While most *Qikirtarmiut* were well enough off, there was also social stratification in the camps they occupied after abandoning Kekerten—a trait that has continued into recent times.

Nowhere did this reveal itself more vividly than during an unplanned whale hunt in Pangnirtung Fiord in 1989. In mid-summer of that year, I was conducting an inventory and assessment of Pang's historic HBC and mission buildings when the hamlet came alive in a flurry of frenzied activity as scores of men sprinted toward their boats on the beach. A pod of forty or so narwhal had been spotted, and all available men in the community (including myself) jumped into boats in hot pursuit. What followed was something that I was fortunate to escape unscathed. Although, in retrospect, I suspect that there was a much greater degree of organization to this hunt than I was able to comprehend at the time. Nearly a hundred men, half of them with rifles, in twenty or more boats, drove the pod toward the head of the fiord. Shots rang out from every direction as boats sped past our bow and stern. After a period of about forty minutes or so, we spotted several boats on a beach. Here, two whales had been hauled ashore and a dozen or so hunters were busily cutting *maqtaaq* off them, helping themselves to small pieces of the delicacy in the process.

But this scene was in striking contrast to the apparent chaos that had just transpired. There was order and structure to the events unfolding before my eyes. This was *anthropology in action*. On the periphery of the activity, teenage boys, passive and observant, watched the flensing operations while gorging on *maqtaaq*. Meanwhile their fathers, older brothers, and uncles cut off slabs of this delicacy and transported them to the boats. The job of distributing the whales, however, was reserved only for the boat owners. Yet in the midst of the flensing a hunter with a captain's hat, and one of the eldest men on the hunt, freely helped himself to the choicest parts of both whales (i.e., the flukes, flippers, and cheeks). This man was probably not the individual who'd shot the whales, although who could tell? Nor was he the richest or most influential man on the hunt; there were younger men on the hunt who held better jobs and had more political acumen on the hamlet council. He was simply the eldest and no hunter had more *issuma* (thoughtfulness) and life experience. Here, in the increasingly contradictory and changing world in which the *Pangnirtarmiut* found themselves, traditional productive relationships and social order were being acted out and reaffirmed through the hunt.

A few years earlier, I had proposed in an extremely perfunctory paper that the social stratification I was witnessing was formalized into a class system and the direct result of participation with British and American whalers in the commercial whale fishery. That I could have been so naive amazes me now.

During my research with Pang's elders, I gradually came to understand that post-commercial whaling period camps of the *Umanaqjuarmiut* on the southwest side of Cumberland Sound did not emphasize leadership and followership to the extent that *Qikirtarmiut* camps did on the northeast side of the Sound. Indeed, almost every feature of social organization—from kinship ties, to marriage arrangements, to local group stability, to individual mobility, to territoriality, to hunting partnerships and strategies—was different. But how could this be when the two groups lived so close to each other and intermarried?

Weeks before accompanying Pang's elders around the Sound to record the social history of their former camps, I re-read David Damas' seminal work, *Iglulingmiut Kinship and Local Groupings* . . . .[11] I had become intrigued with the two organizing principles of Inuit group formation and social relations about which he wrote. I was convinced that *ungayuq* (closeness or affection) and *naaluqtuq* (respect-obedience) possessed considerable explanatory power and possibly held the key to understanding Inuit social organization, both in Cumberland Sound and elsewhere across the Canadian Arctic. Could the structural differences I was observing between the *Qikirtarmiut* and *Umanaqjuarmiut* best be explained, respectively, with reference to *naaluqtuq* and *ungayuq*? In particular, these

---

11 D. Damas (1963). *Iglulingmiut Kinship and Local Groupings: A Structural Approach*. National Museum of Canada Bulletin 196, Ottawa.

concepts appeared to offer a far more credible explanation for the variety of Inuit social formations throughout Arctic Canada than the heavy-handed environmental determinism that has dominated Arctic anthropology and archaeology for decades.

Our culture's fascination with the Inuit has generated a body of literature that distinguishes them as one of the most thoroughly studied Indigenous peoples in the world. As one student of Inuit culture put it, *"rarely has so much been written by so many about so few."*[12] Yet the search for principles of Inuit group formation and social structure has been a frustrating quest for anthropologists. This, in turn, has left many to conclude that the environment must somehow be the ultimate architect of Inuit society. It is absurd to think that the environment does not play a role in shaping Inuit social organization. Nevertheless, the structure of socioeconomic relationships—who marries whom, who hunts with whom, how products of the hunt are shared, etc.—is not as preordained by environmental factors as many anthropologists have supposed.

It became clear to me that during the post-commercial whaling era in Cumberland Sound the *Qikirtarmiut* were governed largely by hierarchical directives (*naalautuq*), while the *Umanaqjuarmiut* manifested egalitarian relationships (*ungayuq*). This realization prompted me to re-examine the late prehistory of the Sound and develop a more nuanced understanding of the three most studied Inuit groups in Canada's central Arctic. Whereas the Iglulingmiut and Netslingmiut were found to be embellishments of *naaluqtuq* and *ungayuq*, respectively, the Copper Inuit were seen to be the antithesis or systemic rejection of both systems. In turn, the implications of these findings allowed me to advance an alternative model of Canadian Arctic prehistory, offer new insights into kinship theory, and advance proposals for the political development of the soon-to-be created territory of Nunavut. Later published as a book,[13] my thesis received a lukewarm reception at best, reminiscent of a ten-point dive at the summer Olympics—*it hardly caused a ripple*.[14] However, if it has accomplished anything it's that we can no longer stereotype and diminish the humanity of the Inuit—or any other Indigenous people for that matter—by explaining away their historical, social, and cultural similarities and differences on environmental factors.

After concluding my doctoral research I continued to consult throughout the 1990s with various regional, national, and international Inuit organizations, as well as federal and territorial commissions. The majority of my time, however, was consumed with undertaking policy research and analysis on a variety of subjects having to do with Indigenous

---

12   C. C. Hughes (1963). Review of James W. Stone's Point Hope, An Eskimo Village in Transition. *American Anthropologist* (65:452-54).

13   M. Stevenson (1997). *Inuit, Whalers and Cultural Persistence: Structure in Cumberland Sound and Central Inuit Social Organization.* Oxford University Press, Toronto.

14   Thanks to Jim Webb for sharing this expression.

governance, traditional economies, and resource use. I also kept my hand in archaeology, undertaking contracts with the Alberta government, and yes Parks Canada. Working under contract with Parks in Yellowknife was entirely different from being an employee and almost restored my faith in the organization—almost! The rest of the decade was spent assisting Indigenous communities to document their traditional knowledge and land-use patterns, and assessing the impacts of industrial resource extraction on their lands, cultures, and economies.

Just before the turn of the millennium, I accepted a ten-year position as aboriginal program manager with Sustainable Forest Management Network at the University of Alberta. At the end of my tenure—yes, I had managed to make it the full ten years, barely—the Aboriginal program's budget accounted for 30 percent of the SFMN's annual seven-million dollar budget. We had also brought together dozens of First Nations with university researchers across Canada to develop and undertake research on forest and resource development issues of importance to their communities. The results of some of this research were published in two volumes from CCI Press.[15] Although the SFMN kept me busy for much of the time, archaeology with First Nations and Métis organizations kept pulling me back. Once an archaeologist, always an archaeologist, I guess. Additionally, every so often, I would undertake planning and policy development, research, and analyses with a range of Indigenous clients, while managing to publish a number of scholarly articles on *wildlife co-management* and Indigenous ecological knowledge.

After my time with the SFMN, my consulting career went into overdrive. Traditional land-use studies (particularly with the Dene Tha' First Nation), socioeconomic impact assessments, land-use planning, and environmental policy development with a variety of Treaty 6 and 8 First Nations and Tribal Councils in Alberta, left little time for anything else. Added to my ever expanding workload was serving as the Treaty 6 appointee on the Lower Athabasca Regional Advisory Council—an Alberta government-funded committee charged with producing a fifty-year land-use plan for Alberta's mineable tar sands and surrounding area. I had been the North Slave Métis Alliance's appointee on the Independent Environmental Monitoring Agency for the BHP *Ekati Diamond* mine, but this was different.

My experiences with Inuit, Dene, Cree, and Métis communities in their entanglements with industry, government, and other stalwarts of my culture have sharpened my view of the world in which Indigenous Canadians are forced to live and defend their rights. Specifically, since becoming an anthropologist, the plethora of systemic barriers that our

---

15   M. Stevenson and D. Natcher (2009) (eds.). *Changing the Culture of Forestry in Canada: Building Effective Institutions for Aboriginal Engagement in Sustainable Forest Management*. CCI Press. M. Stevenson and D. Natcher (2010) (eds.). *Planning Co-Existence: Aboriginal Issues in Forest and Land Use Planning*. CCI Press.

First Peoples confront when attempting to protect their lands and cultures in the face of resource development and other challenges have become permanently etched on my radar screen. In varying detail, some of the more pivotal moments and learning opportunities that Indigenous Canadians'—and those who engage them—allowed me to experience follow.

CHAPTER 3

Where Have all the Whales and Polar Bears Gone?

Dez Damn Buttons!

ANTICIPATING A RECORD RUN OF KING (AKA CHINOOK OR SPRING) SALMON, MARGE HAD just finished several days of hard work repairing fishing weirs and building drying racks at Klukshu fishing village, southwest Yukon, when she heard a knock on her cabin's door. It was a young man wanting to speak with Marge about her previous winter's trapping activities in the Dezadeash River Valley, Kluane National Park, Yukon Territory.

This young man, you see, was researching Arctic ground squirrel ecology and behaviour for his PhD dissertation, and this was his last year of fieldwork. In previous seasons he had live-trapped, tagged, and released hundreds of ground squirrels in the valley without incident. As one might expect, he had gotten to know many of his research subjects intimately. And while he was eagerly looking forward to concluding his field research, it was not without a sense of melancholy. However, when the young biologist arrived in the river valley he was shocked and dismayed to find a lifeless flood plain overrun by tumbleweeds where his ground squirrel colony once thrived. It must have reminded him of a parched landscape out of an old Spaghetti Western.

The budding scientist's subsequent line of questioning of Park personnel over the next few days led him to Marge Jackson—an esteemed Southern Tutchone elder, trapper/fisher, and member of the Champagne-Aishihik First Nation. Years of field research must have evaporated in front of his eyes as Marge pulled open a drawer full of small marked tags, exclaiming, *"Oh yeah, dez damn buttons! I couldn't figure what dey were for! But kept em anyways, just in case."*

Throughout the 1990s and well into the first decade of this century, I continued to develop traditional ecological knowledge research protocols for a variety of Indigenous and multi-stakeholder co-management boards. Most notable among them were the Nunavut Wildlife Management Board, Mackenzie Valley Environmental Impact Review Board, and Cumulative Environmental Management Association (for Alberta's mineable tar sands). I also designed, and in some cases undertook, traditional ecological knowledge studies for both local and regional Inuit hunter-trapper organizations. Some of these, as well as a few I had little or nothing to do with, warrant consideration here, if only to highlight the ever-widening gap between holders of Indigenous knowledge and those educated and cultured in the Western scientific tradition. The story Marge Jackson told me in the summer of 1980 was just a prelude of things to come.

Bear-ly Credible

One project proposal, a Nunavut-wide Inuit knowledge study of polar bear (*nanuit*) that I designed for and with the three regional hunter and trappers organizations in Nunavut—Qikiqtaaluq Wildlife Board, Keewatin Wildlife Federation, and Kitikmeot Hunters' and Trappers' Association—was especially unforgettable. But not for its success. Inuit hunters across Nunavut had grown increasingly upset with the *polar bear management* system being implemented by the Nunavut Wildlife Management Board on the advice of Canada's Polar Bear Technical Committee. Specifically, Inuit felt that the thirteen subpopulations of polar bear identified by scientists did not reflect Inuit experience or reality. Moreover, too many large, older males were being killed under the current management system, potentially compromising the survival capability and reproductive capacity of local *nanuit* populations. At the same time, Inuit hunters were upset over the virtual disregard of their knowledge in setting *total allowable harvests* and other polar bear regulations. After a series of meetings and follow-up consultations with the three regional organizations, I produced a proposal and submitted it with their blessing to the NWMB and PBTC.

The response was immediate and came in the form of a rather curt email from a Dr. Ian Stirling informing me that the PBTC had already considered Inuit traditional knowledge and no more was needed to inform its work. Clearly, whatever Inuit knowledge had been considered by this committee of scientists was not sufficient or of the kind and quality to appease Inuit hunters.

The controversy over the hunting of adult males of various mammal species in Nunavut is not limited to polar bears or beluga. Inuit hunters from Resolute Bay and Grise Fiord, for example, know that Peary caribou numbers in the High Arctic fluctuate dramatically over extended periods of time. They also know that the survival of the herds depends upon maintaining the social structure of small groups in winter whereby hunting is opportunistic and does not select on the basis of age or sex. This practice is in stark contrast to the management approach advocated by scientists and conservation bureaucrats, which seeks to *harvest* only large males while prohibiting the hunting of females and immature animals. Conversely, Inuit hunters know that the selective hunting of large males not only jeopardizes the breeding success of herds, but actually results in the accelerated death of other herd members owing to the loss of dominant males, which defend and lead the herds. Nonetheless, in 2011, Peary caribou were listed as *endangered* under the *Species at Risk Act*. In recent years, Inuit hunters in the High Arctic have been forced to protect their rights and interests by participating in a *co-management* regime that seeks to establish *management units* and *total allowable harvests* for each community.

Where Have All the Whales Gone? Part 2

Another Arctic species that has been a source of much controversy is the bowhead whale (*arqviq*). The bowhead is an amazing animal. Much longer than a Greyhound bus and weighing up to a hundred tons, the bowhead can live well beyond 200 years—making it the longest-living mammal on earth. Indeed, over the past few decades ancient harpoons of prehistoric origin have been found in large bowheads landed by Alaska's Inupiat hunters.

Throughout the eighteenth and nineteenth centuries the bowhead provided the industrial world with whale oil for heat and light and whalebone, the forerunner of petroleum-based plastics. Decades of commercial whaling by British and American whalers in Baffin Bay and Hudson Bay, however, brought the eastern Arctic bowhead perilously close to extinction.

I was not directly involved in the implementation of the Inuit Bowhead Knowledge Study—a traditional knowledge research initiative mandated by the Nunavut Land Claim Agreement in advance of setting quotas to allow Inuit to once again hunt bowhead, much as their ancestors had done for centuries. Even so, I followed closely the implementation of this study and other federal and territorial management decisions related to the bowhead.

For decades, the eastern Arctic bowhead whale was considered by Canada's wildlife conservation bureaucracy to be among the most endangered of all Arctic species. Estimated to have numbered more than 11,000 prior to the onset of commercial whaling in the 1820s, the eastern Arctic bowhead population was determined by biologists in the 1970s to be several hundred at most, and possibly *"less than a hundred."*[16] Subsequently, in 1979 the eastern Arctic bowhead was officially listed as *endangered* and Inuit were prohibited from hunting the animal.

With the bowhead now off-limits to Inuit hunters, interest and enthusiasm in observing, gathering information about, and passing on knowledge of this animal waned. Still, in the hope that one day they might be allowed to hunt bowhead again, a few hunters continued to observe its behaviours and distributions. One of these, Adamee Veevee of Pangnirtung, spent several weeks each spring during the 1970s and 1980s at Cumberland

---

16   R. A. Davis and W. R. Koski (1980). Recent Observations of Bowhead Whales in the Eastern Canadian High Arctic. *Report of the International Whaling Commission* (30):439-444.

Sound's floe edge, monitoring bowhead and recording his observations. Every spring from his lookout near the floe edge, Adamee observed not only more bowhead, but larger groups of whales with more young ones—a trend, as I later discovered, anticipated by the Hudson Bay Company's post journals from decades earlier.

Inuit hunters across Nunavut have asserted for years that bowheads were far more numerous than what Canada's federal fisheries department was willing to admit. In fact, by the 1990s bowheads had become so plentiful in eastern Arctic waters that they had become navigation hazards for hunters from at least seven Nunavut communities. Indeed, during the summer of 1995 a bowhead surfaced on and capsized a boat of American tourists in Isabella Bay near Clyde River, Baffin Island, leaving four dead—only the Inuit guide survived. Yet DFO continued to dismiss Inuit claims as anecdotal and decreed that they could only hunt one whale every thirteen years from the Davis Strait-Baffin Bay *stock*, and one every three years from the Hudson Bay-Foxe Basin *stock*.

But Inuit fought back. With the creation of the new territory of Nunavut just around the corner, and under license from obstinate DFO officials, Nunavut's Inuit resumed in 1996 a limited hunt of one to three bowheads annually. In retaliation, the United States protested, issuing threats to ban the import of Canadian fish products. Meanwhile, the bowhead knowledge study was documenting what Inuit knew all along—the bowhead had made a remarkable comeback throughout eastern Arctic waters.

Even so, DFO's position remained steadfast until the mid-2000s, when scientific surveys and analyses estimated that 14,400 bowheads now inhabited eastern Arctic waters as a single *stock*. In a matter of a few years, Nunavut's bowhead merged into one breeding population and exploded from a couple of hundred animals to over 14,000—a miracle unheard of for one of the largest, slowest-reproducing, and longest-living animals on earth. Technically, whale biologists are 95 percent sure that the population is somewhere between 4,800 and 43,000 animals—such is the accuracy of whale population estimates based on *Science*. With egg on its face, the Fisheries department was forced to concede that the eastern Arctic bowhead was no longer *endangered*, and that up to twelve whales could be hunted sustainably each year without consequence. More recent aerial surveys in 2013 suggested that the population can support an annual loss of fifty-two whales from all sources of human-caused mortality (e.g., hunting, net entanglements, ship collisions, etc.). Still, some whale biologists continue to maintain that Canada is violating international whaling agreements and that Inuit knowledge *"cannot replace science in evaluating a species status and prescribing management plans."*[17] Right!

Pass the Kool-Aid!

---

17 K. J. Finley (2001). Natural History and Conservation of the Greenland Whale, or Bowhead, in the Northwest Atlantic. *Arctic* 54(1):55-76.

Nunavut's annual bowhead hunts continue to this day in the face of ongoing condemnation from animal rights groups and foreign governments.

If the eastern Arctic bowhead controversy sounds familiar, it is because it is. Indeed, it is almost a repeat of what happened in Alaska in the 1970s. Based on government estimates that there were only 1,300 bowheads left in western Arctic waters—down from a pre-commercial whaling population of 10,000 or more—and under pressure from the International Whaling Commission, the USA outlawed the Inupiat bowhead hunt. But whaling captains who possessed generations of knowledge about the bowhead knew that the government was in error. Subsequently, they hired Western-trained scientists with new technology to corroborate their experiential knowledge. It was soon demonstrated that bowheads were far more numerous than government scientists had previously thought, and subsistence whaling was allowed to continue over the objection of anti-whaling organizations.

Another example where *Science*, public opinion, and Indigenous rights are embroiled in controversy concerns the Pacific grey whale. Countless generations of Nuu-chah-nulth on the northwest coast of North America were specialized whale hunters. Commercial whaling in the late-nineteenth and early twentieth centuries nearly exterminated the grey whale from coastal waters, however. In recent decades Indigenous whaling groups in the Northwest have witnessed a dramatic increase in grey whale numbers, while scientific surveys suggest that the population has recovered to near pre-exploitation levels of 20,000 or more. Even so, the Makah, a Nuu-chal-nuth tribe in Washington State, continue to fight public pressure and anti-whaling activists to defend their rights to hunt whales.

The International Whaling Commission has set an annual *total allowable harvest* of 140 for the Pacific grey whale, four of which have been allocated to the Makah. Nevertheless, with the exception of a single whale killed in 1999—the first whale hunt in seventy years—the Makah have been prevented from hunting grey whales by a series of legal court challenges brought by animal rights organizations. Even so, in protest and without the sanction of tribal authorities, several Makah hunters killed a grey whale in 2007, after which they were indicted.

Since 2008, the International Union for the Conservation of Nature has viewed the grey whale as being of virtually no concern from a conservation perspective. However, scientists have now determined that grey whales inhabiting northwest Pacific waters year-round may be a separate subpopulation of several hundred individuals—i.e., those most vulnerable to human activity—distinct from the much larger population that migrates from Mexico to Alaska waters each year. Consequently, the Pacific Northwest subpopulation has been listed as *endangered* by the US government's National Marine Fisheries Service.

Some years ago my friend, Tom Mexsis Happynook—hereditary Nuu-chah-nulth whaling chief, former BC Treaty commissioner, and founding chair of the World Council of Whalers—explained to me the pivotal role whales played in Maa-nulth society. I was amazed at how deep and profound his knowledge and respect were for his people and the whales (grey and humpback) upon which they have depended for centuries.

The Nuu-chah-nulth live a concept called *hahuulthii* (aka *haholthe*). Far more than a land base or a territory occupied and governed by Nuu-chah-nulth peoples, *hahuulthii* is what Mexsis calls a "*big word.*" As Mexsis's son, Tommy, remarked in his master's thesis in anthropology,[18]

> *Words like "hahuulthii" cannot really be translated into English accurately or easily. Unfortunately, in the last several decades, it appears that these words have been simplified, in both their use and translation, possibly for the purposes of treaty negotiations.*

Nevertheless, I understand *hahuulthii* to encompass Nuu-chah-nulth rules, laws, and norms for living sustainably and in harmony with all life forms within the nation's traditional land base. *Hahuulthii* includes not just resource use rights, but specific rights, obligations, and responsibilities that whaling chiefs (*hawit*) play an essential role in fulfilling. After a successful hunt, *hawit* would oversee the distribution of the whale. It was their responsibility to ensure that each family received those parts of the whale to which they were entitled. In so doing, societal obligations were fulfilled and prevailing socio-political relationships were maintained. But whales meant so much more to the Nuu-chah-nulth.

As a hereditary Nuu-chah-nulth whaling chief, Mexsis is expected to pass on his values, wisdom, and knowledge to his eldest son, a responsibility he has fulfilled in spades:

> *In the Nuu-chah-nulth language (Hishuk Tsawalk), hahuulthii literally translates as "the rights of chieftainship." . . . This definition is important in understanding the way that* [my] *people see the world, and implies ownership, but not in the same way that ownership is understood in Canada. Rather, it provides the many places and resources that a hawit needs to serve his people. The hawit has a responsibility and obligation to respect and take care of his hahuutlthii and provide for his people and family.*
>
> *. . . When a whale was being distributed among the people, certain cuts belonged to certain families and you had to be very careful to not cut into another family's piece. In this sense the whale represented the hahuulthii and had to be distributed accordingly. In cases of overlapping territory, or if a whale pulled you into another tribe's territory, then that whale becomes the property of the hawit whose hauulthii you are in . . . who* [in turn] *will be obligated to have a feast*

---

18   T. M. Happynook (2007). *The End of One Journey is the Beginning of Another.* Master's thesis, Department of Anthropology, University of Victoria.

and distribute the whale among his and your people. Having hahuulthii means that the hawit had the responsibility and obligations to respect and take care of his hahuulthii and provide for his people and family.

Whaling within Nuu-chah-nulth society . . . strengthened, maintained, and preserved our cultural practices, unwritten tribal laws, ceremonies, principles, , . . teachings, relationships between families [and] relationships with other nations and communities. . . . People came from great distances often result[ing] in intertribal alliances, relationships and marriages. . . .

To date, despite the central importance of whales to the Nuu-chah-nulth, they, with the exception of the Makah, have refrained from hunting them for almost a century. I recently spoke with Mexsis's wife, Kathy—Mexsis was unavailable owing to health issues—as to why and what impact the cessation of whaling has had on Maa-nulth society and culture. The answers to these questions gave me hope, but left me with reservations.

As part of the treaty they signed in 2006, five Maa-nulth First Nations on Vancouver Island agreed, under increasing public and government pressure, to forgo their traditional rights to hunt whales for at least twenty-five years. Although the treaty preserves the right to hunt whales in the future and is accompanied by an agreement to conduct whale research, the social, political, and cultural impacts of not hunting and sharing whales have been mitigated somewhat by ongoing Maa-nulth ceremonies and rituals, which have become increasingly important in maintaining cultural values, identity, and social relations. Although Kathy felt it likely that a whale would have surely been taken by now had they still lived in their community (Huu-ay-aht) in Barkley Sound, she felt that the overall health of the Nuu-chah-nulth has deteriorated as a consequence of not hunting whales.

Bear-ly Credible: Part 2

Some readers may feel I have been overly critical, even disparaging, of wildlife biologists and conservation bureaucrats in their engagement with Indigenous peoples in the context of *wildlife management*. I would disagree. The so-called scientific methods, models, theories, and data on which this privileged faction relies to stake their knowledge claims, render their decisions, and implement their regulations have had very real and dire consequences on some of the most vulnerable and marginalized peoples in the world. And all for the sake of the construction of knowledge from a uniquely narrow, yet increasingly dominant, cultural perspective that we know as *Science*—not to mention job security, career advancement, or whatever. As Mexsis's son reminds us, "*Science, if we are not mindful, will eventually contribute to the extinction of* [Indigenous] *cultures and traditional ecological knowledge.*" However, I want to conclude this polemic on *wildlife co-management* with one final example of *Science* as a blunt instrument of cultural domination and assimilation.

Polar bears (*nanuit*) on the west coast of Hudson Bay are perhaps the most researched representatives of this species in the world. Conducted over a period from the late 1970s to the mid-1990s, fieldwork by Drs. Andrew Derocher and Ian Sterling from the University of Alberta found this subpopulation to be experiencing marked decreases in reproduction, offspring survival, and body mass. In turn, these findings were directly attributed to global warming, and specifically the loss of ringed seal habitat owing to warmer spring air temperatures and an earlier break-up of Hudson Bay ice.

The conclusions and pronouncements of these researchers have, in large part, fuelled the widespread popular belief that global warming is the greatest single factor threatening not only West Hudson Bay bears, but all polar bears across the Arctic. Indeed, as one astute journalist noted:

> *There has never been a higher profile spokesmodel for the environmental movement than the polar bear: every discussion about global warming has to include a mention of polar bears, every article about the human disregard for nature has to feature a photograph of a sad-looking bear on a tiny speck of ice.*[19]

I am not asserting that global warming is a fiction or that climate change is not one of the most pressing issues of our time. Clearly, the Arctic is warming at a rate many times faster than more temperate zones as ice cover, so essential to ringed seals—the favourite prey of polar bears—decreases with each passing year. This fact I was forced to confront when I boated across an ice-free Cumberland Sound on a warm (by Arctic standards) late October day in 2001. Just fifteen years earlier, Pangnirtung's hunter/outfitters would have surely ridiculed me for thinking that such a journey was even possible. In the last few years community members have been boating across the Sound well into December.

From the late 1970s to mid-1990s nearly 2,800 polar bears in the West Hudson region were live-captured by wildlife biologists, at least 1,100 of which were recaptures. If the 700-1,200 estimate for this subpopulation during this period is even close to being accurate, some scientists claim that as many as 30 percent of all West Hudson Bay bears were captured on two or more occasions.[20] Just as significantly, most live-captures occurred either in the spring when adult females and cubs emerge from their dens or the fall when bears concentrate along the southwestern shore of Hudson Bay as they wait for the ice to form. During both seasons, polar bears are under considerable stress as food is scarce and they are living almost exclusively off stored fat reserves. Additionally, many adult females in

---

19 Z. Unger (2012). The Truth About Polar Bears. *Canadian Geographic* (November/December).

20 M. Dyck et al. (2007). Polar Bears of Western Hudson Bay and Climate Change: Are Warming Spring Air Temperatures the "Ultimate" Survival Control Factor? *Ecological Complexity* 4:73-84.

the spring are still lactating and caring for their cubs. Under these circumstances bears of all ages were pursued, drugged, and handled by researchers. Yet greenhouse-gas-produced global warming was held to be responsible for the observed decline in West Hudson Bay polar bear reproduction rates, body mass, and subadult survival. Clearly, the extinction of this subpopulation of polar bears, and by extension others, was imminent.

Scientific predictions for the demise of this iconic marine mammal, however, have not materialized, either in West Hudson Bay or elsewhere across the Canadian Arctic. Not only have Inuit not observed any decreases in polar bears in all regions of Nunavut, they have seen increases in most of them. Up to 1997, the West Hudson Bay population of bears apparently did not change significantly. Dyck and his co-authors note that bear numbers in West Hudson Bay were relatively stable between 2001 and 2011, *"even as the ice vanished underneath their feet."* Moreover, while any perceived decline in this subpopulation during this period (e.g., in 2004) is difficult to confirm, researchers in 2014 found that these bears were adapting to shorter ice seasons by finding more of their food on land.

Dyck and his colleagues do not deny that global warming is impacting West Hudson Bay polar bears. Rather, they insist that such claims *"must be assessed in a more realistic framework that considers all likely stress factors and their cumulative impacts."* It is simply not acceptable to *"infer a direct cause-and-effect relationship between polar bear mortality and the loss of sea ice* [as] *other factors and their cumulative impacts must be considered, including handling by biologists."* They further argue that other related stress factors (e.g., polar bear populations approaching the carrying capacity of their environments are expected to exhibit poorer physical condition, lower survivorship, and lower rates of reproduction) *"can explain the observed patterns in polar bear population ecology."* Moreover, increased human-bear interactions must be taken into account in a more realistic study and explanation of West Hudson Bay bear ecology.

> *It is difficult to isolate one factor of predominant severity and, consequently, it is simply not prudent to overstate the certainty of any single factor. . . . A full scientific understanding of the issue requires the combined assessment of both the natural and social systems rooted in the problem rather than consideration of either component in isolation. . . . If attention is inappropriately confined to a single mechanism, namely greenhouse warming, opportunities to understand other relevant mechanisms behind changes in bear population and health parameters may be lost in the process. . . . Therefore, we believe it is premature to make "one-dimensional" predictions about how climate change may affect polar bears in general and there is no ground for raising public alarm about any imminent extinction of Arctic polar bears.*

An Inuit-Nanuit Co-management Plan?

In the fall of 2018 the Nunavut government released the final draft of its Polar Bear Co-management Plan. On the face of it, the draft dispels much of the conventional scientific thinking about *nanuit*.[21] Based on four years of study and public consultations across Nunavut, the draft concludes that there are not too few, but too many, polar bears in Nunavut, and that climate change, while real, has not diminished their numbers as scientists have predicted:

> *Although there is growing scientific evidence linking the impacts of climate change to reduced body condition of bears and projections of population declines, no declines have currently been attributed to climate change.* [Inuit knowledge suggests] *that polar bears are exposed to the effects of climate change, but suggest that they are adaptable.*

Furthermore, the plan acknowledges the limitations of assigning boundaries to polar bear subpopulations based on satellite telemetry data and tagging programs. Indeed, these boundaries are recognized to be somewhat arbitrary as bears seemingly cross them at will. Yet they have formed the basis for setting *total allowable harvest* levels and other management actions for over four decades. In contrast, Inuit believe that polar bears travel regularly between different geographic areas of Nunavut and that there may be far fewer subpopulations of polar bears than the thirteen proposed by wildlife biologists.

The draft plan purports to lean heavily on *Inuit qaujimajatuqungit* and to reconcile the rights of Inuit in co-management practice. Indeed, it states that its *"about time that Inuit knowledge drove management policy."* Subsequently, Inuit will soon be allowed to take one female for every male *harvested*. This concession notwithstanding, the plan appears little more than a vehicle to solicit Inuit buy-in for the dominant scientific paradigm of polar bear management, and to further subordinate their knowledge to *Science*:

> *Previous management relied heavily on scientific monitoring and modelling to determine sustainable harvest rates. This scientific approach has been effective and will continue, but now allows for full participation of Inuit. . . . As our understanding of bear populations improves, there will be an ongoing need to review current subpopulation delineation. . . . Maintaining Inuit support for subpopulation boundaries is fundamental to the success of polar bear management in Nunavut.*

Okay then,

---

21   *Nunavut Polar Bear Co-management Plan* (2018). www.nwmb.com

Pass the Kool-Aid!

Particularly disturbing is the fact that virtually nothing has changed since my time with the Southeast Baffin Beluga Committee—more than twenty-five years ago—in the way *wildlife co-management* is undertaken in Nunavut. Even before the creation of the territory in 1999, it was recognized that Nunavut's co-management institutions only *"permitted Inuit to participate in "wildlife resource management"* [on the basis of] *Western standards of management and conservation,* [whereby] . . . *Inuit hunters are subjected to quotas, hunting seasons, and instruction on how to "scientifically" manage their resources."*[22] One would have thought that many of the old tired notions of this colonial institution imposed on Inuit back then would have been replaced with newer ideas and better approaches more sensitive to and accommodative of Inuit experiences and knowledge. Apparently not!

One thing that both scientists and Inuit agree on is that public safety is increasingly at risk as human-bear encounters are far more common today than they were in the past. As recently as the summer of 2018, polar bears killed Inuit hunters in two different Nunavut regions as they attempted to protect their families and property. Nevertheless, while scientists maintain that the loss of sea ice has driven bears inland, resulting in more frequent encounters with humans, Inuit claim that bear populations have increased across all regions of Nunavut. More frequent interactions between humans and bears, in turn, have led to an increase in defence kills, which can reduce a community's *total allowable harvest*. They also led to the loss of thousands of dollars of much-needed income from guided hunts, traditional hunting opportunities, and the transfer of Inuit knowledge, traditional values, and survival skills:

> *It is like ripples in a pond, we lose the hide and the meat and the hunt, but there is also loss of culture and knowledge. We no longer travel to the areas we used to hunt polar bears, so a generation has no knowledge of the land and traditional camping areas, we no longer have sport hunters so we no longer keep dog teams and we cannot pass on that knowledge, we no longer have skins to handle and women cannot pass on the skills to prepare and sew.* (David Irqiut, Taloyoak, Nunavut Polar Bear Co-management Plan 2018)

It would seem to me that the main focus of any comprehensive co-management plan involving the majority of the world's polar bears should have been to discover and mitigate the cause(s) of increased human-polar bear interactions. Is it the loss of sea ice that forces bears to spend more time on land—thus coming into greater contact with people—or are polar bears actually increasing in number throughout their ranges, and if so, why? And what sort of indicators are required to make these assessments? Such an examination can

---

22　T. Rodon (1998). Co-management and Self-determination in Nunavut. *Polar Geography* 22(2):119-135.

only occur via the design and implementation of an approach that does more than just pay lip-service to Inuit knowledge and experience. It would also be prudent to conduct a thorough review of all the assumptions and information sources that led to the establishment of subpopulation boundaries in the first place. Reinforcing an outmoded and oppressive system of *wildlife management* that depends on arbitrarily established population boundaries will not get the job done! By obscuring what is really happening, the ongoing entrenchment of status quo approaches to *wildlife co-management* will only contribute further to the extinction of Inuit ecological knowledge, land-based skills, traditional values, and even polar bears themselves. There is no choice but to find new and better ways to manage human-polar bear relationships.

The Nunavut Wildlife Management Board will submit the final Nunavut Polar Bear Co-management Plan to the territorial cabinet for approval once it receives comments from public hearings. As of April 2020, the plan had not been released to the public. When it is, expect the shit to hit the fans, from both directions.

CHAPTER 4
Where Have All the Caribou and Caribou-Eater Chipewyan Gone?

IT WAS ARGUABLY THE MOST REPREHENSIBLE *WILDLIFE MANAGEMENT* DECISION EVER TO impact Canada's Indigenous peoples. I first learned about the abduction and botched relocation of the Sayisi Dene during my inaugural meeting with the Beverly-Qamanirjuaq Caribou Management Board—a multi-government *caribou management* committee created to protect barren ground caribou from Indigenous hunting and other perceived threats.

Close, But No Caribou

Tim's eyes rolled back in his head as I glanced over to see his reaction. I first met Tim Trottier on a blistering hot summer's day in 1981 on the edge of the Lake One prairie two kilometres south of Peace Point in Wood Buffalo National Park. With our heads buried in an archaeological test-pit high on a bluff overlooking an old bison trial, Doug Proch and I suddenly sensed that we were not alone: "*What are you guys doing?*" Glancing up, we were startled to see a bronzed and chiseled *Grizzly Adams* look-a-like standing over us wearing nothing but a pair of boots and cut-off jeans. Tim, as we soon learned, was a wildlife biologist studying North America's last surviving example of its once-dominant post-Pleistocene predator-prey dyad, frequently following wolves and bison daily for thirty kilometres or more on ankle-busting bison trails. Married to a Cree woman and intimately familiar with Cree culture and Indigenous issues, Tim was the only provincial government biologist on the BQCMB who understood what was really going on. Of course, the few Indigenous board members left in the room had seen this all before.

It was the final day of a BQCMB meeting in Thompson, Manitoba, on a wintery late fall day in 1997, and one of Tim's colleagues was drawing folded pieces of paper out of a ball cap. Two days earlier, before most Indigenous board members had yet to display their displeasure with the proceedings by boycotting the meeting altogether, an aerial photograph of a caribou herd had been circulated briefly to everyone in attendance. A prize for the person closest to guessing the actual number of caribou in the photo was the *carrot* to induce everyone to participate. Neither I nor Stella (Spak)—an anthropologist observing *wildlife co-management* in action for her doctoral research—can recall what the prize was. Nevertheless, it was certainly not attractive enough to entice the majority of the board's Indigenous members to attend the last day of the meeting. Having read all the guesstimates, the government member announced that, to no one's surprise, one of his learned fellows had come closest to guessing the correct number of caribou. No Indigenous guesstimate came within a rifle shot of the correct answer.

Embedded within this spectacle was a not-so-thinly veiled message aimed directly at Indigenous board members: "*We highly educated biologists know caribou, how to count caribou, and our knowledge is superior to yours—so shut up and let us do our damn job!*" I do not know if this sub-text was intentional or not. I hope it wasn't. Regardless, it was received loud and clear: "*Indigenous knowledge of caribou does not measure up to scientific knowledge, and thus cannot be trusted or given any credibility.*" This was not the first time that this message had been delivered. It had been apparently going on for years. Nor would it be the last.

I had been hired by the BQCMB to design an Indigenous knowledge study of caribou—something that the seventeen Inuit, Dene, Cree, and Métis communities dependent on the Beverly and Qamanirjuaq caribou herds for survival had been requesting for years. And this meeting was my first face-to-face encounter with the board. Consecutive aerial calving ground surveys conducted in the 1970s had indicated that both herds were in significant decline. Over the winter of 1979-80 the Beverly herd wintered unusually far south, and an estimated 15,000-20,000 animals were killed in northern Saskatchewan alone. Subsequently, federal and provincial authorities, as well as First Nation communities, came under heavy national and international condemnation to stop the hunt. While government board members (except Tim) were certain that both herds would soon become extinct if hunting was not significantly reduced, Indigenous board members believed that caribou were using different parts of the range, and may even be increasing in number. Out of this manufactured crisis the BQCMB was created in 1982.

Later in the decade, government biologists were at a loss to explain why herd population estimates were stable when recruitment levels—the number of calves surviving beyond the first year of life—indicated that numbers should be rising. In 1993 a survey of the Beverly herd estimated that it had dropped below the board's arbitrary crisis point of 150,000 animals. Apparently, most females had calved well before reaching the calving grounds. A board-sanctioned, multi-government calving ground survey the following year involving two Indigenous board members (Billy Shot and Pierre Robillard), however, revealed the

Beverly herd to be 276,000 (+/- 111,000) animals and the Qamanirjuaq herd 496,000 (+/- 105,400) animals.

In the late 1980s other phenomena such as forest fires and mining began to attract the attention of the BQCMB as factors influencing caribou numbers in any given year. Even so, board management recommendations continued to focus on the Indigenous hunting of caribou. This was the low-hanging fruit about which it could reasonably do something. By 1997, under mounting pressure from Indigenous members, government representatives were forced to consider that an Indigenous knowledge study of caribou, not just limiting the Indigenous *harvest*, might be of value.

The opportunity to design a traditional knowledge study for the BQCMB was hard to turn down. After all, it was one of the first efforts by one of the first *wildlife co-management* boards in Canada to meaningfully access and incorporate Indigenous knowledge into management decisions. In spite of the fact that the study was grossly underfunded, I accepted the contract and challenge head-on. My engagement with Indigenous board and community members, however, was limited to two BQCMB meetings, an associated informal sidebar meeting, and a single trip to Wollaston Lake, Saskatchewan.

Even so, I managed to design a study that addressed most of the concerns, knowledge gaps, and information needs of user communities. Nevertheless, while the proposed study was supported by Indigenous board members, federal and provincial government members (except Tim) rejected it for being too expensive and too focused on knowledge that government representatives felt was irrelevant. Subsequently, the board chair dictated that I revise it to address non-Indigenous board member priorities. To do so, however, would have breached my ethical obligations to Indigenous members and their communities, so I declined and walked out the door. Many months later, Stella Spak observed in her doctoral dissertation that with my refusal to acquiesce to the board chair's demand the BQCMB "*got more than they bargained for.*" Although I had been, and would be in the future, challenged by government, industry, and even Indigenous clients to abandon my ethics in order to serve their interests, this was the first and only time I walked away from a contract.

Genocide of the Sayisi Dene: Manufactured Caribou Conservation Crisis Meets Administrative Convenience

During the 1997 BQCMB fall meeting in Thompson, another event was unfolding in the room next door—the formal release of Ila Bussidor and Bilgen-Reinart's *Night Spirits*. The book is a tragic tale of the forced removal of the Sayisi Dene from their traditional homeland and community of Little Duck Lake, Manitoba, to Churchill. A suggestion to cut our meeting short in order to attend this seminal event was unanimously rejected by government board members (except Tim)—a decision I found ironic, but not surprising. Clearly, in their minds there were more important matters that needed attention.

In a review of *Nights Spirits*, Ovide Mercredi, former Grand Chief of the Assembly of First Nations, remarked:

> *Ila Bussidor's story ... is so deeply personal that once told, her people will enter into a new journey; a healing journey that will involve atonement on the part of the federal government. Canadians will weep. The Dene will heal.*

Six hundred and seventy thousand (670,000)—that's how many caribou populated the barren grounds in the summer of 1947 according to government scientists. Repeating the aerial survey in the summer of 1955, only 277,000 were counted. In less than eight years, nearly 400,000 caribou had disappeared. Federal scientists and officials were perplexed and understandably concerned about what could be causing this precipitous decline.

Looking to land their ailing Norseman in early October of that year, a small group of government officials flew low over the Sayisi Dene settlement of Little Duck Lake, a prime fall hunting camp and sacred caribou crossing. What they witnessed shocked and appalled them: two dozen men and boys in canoes near the rapids shooting and harpooning caribou. By the time they landed, the hunters had disappeared leaving "*hundreds of dead and dying animals*" on the shore of the narrows. The cause for the alarming decline in barren ground caribou had been found. To embellish the point, one biologist graphically reported that, "*Orgies of killing still take place at several crossing points ... their bloated bodies crowding the shores of northern lakes whose waters flowed red a few days before.*"

Prior to the mid-1950s, the Sayisi Dene (people of the east), known to anthropologists as the Caribou Eater Chipewyan or *Edthen-eldeli-dene*, were a vibrant self-sufficient people with minimal contact with the outside world. Dependent on caribou, fish, and fur trapping, these people endured a hard life in the bush, but it was a rewarding existence as everybody thrived and got along:

> *In Duck Lake, our people never suffered shortages. We had a lot of caribou meat, game, fish. At the trading post, we could get tea and flour for bannock to supplement our diet. I remember how well our people were dressed. The women would buy fancy cloth at the trading post and make the most beautiful dresses. Men wore beaded caribou-hide or moose-hide jackets. Their gloves and footwear were decorated with beads.*
>
> *... We prepared and preserved the caribou meat so well that it lasted us through the winter. We made lots of pemmican and dried meat. In the fall the men went on their hunting trips, they would leave supplies of caribou frozen under the*

snow. Anyone could go there, feel under the snow with a long stick, and take what they needed.

The well-being of children was always a priority for the community. Nobody spoke harshly to children, we never punished them, yet they were well disciplined by their parents and grandparents, raised with good values. They were always respectful toward their parents and towards elders. The children played outside, warmly dressed in their caribou-hide jackets, pants, footwear, and mitts. When it was time to eat, the parents would call them in. In the evening, they could play for a little while and then they were told it was bedtime. They went to bed without argument. . . . Almost immediately the kids would go in. No one stayed out to run around late at night. Night time was quiet time.

When I put my children to bed, it was my time to do the work that was unfinished during the day. I could prepare caribou hides, I could sew in peace. I loved that quiet time. Adults were also respectful towards each other. We respected each other's ways. People had space. (Betsy Anderson, *Night Spirits*)

For Ila Bussidor and the Sayisi Dene, what the government officials witnessed on the shores of Duck Lake was not wanton slaughter, but

a centuries old method of survival; . . . leaving carcasses to be buried under the winter snow was a time-honoured, reasonable way of storing meat, in a land where winters were long and harsh, and where the people could never be sure of enough food for their families.

During the late 1950s Canada was in the throes of implementing a policy of assimilating its Aboriginal peoples into Canadian society, *"for their own good."* As part of this project, the federal government had contemplated for several years the relocation of the Sayisi Dene to Churchill. The town was booming, fur trapping was in a downturn, and it would be far easier to deal with them if they were concentrated in one place rather than pursuing a semi-nomadic existence in the bush. Nevertheless, in the absence of any concrete plans, funding, or infrastructure, local government officials were engaged in other priorities. The perceived caribou conservation crisis precipitated by the *Duck Lake massacre* in 1955, however, moved the relocation off the back-burner and into high gear. The following summer government planes descended on Duck Lake to abduct and relocate the Sayisi Dene. What followed was unimaginable and deeply shameful.

Dumped with their dogs on a gravel bar on the shores of Hudson Bay with few belongings and fewer supplies, the Sayisi Dene were left to fend for themselves. Promised building materials and canoes before winter set in, the Sayisi Dene were relocated to North River, forty kilometres to the north. But the supplies never arrived and they were forced to overwinter in flimsy canvas tents and rotting log cabins. The following spring, they were moved back to Churchill. Here, the once proud and independent Sayisi Dene had no choice but to scrounge off the town garbage dump for food scraps and wood to build and heat their make-shift dwellings. After much wrangling amongst government officials, the Sayisi Dene were forced to move once again, this time to Churchill's outskirts adjacent to the town's cemetery. It was a gross affront to Sayisi cultural norms and spiritual beliefs. Surrounded by the *spirits of the dead*, Camp 10 became the new home of the Sayisi Dene. In order to ensure that they would not escape back to their homes at Little Duck Lake to resume their dependence on caribou, the RCMP rationed their ammunition and shot their dogs.

The tightly packed, make-shift shacks in which the Sayisi Dene were now forced to live were cold, draughty, damp, and in stark contrast to the cozy log cabins they were forced to abandon. Around 1967 a new housing project known as Dene Village was built for them south of town. The demoralized Sayisi Dene soon became residents of what one government official called Canada's "*worst slum.*" Without access to local jobs and unfamiliar with Churchill's cultures and languages (Inuit, Cree, English), the Sayisi Dene endured racism, sexual assault, physical assault, and discrimination. Unable to hunt or support themselves, they continued to rely on the town dump for survival. As they sank into a tragic vortex of dependency, poverty, alcoholism, violence, and crime over the next two decades, nearly half of the 250 Sayisi Dene died horrible, unnatural deaths from domestic violence, suicide, house fires, exposure, drownings, and hit-and-runs. Few of these deaths, however, were ever investigated by local authorities.

An arbitrary and discriminatory federal government decision to relocate the Sayisi Dene against their wishes, implemented by an unprepared and uncaring bureaucracy, had catapulted them into a life of squalor, violence, anomie, and despair. As Ila Bussidor laments in *Night Spirits*, it was "*nothing less than genocide.*" Arguably, no prior or subsequent *wildlife management* decision in Canada or forced abduction and relocation of this country's original inhabitants has had a more devastating and unintended impact.

I struggled to read and comprehend the powerful, heart-wrenching stories of the Sayisi Dene in *Night Spirits*, and vacillated over whether to include them in this book. To even begin to fathom what happened to the Sayisi Dene, one must read the book in its entirety, and then read it again. Recognizing that words will never capture the true extent of their pain and suffering, but in the hope that by continuing to share their story their nightmare will never be forgotten or repeated, and that true restitution will eventually be achieved, a few excerpts from *Night Spirits* are warranted:

> *My father was a tall handsome man. He was always well dressed, and he usually wore a beaded jacket made out of caribou hide. The hood of his jacket was*

trimmed with wolf fur. His moccasins and gloves were also made out of caribou hide and beautifully decorated with beads. He was a leader and carried himself with pride and dignity.

I have a memory from when I was ten years old. An old couple, Sarah and John Kithithoe, were going to the dump . . . and asked if I wanted to go. We were at the dump all day, collecting food (things like wieners and baloney) and anything else that was useable. . . . It was a good ten or twelve kilometre walk. [When I got home] my dad was standing by the window. I saw that he was crying. "I was a proud man," he said. "I hunted and trapped for my family. I was so proud. I never wore clothes that were even a little damaged. But today my little girl brings food home from the garbage dump so I can eat."

I watched my parents become broken people and die tragically. I witnessed the burning of our house, while they were trapped inside, drunk. When they died, a big part of my spirit died with them. I remember watching other house fires. People died in all of them. My memories of this time are filled with sadness. I know my spirit was injured by the tragic deaths, by alcohol and drug abuse, by violence, from being sexually abused by drunken men. And, I wasn't the only person who suffered these injuries. All Sayisi Dene, especially those of my generation, have a personal account of brutal hardship and despair. . . . As children, we watched as our parents were destroyed, unable to bear the weight of a way of life that did not belong to them. We witnessed people being beaten, murdered, people of all ages dying in house fires, young women and girls being raped and beaten. Men and women froze to death every winter. There were countless victims of hit-and-run accidents. . . . We were reduced to humiliation . . . [and] cruel discrimination from . . . whites, the Inuit, the Métis and Cree. . . . Along with our independence, our innocence, and many lives, we lost immeasurable potential. We lost the potential of generations of children yet to be born, and the knowledge of our elders and parents, who took their wisdom with them when they died in Churchill. (Ila Bussidor, *Night Spirits*).

Pehaps no personal story more succinctly encapsulates what happened to the Sayisi Dene as Betsy Anderson's:

Of my eleven children, nine have died alcohol-related deaths during our days of poverty in Churchill. I often wish I had pictures of my children who died, so I could look back and remember what they looked like. (Betsy Anderson, *Night Spirits*)

Healing and Sayisi Dene Relocation Claim Settlement

By 1970 surviving members of the band had had enough. After two years of preparations, half the Sayisi Dene, led by Peter Cassie and other leaders, packed up their few possessions and headed home to the bush to live much as their ancestors had done for generations. Shortly thereafter, other members followed, first to Duck Lake, then to Tadoule Lake, where they now reside. Located eighty kilometres south of the tree line, Tadoule Lake is one of the most northern isolated settlements in Manitoba, reachable only by plane, dog team, snowmobile, or canoe. With an on-reserve population of around 380 and a somewhat larger off-reserve population, the Sayisi Dene have been unable to escape the nightmare of their years in Churchill. Without the knowledge and guidance of elders and traditional land-users who died needlessly in Churchill, they have struggled to heal and to find the dignity, meaning, and value that shaped the lives of earlier generations.

In 1999 the Sayisi Dene filed a relocation claim with the federal government. In no rush to negotiate the claim, Canada did not enter into exploratory discussions until a decade later. Three years on, settlement negotiations began. In the interim, Manitoba apologized to the Sayisi Dene for its role in the relocation promising them 13,000+ acres of provincial Crown land over and above any federal treaty lands as compensation. Canada finally apologized to the Sayisi Dene in 2016 signing an agreement that provided them with $33.6 million to be paid into a trust for current and future generations.

Few would agree that this amount and years of government stonewalling is sufficient recompense for the loss of so many deprived of their lives and *"immeasurable potential."* One can only speculate about what the settlement might have been had nearly half of all band members, many of child-rearing age, not died tragically in Churchill at the hands of the government.

A New Age BQCMB?

Every six years or so the BQCMB relies on a multi-government funded calving ground survey to achieve its primary mandate of determining *"how many caribou can be safely harvested without endangering the size of the herd(s)."*[23] In 2007, very few caribou were observed on the Beverly herd's calving grounds when there should have been thirty to forty animals per square kilometre. The following year, the Beverly caribou herd was estimated to be 50 percent lower than in 1994, while the Qamanirjuaq herd was determined to be 30 percent lower. A June 2009 calving ground survey on the Beverly calving grounds found fewer than half the number of breeding cows counted in 2008. From 2007 onward, summer surveys

---

23   *BQCMB Newsletter* (1999).

have spotted fewer and fewer caribou on the Beverly calving grounds, raising concerns about the fate of the herd. In 2014, the Qamanirjuaq herd was estimated to be 264,700, down significantly from the 2008 population estimate of 344,100. Subsequently, barren-ground caribou are currently listed as *threatened*, and animal welfare organizations have become increasingly embroiled in the controversy.

While the BQCMB considers calving ground surveys to be "*the most important information for managing caribou,*" tagging caribou has provided the board with additional information for decades. Tagging, however, continues to be problematic for Indigenous user communities; such interference is a violation of traditional Dene and Inuit relationships with caribou. Perhaps surreptitiously, perhaps not, soon after the Sayisi Dene's were relocated to Churchill, the sacred caribou crossing at Duck Lake was targeted as the principal location from which barren ground caribou were tagged.

Collaring studies, first undertaken in 2006, like tagging, initially found little support among Indigenous user communities. Ironically, albeit fortuitously, collaring soon began to call into question the utility of counting caribou and calving ground surveys altogether. As Tim Trottier conceded in a 2006 BCCMB newsletter:

> *We have total overlap with collared animals from the Beverly herd and two other herds, possibly three other herds. . . . We've got Beverly animals that are located pretty much with a bunch of Ahiak collared animals and they're on what we think of as Bathurst range. . . . Qamanirjuaq caribou are also roaming the centre of the Beverly range. . . . Not only are we not sure what the [Beverly] herd population size is, we're not even sure where they're at.*

It turns out that strict herd fidelity to specific calving grounds, long the cornerstone of board management decisions and recommendations, was less a substantiated fact than an erroneous and culturally biased assumption. At the same time, given the great variation (and large standard deviations) observed between consecutive calving ground surveys, some researchers affiliated with the BQCMB began to question the rationale of counting caribou altogether relative to other indicators of herd health, behaviour, composition, and discreteness that Indigenous hunters may possess.[24]

Even though collaring continues to provide counter-intuitive information about barren-ground caribou movements and behaviour, government Board members (except Tim) appear reluctant to examine critically their rationale and methods for determining caribou herd size and fidelity. Nor have they created the space for Indigenous user knowledge in their deliberations. For example, while the cost of calving ground surveys ballooned from about $200K to $500K between 1999 and 2008, the board struggled to find even

---

24   A. Kendrick (2000). Community Perceptions of the Beverly-Qamanirjuaq Caribou Management Board. *Canadian Journal of Native Studie*s XX(1):1-33.

$5K to conduct interviews with Indigenous hunters and elders. With various federal and provincial government sponsors of the BQCMB unwilling or unable to fund research on Indigenous knowledge, the latter is forced to play a handmaiden's role to *Science*. According to a board newsletter, the best it can do is "*encourage user participation in caribou movement and distribution research in order to validate the research of caribou biologists.*"

One positive of the BQCMB's work concerns the issue of fire control. Most Indigenous hunters possess detailed knowledge of winter caribou behaviour and movements. They have made it clear that fire suppression in productive winter feeding grounds is crucial for caribou survival. Even so, early attempts by the BQCMB to convince government ministers about the need for fire control in older-growth forests were ignored. Meanwhile, the board continued to encourage government personnel to work with the user communities to identify corridors between burns as critical routes for caribou migration and winter feeding areas. By 1991, a sub-committee of the board, relying on Indigenous knowledge, began to identify caribou migration corridors and older forest areas with user communities. The board's role in changing fire-management priorities, and delineating and protecting calving grounds and other critical caribou habitat from industrial development, must be regarded as achievements in a complicated inter-jurisdictional context. However, the BQCMB continues to invest a great deal of time, energy, and resources from federal and provincial agencies to count caribou and to communicate the principles, methodologies, and benefits of Western scientific caribou research to user communities.

During the drafting of this chapter I contacted Tim—currently the longest-serving government board member. We hadn't spoken in nearly two decades, but it was as if time had stood still. As we reconnected, I learned that the fluctuating status of the Beverly herd (to which the Ahiak herd is now assigned), the commercial *harvesting* of caribou for inter-settlement trade, and the role of climate change had been added to the board's research priorities. I also found out that the traditional cooperative hunts at select water-crossings are no longer undertaken due partly to temporal and spatial changes in caribou distributions. Barren ground caribou are not only more dispersed than decades ago, they do not penetrate the treeline until much later in the fall, if they arrive at all—perhaps a consequence of global warming? Hunting pressure has further declined owing to the increased energy and financial costs required to hunt caribou. Yet the Committee on the Status of Endangered Wildlife in Canada in 2016 became so concerned about barren ground caribou that it listed the species as *threatened*. At the same time, the BQCMB remains perplexed by the movements and distributions of caribou herds. In 2017, collaring studies once again revealed a 100 percent overlap of the Beverly and Bathurst caribou herds.

As we spoke, I sensed Tim's lingering frustration with the BQCMB's ongoing effort to control Indigenous hunting vis-a-vis its inability to find a larger role for Indigenous voices and traditional knowledge in its deliberations. Although Tim felt that this situation had improved somewhat since the 1990s, I wondered what makes a well-intentioned and culturally sensitive scientist serve so long on a *wildlife co-management* board unable to give even minimal consideration to user knowledge and concerns? For that matter, I mused about the role of Indigenous board members and what they get out of their continuing involvement with the BQCMB.

Tim responded that he continues to serve as a board member after all this time because no other similar entity exists to address the issue, and that, in his absence, *"things might get worse."* I also sensed that Tim still retains a measure of hope that things will get better, hope that new information and knowledge—Indigenous or otherwise—will emerge that will result in more informed, nuanced, and equitable management decisions.

I do not know for sure why Indigenous board members continue to attend BQCMB meetings, at least occasionally. Based on my former engagement with them, I suspect that it might have something to do with the fact that through their participation on the board they ensure that their families and communities will always be able to hunt caribou, regardless of what the *Science* says!

Postscript: On Knowledge and Humility

A few years ago while channel surfing, I stumbled upon an anthropologist recounting a story about an Indigenous elder putting a young wildlife researcher in his place after he had dismissed the elder's knowledge. Although I wasn't paying close enough attention to catch the story's original source, characters, or details, it did sound suspiciously like Carl Sandburg's poem *Circles in the Sand*. Populating the following allegory with Dene and caribou, its key message is still fresh in my mind:

> *Fresh out of graduate school, a young and enthusiastic biologist had arranged to meet a knowledgeable Dene elder on the sandy shore of a northern lake to talk about caribou. After explaining what his research project was about and what he wanted to know about caribou, the scientist turned to the elder in the hope that he might be enlightened. The old man proceeded to talk about the importance of caribou to his family and community, how he knew when and where to hunt caribou, how and why caribou needed to be respected and shared, what would happen if they weren't, and many other things that the biologist was not concerned with. After what seemed to be an insufferably long time, the young scientist interrupted the elder, stating that he had heard enough. Grabbing a stick, he began to draw two circles in the sand, one many times larger than the other. Pointing to the smaller circle, he proclaimed without hesitation: "This is what*

you Native people know about caribou." Pointing to the larger circle, the young man stated emphatically: "This is what the white man knows about caribou."

Looking askance at the young man, the elder reached for the stick and walked in the opposite direction. After about a minute or so, he stopped and began to draw an expansive circle that soon dwarfed the two smaller ones. Upon his return minutes later, the elder looked squarely at the young man and said: "You see that big circle? That is what the Dene and the white man don't know about caribou!"

Postscript #2: A Chance Encounter

A dozen years after my awkward involvement with the BQCMB, I and a diverse cohort of Sustainable Forest Management Network researchers from universities across the country had the good fortune of accidentally running into Ila Bussidor and northern Manitoba's federal Member of Parliament, Tina Keeper, at the Winnipeg International Airport. Each summer during my tenure with the SFMN it held a two-to-three-day workshop with one of its First Nations' partners. The purpose of this annual event was to familiarize newly funded professors and graduate students with Indigenous research needs, issues, and protocols. In 2006, the Pikangikum First Nation and researchers from the Natural Resources Institute, University of Manitoba, were the hosts of the event.

It was a cold, blustery late summer's day as our small group huddled on the tarmac near the charter aircraft that would soon take us to Red Lake, Ontario. We were en route to Pikangikum traditional territory where we had arranged to meet with elders and land stewards of the nation. Pikangikum was involved in a sustainable forestry management initiative to create a viable economic future for its youth, and to erase its reputation as the *suicide capital of Canada*. Chief Bussidor and the former *North of 60* actor were on their way to Tadoule Lake to consult with community members about the federal government's relocation claim. This was one of those teachable moments that only comes along . . . well, almost never, and Ila and Tina did the best they could in the short time we had together to tell the story of the Sayisi Dene. Upon parting and going our separate ways, few people in our small party spoke, or had a dry eye.

CHAPTER 5
Listening to the Silence

For God's Sake, Let's Keep the Science Clean!

THE TENSION IN THE AIR WAS PALPABLE. CLOSE TO $5 MILLION IN RESEARCH FUNDING WAS on the table, and everyone was holding their breath as Dr. Stan Boutin, an internationally regarded University of Alberta wildlife biologist, was about to deliver his proposal evaluations. The Research Planning Committee of the Sustainable Forest Management Network was in the process of concluding its annual adjudication of two dozen or so research proposals from academic, forest industry, environmental, and First Nation partners across Canada when Stan emphatically made the above declaration. He was referring to several research proposals that proposed to access and integrate the traditional ecological knowledge of First Nation elders and land-users into what were predominantly science-driven forest research projects.

I do not know the motivations behind Stan's dictum. But I suspect that it had more to do with the lack of a professionally recognized methodology that could accomplish this task without somehow infecting the sanctity of Western scientific knowledge, rather than an outright dismissal of the value of Indigenous ecological knowledge per se. Even so, I was initially stunned at what seemed to be a callous off-handed remark, as were several First Nation and social scientist members on the committee. Even a suggestion by Jim Webb (Little Red River Cree First Nation Chief Johnson Sewepagaham's proxy at the meeting) encouraging Stan "*to think of Indians as ground squirrels*" so that he might grasp the merit of these proposals was not enough to sway Stan's opinion, though it did elicit more than a few laughs.

In retrospect, however, I have come to see that Stan might not have been wrong. I have no problem with "*keeping the science clean*." After all, if the shoe was on the other foot, if I was an Indigenous person who depended on my ecological knowledge and wits to survive and feed my family, I might feel the same way. But *keeping the science clean* presupposes a space for Indigenous ecological knowledge that does not exist. So where does that leave it?

First of all, although Indigenous knowledge has failed to make any headway into the hallowed halls of *Science*, it has been remarkably successful at sustaining Indigenous peoples, cultures, and societies over the millennia. Clearly, Indigenous knowledge systems have withstood the test of time and, incredibly in many cases, oppressive colonial regimes. Yet it has failed to make even small inroads into *wildlife co-management*, environmental impact assessment, land claims negotiations, and other venues where legislation mandates its consideration and use.

Co-management: Taking the *Indigenous* Out of Indigenous Ecological Knowledge

I know of no example in Canada where *wildlife co-management* has lived up to its advanced billing or met the expectations of Indigenous participants. Perhaps the southeast Baffin beluga case comes closest, not because Inuit knowledge was given parity in decision-making, but because of the resolve of Inuit hunters to defend their rights against the fallacious assumptions and duplicity of DFO personnel. Analyses of the systemic barriers that keep Indigenous participants on the sidelines of co-management are few and far between. A recent study of the Porcupine Caribou Management Board, however, identified several factors that prevented the successful application of Indigenous ecological knowledge into a regulation that would have allowed the "*leaders to pass.*"[25] Not often considered in such analyses, however, is the likelihood that Indigenous participants find it virtually impossible to penetrate a value-driven system of *wildlife management* fundamentally at odds with, even contemptuous of, Indigenous knowledge and management systems.

The incorporation of Indigenous peoples and their ecological knowledge into decision-making with provincial, territorial, and federal government authorities has been the raison d'être of *wildlife* and environmental *co-management* in Canada for decades. As the rights of government and industry to take up land and extract natural resources come into increasing conflict with the constitutionally protected rights of Indigenous Canadians, *co-management*—whether created under a land claim, a resource-use crisis, or a multi-stakeholder environmental management agreement—is seen to be a fair compromise. Even so, never have the rights, interests, knowledge, management, and conservation systems of Indigenous peoples achieved anything close to parity with those of settler society. In all three types of co-management arrangements, the state-sponsored, scientifically-driven institution of

---

25   E. Padilla and G. P. Kofinas (2014). "Letting the Leaders Pass": Barriers to Using Traditional Ecological Knowledge in Co-management as the Basis of Formal Hunting Regulations. *Ecology and Society* 19(2):7. http://www.ecologyandsociety.org/vol19/iss2/art7/

environmental resource management has played a pivotal role in marginalizing Indigenous participants and their authority over, knowledge about, and responsibilities to their lands and resources. Attempts to force Indigenous knowledge into the established methods, data sets, and theories of Western scientists have been particularly effective in disenfranchising Indigenous peoples, muting their voices, and hamstringing their knowledge contributions. In fact, it would be difficult to conceive of a more covert and insidious form of cultural oppression and assimilation than Canadian *wildlife co-management*.

The usual process by which Indigenous knowledge is accessed and applied in co-management is replete with systemic defects and unethical practices. Only those aspects of Indigenous knowledge that are acceptable to those *cultured* in the Western scientific tradition are considered worthy of consideration. The rest is dismissed as anecdotal and irrelevant. The practice to date has profound implications for the widespread failure of *co-management* with Indigenous peoples on many fronts, and goes something like this:

Step 1: The conservation crisis is almost always identified by wildlife managers, environmental scientists, research biologists, and the like. Seldom, if ever, does the emergency originate with Indigenous resource users.[26]

Step 2: The research protocols (methods, questions, relevant data, etc.) used to address the crisis are normally established by the same actors.

Step 3: Indigenous translators with variable proficiency and/or experience in either or both cultural systems are frequently hired to assist in interviews, data collection, and to interpret and translate culturally loaded and nuanced concepts originating in the language of one culture into the language of the other.

Step 4: Indigenous knowledge holders are then interviewed using recording formats (e.g., questionnaires, maps, audio/video) required by non-Indigenous authorities.

Step 5: These formats are then transcribed and cherry-picked—usually by the same actors—to filter out specific tidbits of environmental information that most parsimoniously fit with their beliefs and theories, obliterating the contextual richness and complexity of Indigenous knowledge and narratives.

Step 6: This dumbed-down decontextualized information—especially that easily quantified or represented on maps—then becomes the authoritative reference upon which management decisions are taken, effectively excluding Indigenous peoples and the full breadth and depth of their knowledge from decision-making.

The end result is that neither Indigenous peoples nor their knowledge make any real or significant contribution to the way resources are *managed*, frustrating both those who possess this knowledge and, sometimes, even those mandated to use it. At each step of the

---

26 This list has been extracted from my paper, Decolonizing Co-management in Northern Canada. *Cultural Survival Quarterly* 28-1 (March 2004).

way there is a progressive and cumulative loss of knowledge and context. Not only are specific elements of Indigenous knowledge increasingly separated from the broader cultural and social contexts where they more properly reside, its holders are increasingly divorced from knowledge that they constructed and once owned and controlled, effectively excluding them from any meaningful role in decision-making. In this all-too-common scenario whatever aspects of Indigenous knowledge are deemed worthy by environmental managers are valued primarily for their contributions to *Science*. It is thus remarkable that Indigenous peoples would want to share their ecological knowledge at all, especially since their political representatives have insisted for years that it be given full and equal weight with *Science* in environmental management decisions that impact them directly. As Rosemarie Kuptana, former president of the Inuit Tapirisat of Canada, has stated:

> *Our traditional ecological knowledge is too often taken out of context, misinterpreted, or misused. What wildlife managers, biologists, and bureaucrats understand, or think they see, is interpreted within their own knowledge and value systems, not ours. In the process, our special ways of knowing and doing things—our local systems of management—are crushed by scientific knowledge and the state management model.*[27]

There is no doubt that many Indigenous peoples have developed extensive knowledge about their environments, including the spatial and temporal distributions of many species, and the factors that influence their composition, behaviours, and relationships. Such knowledge, being the product of both personal experience and knowledge passed down from previous generations, may reveal much about changes over time and space in various species and habitats. At the same time, many Indigenous peoples have witnessed the specific and combined impacts of natural and human disturbances on critical resources. Although environmental co-management would benefit from this kind of information and knowledge in order to make informed decisions over broad time and spatial scales, this alone may not be sufficient.

The ongoing decontextualization of traditional ecological knowledge in the absence of considering how it is valued and understood by Indigenous peoples—i.e., within its broader socio-cultural context—is ethically bankrupt, not to mention politically, culturally, and ecologically amoral. Through its progressive dumbing-down, the traditional knowledge of Indigenous peoples assumes a subordinate role to Western scientific knowledge while failing to meet the needs, rights, and interests of its creators. As a consequence, Indigenous ways of knowing, seeing, and relating to the natural world are devalued and

---

27 R. Kuptana (1996). *Indigenous Peoples' Rights to Self-determination and Development: Issues of Equality and Decolonization.* Keynote Address to International Seminar on Development and Self-determination among the Indigenous Peoples of the North, October 5, University of Alaska, Fairbanks.

ultimately dismissed. This process not only reflects the predominant position of *Science* in environmental decision-making, but strengthens the existing institutional arrangements and asymmetrical power relationships that support it.

The imposition of state management concepts and procedures on Indigenous participants in co-management is often met with resistance, which may take the form of direct confrontation—think Meeka Kilabuk. More frequently, resistance is expressed in more subtle and indirect ways, such as non-engagement and non-attendance at meetings, a behaviour routinely misinterpreted by non-Indigenous actors. Recall the decision by some Indigenous members of the Beverly-Qamanirjuaq Caribou Management Board to boycott its Thompson, Manitoba, meeting in favour of spending time together in a local establishment. This act was not interpreted by government board members (except Tim) as resistance, however, but support for the general stereotype they had already manufactured in their minds about Indigenous peoples. Indigenous refusals to abandon their ways of relating to and thinking about animals, or to adopt the lexicon and concepts of state managers, also fuel this stereotype. While direct forms of resistance are not usually sustained for any length of time because of the transactional costs involved and/or the failure to achieve any meaningful changes to *co-management* practice in the short-term, indirect forms of resistance may not even be recognized by colonial agents for what they really are because of their subtlety. Inevitably, neither direct confrontation nor indirect resistance have been effective tools for Indigenous participants to get their viewpoints across or to affect change in *wildlife co-management,* environmental management, or environmental impact assessment.

The Political Football in Environmental Impact Assessment

I was in the process of writing a journal article one spring day in 1994 when the phone rang. It was my former doctoral thesis committee member and friend, Dr. Milton Freeman. The federal environmental review panel for Broken Hill Proprietary's proposed diamond mine at Lac De Gras in the Northwest Territories had recently issued a directive to BHP to give traditional knowledge equal consideration with scientific knowledge in assessing the impacts of its project. Milton had been contacted by a BHP representative seeking advice on who could undertake this challenge, and he wanted to know if I might be interested. If I accepted, it meant that I would be working directly for BHP to access Indigenous knowledge from a diverse cohort of Inuvialuit, Dogrib Dene, Yellowknives Dene, and North Slave Métis communities. After short deliberation and against my better judgement, I phoned Milton back later that evening to say I was interested. After all, this opportunity was one of the first efforts in Canada to meaningfully incorporate Indigenous knowledge into environmental impact assessment. The following day my brief and painful relationship with BHP began.

After reading the review panel's guidelines, the scope of BHP's environmental impact assessment and the potentially enormous effort and associated costs involved came into focus. To think that there would be enough money to design and carry out a traditional knowledge study on an equal footing with *Science* was an exciting prospect. In retrospect, I must have been dreaming. The budget for traditional knowledge at the end of the day was little more than an afterthought, amounting to less than five percent of that allocated for environmental studies. Sometimes *equal* does not mean *equal*. Moreover, working under strict deadlines with a half dozen culturally diverse Indigenous communities to access their members' knowledge gave new meaning to the word challenging. Although I had gotten to know from previous work a small cadre of Inuvialuit traditional knowledge holders, I had only passing familiarity with elders and hunter/trappers from the other Indigenous groups, and they with me. It often takes years for an outsider to build trust with a single Indigenous community, let alone several culturally disparate ones as community members need time to open up to outsiders and to feel comfortable with sharing their knowledge, values, and understandings of the world. Consequently, most Indigenous parties were hesitant to participate in such a study—some even refused. The very best I could do in the fourteen months afforded me was to consult with the affected communities and to develop a culturally appropriate research methodology that would access their knowledge and address their concerns at some point in the future should funds become available.

Fast forward to the eve of BHP's Environmental Review Panel technical session on traditional knowledge in Yellowknife. It was an event that territorial media and residents had been eagerly anticipating for months since BHP's diamond mine had the potential to inject hundreds of millions into a sluggish territorial economy. But first, it had to clear this one last hurdle.

My last meeting with BHP officials the night before the session remans indelibly imprinted on my brain. Frustrated with the whole idea of traditional knowledge and the possibility that it, perhaps more than anything else, could derail BHP's plans to build Canada's first diamond mine, a senior mine executive told me that I would have to introduce myself as a BHP representative at the upcoming session. My response that *"I would introduce myself, not as a representative, but an independent consultant hired to provide expertise and advice to BHP, and that my views did not necessarily reflect those of the proponent"* ignited her fury. Minutes later, she stormed out of the room, exclaiming, *"FUCK TRADITIONAL KNOWLEDGE! This mine is going through, whether you like it or not!"* I was in the process of changing my airline ticket back to Edmonton that night when BHP's mine manager (Bruce Turner) phoned, acquiescing to my position. My participation in the session was back on.

Incidentally, a handful of Indigenous peoples have shared with me some of the tactics that Canada's mining industry uses to gain their favour. A meeting between Diavik Diamond Mines and the North Slave Métis Alliance in the late 1990s stands out. Prior to the meeting, a couple buckets of fried chicken and a case of alcohol arrived at the NSMA office. After the prayer and introductions, the Diavik representative's enthusiastic request, "*Come on, boys, drink up, we gotta get this deal done!*" was met with an awkward silence and blank stares. He could not have known that the NSMA president and most council members present were recovered alcoholics and had been sober for years.[28]

There can be no better illustration of settler society's growing rancor towards Indigenous efforts to protect and assert their rights in the face of unbridled resource development than Widdowson and Howard's malicious treatise *Disrobing the Aboriginal Industry: The Deception Behind Indigenous Cultural Preservation*,[29] born the following day during the federal review panel's session on traditional knowledge. A Donner Book Prize nominee and cult classic in some industry and government circles, *Disrobing…* begins:

> *Despite the expectations that had been raised about the incorporation of traditional knowledge into environmental assessment, and the praise heaped upon the panel for issuing a directive to equally consider it, we were surprised when the technical session on traditional knowledge proved to be nothing more than a compilation of jejune platitudes interspersed with various intellectual dodges. Not only had the panel chosen to avoid establishing criteria and standards to evaluate traditional knowledge research, . . . no one at the session seemed to be able to identify what traditional knowledge was, let alone how it could be applied. Instead, BHP's anthropological consultants spent a great deal of time explaining that it had been difficult for them to obtain traditional knowledge because it could not be separated from its "cultural context." These anthropologists explained that traditional knowledge meant different things to different aboriginal groups, and it would take many years to document. BHP then made the extraordinary statement that it would pay for traditional knowledge research despite not understanding what it was.*
>
> *. . . The presentations made by aboriginal groups, the government of the Northwest Territories, and the Department of Indian and Northern Affairs were also unable to shed light on the methodology of traditional knowledge or how it would assess the environmental impacts of a diamond mine. Nevertheless, it was taken for granted that there was a great deal of information that could be*

---

28 Thanks to Clem Paul and Bob Turner for sharing this anecdote.

29 F. Widdowson and A. Howard (2008). *Disrobing the Aboriginal Industry: The Deception Behind Indigenous Cultural Preservation.* McGill University Press.

acquired and that government and industry should further increase their allocation of funds to collect aboriginal peoples' special knowledge. A spokesman for the Department of Indian and Northern Affairs claimed in his presentation that a "huge data base" of traditional knowledge already existed that could be used for future research. And while a great deal of concern was expressed about combining traditional knowledge with scientific studies, since there was potential for destroying the "cultural context" of traditional knowledge and infringing upon the "intellectual property rights" of various aboriginal groups, there was no attempt to elucidate how the different "knowledge systems" or "worldviews" could be incorporated to more fully understand ecological processes.

As disinterested observers, we were astonished at how the panel, BHP, the government and aboriginal groups were so confident that traditional knowledge was essential to the environmental assessment process when they didn't even seem to know what it was or how it could be used. After all, no one had recognized the necessity of traditional knowledge until the panel had directed that it be considered. In order to try to understand the nature of traditional knowledge and how it differed from science, we asked a number of questions both publicly and informally at the panel review. It was to form the basis of our understanding of aboriginal policy because it inadvertently uncovered the subterfuge. And the extensive chicanery was only the tip of iceberg where aboriginal policy was concerned.

The acceptance of this continuous obfuscation in a forum that was devoted to understanding traditional knowledge's importance was not the only surprising circumstance that occurred. After the session was over, a number of people expressed support for our questions that attempted to clarify the difference between traditional knowledge and science. Two BHP representatives also admitted to us confidentially that they were glad these questions were asked, since the company was prevented from raising similar questions. And finally, one of the panel members approached us and expressed his gratitude for the questions, reiterating that there was apprehension about discussing traditional knowledge openly.

The panel's hearing exemplified a well-known pattern of behaviour in the North; publicly, everyone declared unconditionally that traditional knowledge was a valid and essential source of information for environmental assessment and that it could enhance the scientific research that was being undertaken. When questions were asked about what this information was, or how it could be incorporated with scientific methods, however, no clarification was available. And although ... many people had concerns about traditional knowledge's usefulness, no one gave voice to them publicly, even in a forum that had been specifically tasked with discussing how to incorporate traditional knowledge into the environmental assessment process currently being undertaken by BHP.

Armed with a bunch of maliciously worded and appalling chapter titles, Widdowson and Howard go on to attack the integrity of traditional knowledge and the role of consultants in perpetuating the ruse on all Canadians. These included *Traditional Knowledge: Listening to the Silence; Environmental Management: The Spiritual Sell-Out of "Mother Earth"*; and *The Aboriginal Industry: Weavers of Illusory Silk*. Embittered, emboldened, and undeterred they then set their sights on policy initiatives in other arenas: *Self-government: An Inherent Right to Tribal Dictatorships; Justice: Rewarding Friends and Punishing Enemies; Child Welfare: Strengthening the Abusive Circle; Health Care: A Superstitious Alternative*; and *Education: Honouring the Ignorance of Our Ancestors.*

Agents of the Colonial Order in Sheep's Clothing

I was tempted to spend the remainder of this book rebuking Widdowson and Howard's racist, misleading, contradictory, and bigoted tirade. After all, I was the lead anthropologist that was the focus of their vitriol. However, I thought better of it. Besides, I had written about their sophistry back in 1997.[30] Moreover, many academics had already beaten me to the punch—and punch they did. No rebuke of *Disrobing the Aboriginal Industry* has been better articulated or harder-hitting than Mohawk scholar and University of Victoria professor Taiaiake Alfred's crushing take-down,[31] a lightly edited version of which follows:

> *From the excited, glowing reviews of Disrobing the Aboriginal Industry I had seen in The National Post, and as a critic of parasitic white lawyers and consultants, sell-out aboriginals, and collaborationist Aboriginal politicians, I was prepared for a hard-hitting critique and useful deconstruction of the complex of injustice that has been built up around Indigenous-state relations in Canada. Instead, I found a collection of distortions, omissions, and exaggerations....*

---

30 M. Stevenson (1997). Ignorance and Prejudice Threaten Environmental Assessment. *Policy Options* 18(2):25-28.

31 T. Alfred (2010). *Redressing Racist Academics, Or, Put Your Clothes Back On, Please!: A Review of Widdowson and Howard's, Disrobing the Aboriginal Industry.* https://bermudaradical.wordpress.com/2010/08/20/redressing-racist-academics-or-put-your-clothes-back-on-please-a-review-of-widdowson-and-howard's-disrobing-the-aboriginal-industry/

For those who are not aware . . . Widdowson and Howard are a pair of "academics" in Canada who simultaneously attempt to pass themselves off as Marxists, while at the same time gleefully joining up with the centuries old colonial-imperial project in putting an end to indigenous peoples as distinct cultural and national entities. . . . They and their work is an insult to both the 500 year-old Indigenous resistance to colonialism as well as legitimate Marxists and socialists who have been there standing side-by-side with Indigenous warriors. Anyone seriously concerned with the construction of another world, one not based on colonialism-imperialism, racism and capitalism would do themselves some good by recognizing Widdowson and Howard for what they are, "agents of the colonial order in sheep's clothing."

Evidently, Widdowson and Howard get up in the morning and eat a dog's breakfast of outmoded communist ideology and rotten anthropological theories washed down with strong racial prejudices inherited from their own unexamined colonial upbringings, all of which would turn anyone else's stomach. Their ideas are . . . a ragtag collection of theoretical frames, which taken together form a methodological approach remarkable mostly for its inability, like the authors who employ it, to comprehend indigeneity outside of being the object of colonization and empire. To wit: elements of Darwinian evolutionary stages theory, bits of Hegelian historical determinism, and a reliably unsophisticated view of capitalism is a necessary destructive-progressive force leading to the realization of a communist utopia wherein exists a scientifically planned and state organized global society made up of human beings who are worthwhile only to the extent they are "productive." Thus it is understandable how the authors can, or must, advocate for the destruction of the natural environment by industrial development, and why they must hate and seek to destroy the people most closely connected to and committed to the preservation of nature in the face of capitalist exploitation of the land. . . .

. . . Instead of attacking Indigenous people, they attack the "Aboriginal industry." But their cover is blown the instant you realize . . . that their notion of culture is equated to ethnicity and that their "Aboriginal industry" includes and embodies just about every Indigenous writer and representative in the country. There is nothing novel or insightful in their conceptualization of an "Aboriginal industry." In fact, the idea is lifted from the Métis scholar Howard Adams' seminal work in Prison of Grass and my own work on the subject—Peace, Power, Righteousness—both of which have a sustained focus on the cooptation

of First Nations leaders and "comprador" Aboriginal leadership and the problem of parasitic white professionals.... As a critique of this problem, the book is boring drivel that anyone working in this field has heard and read many times over by now. And if this was the point of the book, I could stop my review right here. But their point is not to illuminate, it is to denigrate, and the book is voluminous in this objective.

If Widdowson and Howard were serious Marxists concerned with the oppression of Indigenous peoples ... they would no doubt have focused on the economic and political relations that are at the root of the problems besetting Indigenous peoples and Canadian society as a whole. So, where is the analysis of Canada as a colonial regime and the broad consideration of Indigenous-state relations and the history of imperialism that forms the backdrop to any serious discussion of Canadian history and of Indigenous issues?

This book really is a shoddy piece of trash posing as serious analysis and pretending to respectability. And I use the word "pretending" advisedly; it is common knowledge among people who work in the field academically and professionally that Widdowson and her husband worked diligently for a number of years to integrate into and gain access to the profits of the "Aboriginal industry" for themselves. But they were unsuccessful. They could not gain acceptance and a permanent position in the very structure of land-claims negotiation in the NWT which forms the main target of their polemic. Finding themselves shut out of the profits and unable to gain the respect of colleagues because of their unprofessionalism, lack of skill, and social ineptness, they took to hysterically attacking the structures and people who denied them.

Widdowson and Howard see the dissolution of Indigenous culture and the assimilation of Indigenous people into the white mainstream as the best thing that could possibly happen in Canada. They hold up the Métis, in contrast to First Nations and Inuit, as having "principled leadership," and because of their being assimilated, "it is with them that hope for real change lies" (p. 256).... So it becomes clear that the extermination of any meaningful sense of indigeneity, [accompanied by the] championing of the industrialization of Indigenous lands as the guarantor of a healthy, stable and prosperous future ... is Widdowson and Howard's end objective. Basically, their fundamental prescription is idiosyncratic and asinine, and it renders [them] ... as blind fools, especially given the global financial and political realities facing the world today.

It would be easy to refute [their]... *derogatory and unsubstantiated attacks... but serious engagement with the substance of such insulting slanders would dignify their book. Instead... the scientific literature will disabuse anyone of the notion of Widdowson and Howard possessing scholarly integrity. Indeed* [it] *goes even further in debunking the authors' central arguments as the scholarly consensus supports many of the Indigenous teachings and oral histories that Widdowson and Howard debase as mere superstition in their book.*

Most of the book consists of uninformed and ideologically-driven assertion. There are significant chapters on subjects in which the authors have no expertise at all and have done no research, save for their own unique methodological innovation: web surfing and Internet chat room analysis. ...Unverified personal anecdotes are also repeatedly given as proofs. ...Their writing throughout the book conveys a profoundly wilful ignorance of both Indigenous realities and scholarship on Indigenous issues, [and] *... is also both insensitive and oblivious to the extensively studied experiences of colonized peoples, the social phenomena of acculturation, the anomie resulting from state-induced social suffering and the psychological and social effects of oppression in a colonial regime.*

... Their section on education argues against the teaching of Indigenous languages, which they view as inherently backward and inferior to European languages as communicative tools in the modern era ... [and] *since European languages are superior, Indigenous languages should be left to die off.*

The chapter on environmental management ... is a recycling of hostile email exchanges in which actual experts in the field tell Widdowson and Howard that they don't know what they are talking about. This makes it the most truthful and satisfying part of the book. It's topped off by the authors telling us what Indigenous people think about the environment, and then criticizing their own cartoonish representation of Indigenous philosophy.

... In the chapter on traditional knowledge they say that [it] *"is immune from questioning and resists its methods being assessed." It is assumed to be "held by people with revered qualities, usually elders, whose views must be critically supported" (p. 240). Beyond citing the work of other white academics on the subject and duplicitously reading into and distorting their words—by using supportive statements declaring respect for Indigenous people and knowledge to support their own hostile position—no evidence is provided from Indigenous people to back up their spurious claims. They also say that Indigenous people are opposed*

to science (p. 248). This is yet another ridiculous statement lacking supporting evidence. The reason they cannot provide evidence for their claims is that the processes of knowledge generation and transmission among Indigenous people in no way resembles Widdowson and Howard's caricature. Their method here, clearly, is to try to generate an understanding of Indigenous knowledge that has little relation to actual Indigenous beliefs and which serves their own critical purpose. They attempt to do this by using fragmentary quotations gathered unsystematically and without the benefit of a human subject ethical research oversight framework. They then decontextualize the information and transpose it into unrelated discussions so as to distort and belittle the information's significance. . . . What is important to Widdowson and Howard is the rejection and denigration of any and all attempts by Indigenous people to speak for themselves and to defend their ideas. . . .

Reminiscent of a nightmarish succession of under-researched, badly-written, unedited and emotion-laden undergraduate-level papers, this book wears you down in the end. . . . Suffice to say by this point that if you're a person who rejects the notion of global warming and doesn't believe that the Holocaust ever happened, you'll really enjoy this book. For a sane person, Disrobing the Aboriginal Industry is nothing more than a piece of garbage picked from the dustbin of history by two ignorami scurrying on the margins of academia clutching Marx's The Eighteenth Brumaire of Louis Napoleon and stooped low under the weight of their personal and professional frustrations.

Believe me, the frustrations go both ways!

CHAPTER 6

Breathing with the Authenticity of the Unseparated: Knowledge That Connects

MEEKA (MIKE) AND I WERE IN TROUBLE, DEEP TROUBLE. AND WE KNEW IT. ON A -40 DEGREE day in late February, 1997, our snowmobiles and *qamutiit* (sleds) were slowly sinking through a bed of disintegrating ice as we attempted to ascend a precipitous mountain pass on the west side of Cumberland Sound, south Baffin Island. Four days earlier in Pangnirtung, Meeka had asked me if I wanted to help take her nephew's snowmobile and *qamutit* back to Iqaluit. I was in Pang working with Inuit elders developing interpretive concepts for the new Angmarlik Cultural Centre and museum. I had never experienced a mountainous Arctic landscape in late winter (*upingaaqsaaq*) before, so jumped at the opportunity. Three days before, Meeka had descended this steep mountain valley pass, navigating without incident a series of frozen rapids and waterfalls. You see, it was a short-cut that eliminated two hours of commute between the two communities, and Meeka could not bear the thought of wasting time by going the longer, but less risky, way around. Going up was a different story.

Outfitted in polar bear skin pants (*qarliq*), a caribou skin parka (*kulitaq*), and seal skin boots (*qammiit*), I struggled to help Meeka pull our machines and sleds out of the slush before they and we disappeared into what awaited us below. But as the sun continued to beat down upon us, we both began to sweat—a grave mistake in -40 temperatures—forcing us to remove our parkas. We were soaking wet inside and out—another transgression in such temperatures. With Meeka continually barking out instructions, we eventually managed to free our machines and sleds, turn them around, and race downhill leaving behind a beautifully made untethered *kulitaq* gifted to her by her aunt—a loss for which Meeka still blames me. Twenty minutes later at the base of the mountain range, we stopped to recoup, make tea, consume the only food we had—Smarties and Pilot biscuits—while enduring an alternating regiment of removing our parkas, beating the ice off them, freezing, and putting them back on. Two hours later, half-frozen and disoriented, we continued on our way to Iqaluit, arriving thirteen hours behind schedule, frostbitten, and exhausted.

Most of my nine lives were spent that day. But to Meeka it was *aijungilaq*, "*that's the way life goes*" in her dialect. Her father Jamasie, who had begun to worry, was less conciliatory and reprimanded Meeka for damn near killing me. You see, we had made the near-fatal mistake of travelling over fresh water during a full moon in late winter while the sun shone brightly overhead. Jamasie had expected Meeka to know that one ought never travel during *upingaaqsaaq* over frozen rapids, ponds, and streams when tidal forces and the gravitational pull of the moon are greatest. Apparently, immediately after a full moon, fresh water ice crystals and layers in Arctic streams can separate under direct sunlight, which then act to magnify the sun's rays on lower ice layers, creating life-threatening situations for those who don't know any better. We now know better.

Oral history passed down through generations of Indigenous peoples has proven extremely reliable over the centuries. Recently, I sat in amazement as I listened to Baptiste and Robert Metchooyeah regale me with stories that their father (Paulis) had told them about how the Dene Tha' barely survived a summer many generations ago when their lands were blanketed with snow and nothing grew. While neither knew the year that their people almost starved to death, I soon deduced that it was 1816. During the previous year, the Indonesian volcano Mount Tambora erupted, causing a worldwide deep-freeze in the northern hemisphere known colloquially as *the year without a summer*.

The oral history of many First Nations record devastating natural disasters that have been correlated with dated geological events. The January 1st, 1700, tsunami that wiped out many Maal-nuth villages on the west coast of Vancouver Island (and many more Japanese villages ten hours later) being one of many. In the groundbreaking Supreme Court of Canada *Delgamuukw* decision,[32] 3,000 years of oral history recorded in stories and song played a key role in establishing the Aboriginal rights and title of the Gitxsan and Wet'suwet'en peoples in the eyes of Canada.

Indigenous peoples are experts at constructing and passing on knowledge that has allowed them to thrive in their chosen environments for millennia. I could go on citing examples about how ingenious our First Peoples are in this regard. But such examples really do not get at the heart of the differences between Indigenous knowledge and *Science*. So what's the deal with Indigenous (traditional and/or ecological) knowledge, anyway?

---

32   *Delgamuukw v British Columbia*, [1997] 3 SCR 1010.

More Than Numbers

One thing I learned early on from Inuit hunters and elders is that Indigenous ecological knowledge is more than numbers, much more. For example, the counting system of most south Baffin Inuit before contact with Qallunaat was *ahtauasuq (1), maqguq (2), pingasut (3), tisimat (4), talimut (5), amisuq* (many), and *amisuraluq* (way more than many). It may come as a surprise to some that most hunter-gatherer peoples did not possess what could be called sophisticated counting systems. Numbers simply were not important, or needed. There is archaeological evidence that ancient African hunters 20,000 years ago kept tallies—probably of game animals or group members—that far exceeded the number of fingers on both hands (usually ten). But numbers, and counting, didn't truly come into being until the rise of market economies and cities some 6,000 years ago in Sumaria.

Environmental resource managers and conservation bureaucrats—particularly those charged with conserving *wildlife* and setting *total allowable harvests*—depend largely on numbers or interval data sets to make decisions. Often this is accomplished to the exclusion of other types of knowledge and sources of information. The old materialistic saw that *"what cannot be counted, does not count"* did and does not apply in most non-literate societies. Rather, there were and are far more important observations to make, and much more nuanced and detailed information to gather, process, and share.

Nowhere is this more clearly demonstrated than in the 1922 effort by Danish ethnologist Knud Rasmussen to solicit from seven Netsilingmiut hunters the number of seals each had killed during the previous winter (*ukiaq*). Rasmussen's initial attempt to obtain this information was unsuccessful. However, it soon dawned on him to supply each hunter with a pencil in order to draw every seal each had procured over the preceding months.

Rasmussen's caption for the following figure reads:

> *I was greatly interested to learn how many seals and caribou the various hunters had caught in a season. None of them, of course, had the figures. It occurred to me to let them draw their catch, and it proved that all the various recollections associated with the occasions on which they made a kill, and their being able to remember whether it was a large or small animal, made it possible to draw up a fairly correct hunting score. The . . . pictures show columns of seals caught by various hunters from the time when they first began to hunt at the beginning of winter and until they ceased in spring.*[33]

---

33 K. Rasmussen (1931). *The Netsilik Eskimos: Social Life and Spiritual Culture*. Report of the Fifth Thule Expedition 1921-24, Copenhagen.

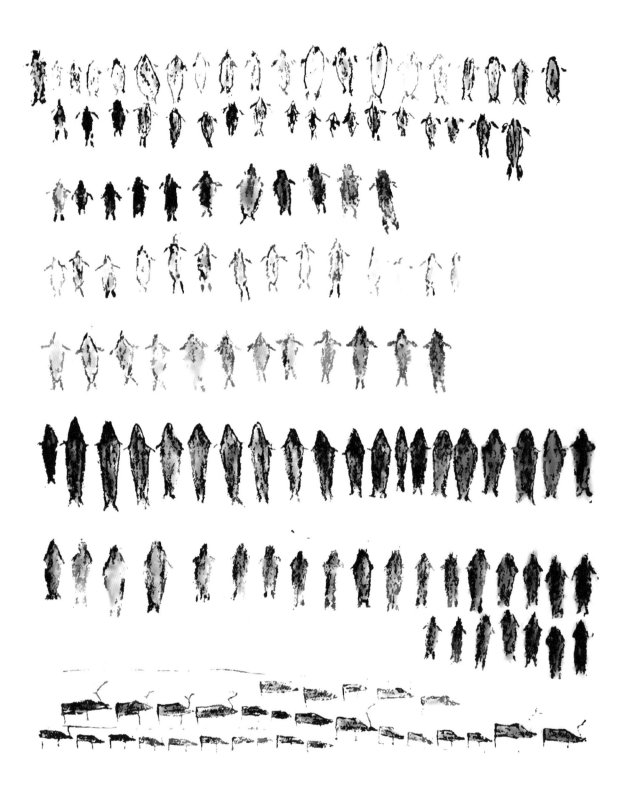

What each hunter drew with an implement they likely never handled before was not only the exact number of seals each had killed in sequence, but a wide range of variation in the size, shape, and coat colour of ringed (*netsiq*) and bearded (*ujuk*) seals within each tally. Had Rasmussen queried each hunter about what these differences meant, had he not been so preoccupied with numbers, he might have learned something about the age, sex, physical condition, stomach contents, and so forth of each seal. He might have recorded each seal's kill location, ice conditions, and the level of effort needed to procure it—lines of inquiry that might have revealed changes in these characteristics over time and space. He might have even found out how each seal was used and shared within the camp—a critical consideration in Nesilingmiut society with its rigid rules for sharing seals—thus revealing something about social group structure and organization.

A somewhat related story was told to me by Livee Kullualik, Jamasie Mike's son-in-law, during my days in Pangnirtung. Many decades ago when Jamasie was just a lad, he was asked by the Hudson's Bay manager to count over a specified period of time—I think it was about a week—all the char he could net at the Kulliq River mouth across the inlet from Pangnirtung. Not yet familiar with the white man's counting system but eager and undaunted, he accepted the task head on. At the end of each day he presented the HBC manager with a bundle of willow sticks matching the exact number caught and calibrated to the length of each fish.

Numbers have been the *sine qua non* of *wildlife management* since, well, forever. While numbers are needed to calculate the size of *wildlife* populations of interest, boundaries for these populations must also be established. But what comes first, the chicken or the egg? This where it gets sketchy. Usually a grab bag of information—from genetic to biophysical to locational to behavioural—is used to arrive at best guess estimates of boundary parameters. Then the counting begins. The resultant *management units* are then managed and conserved via a host of measures—e.g., *harvest* quotas, predator control measures, habitat alterations, etc.—in order to maintain viable *wildlife* populations. Anything approaching reality is a really a matter of blind faith, if not willful ignorance, which renders the whole exercise rather suspect.

Against this backdrop, the knowledge of Indigenous user communities is often disparaged and dismissed as anecdotal by decision-makers, an irony that has not escaped some observers: "*Western scientists should not criticize what they see as unsubstantiated judgements in native science based on . . . generations of experience, when they are speculative about their judgements based on few measurements made over a short time-scale.*"[34]

---

34   C.B. Crampton (1991). Native Conservation in a Northern Canadian Landscape. *Environmental Conservation* 18:67-68.

I am not saying that numbers do not have their place. Some mathematical constants such as pi (π, 3.14159...), the Golden Ratio (1.61803399...), and the Fibonacci sequence (1, 1, 2, 3, 5, 8, 13, 21, 34...), among others, seem to be universal descriptors of nature. Judging by my experience on the southeast Baffin beluga committee, Feigenbaum's constant (4.669) appears to be a favourite tool for wildlife biologists to cut through all the chaos of reality in order to invent population estimates for various animal species. Mathematics has even predicted and revealed some of the most fundamental building blocks of our universe, though no one yet has really figured out what quantum mechanics or gravity are all about. Nevertheless, we must ask ourselves: do numbers reveal the truth about nature, or do they reveal the truth of how we perceive nature? Physicists, for example, have chosen to study the universe building upon historical mathematical formulae and theories, forcing them to think in certain prescribed ways. Not only may we not be able to see most of nature's patterns—especially those within complex ecological systems—relying on numbers and mathematical manipulation, our quest to explain *nature by numbers* may blind us to a whole universe of patterns and interconnections invisible to mathematical prediction and numerical gymnastics.

If used indiscriminately and without reflection, numbers, like language, can be a very oppressive tool that marginalizes Indigenous peoples and subverts what they have known and practised for generations. Recall the caribou numbers guessing game during the Thompson, Manitoba, BQCMB committee meeting. This travesty had the effect of validating the scientific expertise and authority of those using this sleight-of-hand trick, while emboldening them (except Tim) to challenge the experiential knowledge of Indigenous board members and those whom they represented.

No, It's Not Just Like Gardening! Or Who Talks Like That, Part 2

I had been looking forward to her presentation for some time. As one of Canada's leading ethnobotanists, her research with several First Nations, including the Secewpmec, was bound to be informative and thought provoking. It was. She had an excellent reputation as a researcher and had earned the respect and trust of colleagues as well as those Indigenous groups with whom she worked. Near the end of her talk at the University of Alberta she spoke about a First Nation elder on the central coast of British Columbia who tended a plot of land at the head of a large coastal inlet. After querying the elder about his efforts to enhance the growth of certain plants through weeding, thinning, and other activities, she concluded that what he was doing *"was just like gardening."* After a moment of reflection, the elder replied, *"Yeah, I suppose, it's just like gardening."* And that was that!

"But, how can this be," I mused. The First Nation to which this elder belonged had no agricultural or gardening heritage, at least none prior to contact with Europeans. His people traditionally had no worldview in which man holds dominion over nature, a notion that lies at the heart of the British colonial gardening tradition. On the surface, *gardening* and what this elder was doing might have seemed similar. They're not.

So let's examine the nature of the interchange between the elder and researcher at the moment of her discovery. First of all, the elder not only shared his knowledge in a language that was not his original tongue, he was forced to respond affirmatively to the researcher using a concept foreign to his First Nations' lexicon. The researcher then interpreted what the elder said from her own Eurocentric framework with all its inherent cultural bias and baggage. Nevertheless, with this newfound insight that what this elder was doing was *"just like gardening,"* a cultural bridge and a sense of common connection and humanity was built. *"You are just like us and I am just like you"* was the connotation of her remark.

But as quickly as this cultural bridge was built, it came crashing down. Because this researcher perceived what this elder was doing was nothing more than *gardening*, there was no need to learn more, to ask questions that lie beneath the surface, to figure out what was really going on, to explore how his activities were related to other aspects of his existence. *"Because I know gardening, I know you"* was the subtext of her response. A formidable barrier to a deeper understanding of the significance of the elder's actions had been erected and a learning opportunity was lost. I do not know if the elder's response was meant to dissuade the researcher from probing deeper—a possibility suggested by my experience with Inuit and First Nation elders. Often, Indigenous elders do not share their knowledge freely with outsiders until they feel comfortable that the receiver is able to deal with it in the best interests of the community. Maybe the elder felt she was not ready? I don't know.

What questions might our researcher have asked? How about the social significance of what this elder was doing? What roles did his *gardening-like* activities play in maintaining social relationships, fulfilling social obligations, and so on? Did these activities have a property dimension whereby rights of access were inherited, limited, or controlled? How far back in time do they extend? Are they recorded in oral tradition? Were there other ecological, economic, cultural, and symbolic dimensions to the elder's activities? These are the kinds of knowledge that the elder might have shared had he had the opportunity.

Increasingly, so-called *experts* with minimal training in the humanities and social sciences, and with little understanding of Indigenous cultures or settler-colonial history, are being called upon to document Indigenous knowledge and traditional land-use activities on behalf of industry, government, and even Indigenous clients. With formal education in disciplines such as biology, environmental sciences, geology, chemistry, engineering, etc., these individuals rarely come equipped with the tools to examine their own deeply held cultural biases. As a consequence, they frequently extend pernicious cultural concepts, language, values, and motivations to Indigenous peoples, fully unaware of the harm they may be inflicting. If this were not disconcerting enough, some social scientists are even more culpable for their ongoing and unexamined efforts to force the language and concepts of environmental resource management onto Indigenous experience, while ignoring the damage that can result. As multidisciplinary scholar Gregory Bateson reminds us, *"we have been trained to think in ways we hardly notice . . . even the language we speak pushes our minds into particular ways of defining and identifying our world."* Without adequate skills to deconstruct Western scientific epistemologies and ontologies, to filter out of their formal educations what is and is not in the best interests of the Indigenous communities with whom they work and/or represent, these actors often wind up becoming unwitting and insidious agents of assimilation and cultural genocide for the dominant culture.

Managing resources, harvesting animals, and *conserving stocks* are concepts that likely did not emerge among most Indigenous peoples. Yet, in order to make any headway with environmental resource managers, Indigenous Canadians have been forced to adopt these deeply rooted Judaeo-Christian-capitalistic tropes. In doing so, they engage with environmental authorities and institutions at considerable cost to themselves, their communities, and, arguably, even the species and habitats upon which they depend. Unfortunately, the whole process often finds no effective local opposition, at least not initially, by virtue of the fact that they are finally engaging environmental authorities in good faith to make sound decisions that affect their lives. The institutionalized concepts, terms, and procedures that have come to frame the dialogue and dominate the discourse between environmental managers and Indigenous peoples are, however, for the most part, antithetical to the latter's values, concepts, and understandings. Greenlandic scholar Ingmar Egede spoke emphatically about this years ago:

> *The concept of wildlife is taken from a farming culture. . . . My reason for questioning these concepts is that the policy makers, the biologists and administrators outside our world are foreign to hunting and hunting cultures. . . . So ban the concepts of "managing stocks," the concepts like "harvesting", the concepts of "wildlife"* [and] *through the process of changing your vocabulary, you may be understood better by the people you serve . . . or* [who] *hired you to create a sustainable culture for themselves and the generations to come.*[35]

As environmental resource management frequently necessitates the collection of quantitative information beyond that normally held or considered important by Indigenous peoples, it plays a key role in the systemic rejection of more nuanced qualitative ecological

---

35   I. Egede (1995). Presentation at *Conference on Circumpolar Aboriginal People and Co-management Practice.* November 20, Inuvik, NWT.

knowledge. Contrary to traditional Indigenous beliefs that animals exist on an equal footing with humans—and thus deserve the same respect and treatment—adoption of scientific concepts and language subverts customary and sustainable systems of Indigenous knowledge, management, and conservation by placing control of the relationship entirely in human hands.

What Are We Managing and Conserving?

On a lazy late summer's day in 2006 I stood on the edges of the Whitefeather Forest north of Red Lake, Ontario, accompanied by several Pikangikum First Nation elders and a small group of Sustainable Forest Management Network researchers from across the country. We were guests of the Pikangikum First Nation and had gathered together to gain greater perspective into how its elders and land stewards perceived current forest practices, and how they understood and related to their lands. Elders Jake Keesic, Charlie Peters, Oliver Hill, Reggie Peters, and Matthew Strong, spoke at length about the destructive effects of roads and clear-cutting on Pikangikum's traditional territory. In particular, the sacred nests of the *Thunderbird*—30-100m (wide) x 10-30m (deep) circular boulder field depressions—were being destroyed at an alarming rate. The reverence with which these Anishanaabe elders spoke about this sacred icon, and the evident torment they felt over the blatant and wholesale destruction of its nests by the forest industry, was initially met with blank stares and side glances by our small academically trained cohort. However, for some of us, these initial reactions gradually began to dissipate as we began to comprehend, at least peripherally, the role that the Thunderbird played in the cosmology and lives of the Pikangikum people.

You see, as an agent of the creator, Thunderbird at the beginning of time created lightning and thunder. Lightning strikes ignite forest fires that, in turn, burn old forest growth and generate new growth. This never-ending cycle sustains and is the foundation for all life in the forest. For Pikangikum's elders and many Anishanaabe, there can be no greater sacrilege, no greater desecration of their lands, no greater form of cultural genocide, than the destruction of Thunderbird nests. The sacred cycle of life that sustains the lives and culture of the Pikangikum people is incrementally and effectively obliterated with the eradication of every Thunderbird nest.

This was not directly explained to us—that is not the Anishanaabe way. We had to learn it the hard way, on our own time, in our own way. But the insight that this special learning opportunity provided into how the Pikangikum people think about and relate to their lands—how everything is intimately interconnected and interdependent—was profound. Indeed, it began to chip away at our singularly Western scientific view of Thunderbird nests as mere geomorphological remnants from the last glaciation that could be destroyed with the wave of a forest manager's hand. There was a special significance and value to the Pikangikum view of Thunderbird nests that was more aesthetically appropriate, culturally relevant, and ecologically grounded than the sterile scientific cliché.

Whenever interviewing Indigenous elders, hunters, and land stewards our conversations often get around to discussing how their systems of management and conservation differ from those in which they are often forced to participate. And, ever since my Southeast Baffin beluga committee experience, I have been compelled to ask: "*What, if anything, do you manage or conserve?*" The discussion that inevitably follows lands on the fact that it is their "*relationships*" to their lands and resources, not resources per se. For example, during a SFMN researcher retreat hosted by the Shuswap Tribal Council in 2007, treasured Secewepmec elder Mary Thomas acknowledged that if her people could be said to manage anything, it was their "*connections*" to their lands. She further lamented that she could no longer sustain her "*connection*" to her medicinal plant and berry-picking areas because of over-grazing by free-ranging cattle—a loss that produced a variety of adverse ecological, social, cultural, and economic impacts on Mary and her family.

Over the years, I have come to realize how profoundly different the two management systems are. One obsessed with numbers, data, and circumscribed information about specific resources wherein human beings are seen as largely extraneous to the resource(s) needing to be *managed* and *conserved*. The other focused on maintaining relationships with, and responsibilities to, the natural world, while fulfilling obligations to current and future generations. I have also seen how virtually impossible it is for people educated, cultured, and socialized in *Science* to accept Indigenous systems of knowledge, conservation, and management as valid in their own right. Yet some more *progressive* wildlife biologists working with Indigenous peoples have told me that "*traditional knowledge is acceptable only so long as it provides useful information and does not include anything related to spirituality.*" Oh, right! Okay then!

Pass the Kool-Aid!

Relationships That Connect

The realization that all components of an ecosystem, including human beings, are interrelated is so fundamental to ecological thinking that biologist-turned-anthropologist-turned-philosopher Gregory Bateson proposed that, "*relationships should be used as a basis for all definitions, and this should be taught to our children in elementary schools, [and that] anything should be defined not by what it is in itself, but by its relations to other things.*" This, of course, is not what is taught today, even in most post-secondary institutions. The discipline of ecology, where one might expect a new theory of ecological relationships to emerge, has been slow to embrace and explore the space that Bateson,[36] Terrance Deacon,[37] and others so clearly saw. As some anthropologists have observed: *"The problem with the simpler, mainstream, gene-centric story of biology is that it tries to impose a linear narrative on a dynamic that in reality has no obvious beginning or end."*[38] Ecology has not escaped the cultural shackles of Western science, and, not unexpectedly, some of its practitioners have divided ecological relationships into distinct categories, which are then subdivided into even smaller subsets, each having additional multiple and separate functions. Clearly, this is not what Bateson was talking about. Rather,

> *What has to be investigated and described is a vast network or matrix of interlocking message material and abstract tautologies, premises and exemplifications. . . . But, as of 1979, there is no conventional method of describing such a tangle. We do not know even where to begin. . . . As every schoolboy ought to know . . . logic is precisely unable to deal with recursive circuits without generating paradox and that quantities are precisely not the stuff of complex communicating systems. In other words, logic and quantity turn out to be inappropriate devices for describing organisms and their interactions and internal organization.*

Bateson's approach to what really matters is radically different from *Science*'s materialistic preoccupation with separating things from other things and then taking them apart to see what makes them tick, leaving him to ask, *"What is it about our way of perceiving that makes us not see the delicate interdependencies in ecological systems that give them their integrity?* Bateson's focus was on the relationships between things in their context. As he maintained, *"We live in a world that is only made of relationships, and without context, our words and actions have no meaning."* . . . *"The arbitrariness of the kind of separations created by defining things without reference to their relationships to other things"* was one of Bateson's greatest insights. As his daughter reminds us in *An Ecology of Mind*,[39] *"when we define something as separate from something else, we create limits to our ability to see these interrelationships and dynamics."* According to Nora Bateson, this is why we must challenge the authority of those who refuse to see these relationships *"until it breathes with the authenticity of the unseparated."*

---

36 G. Bateson (1972). *Steps to an Ecology of Mind.* Ballantine Books, New York. G. Bateson (1979) *Mind in Nature: A Necessary Unity*, E. P. Dutton, New York.

37 T. Deacon (2012). *Incomplete Nature: How Mind Emerged from Matter.* Norton, New York.

38 H. Sinding-Larsen (2013). *The Patterns which Connect: Gregory Bateson and Terrance Deacon as Healers of the Great Divide between Natural and Human Science.* http://www.uio.no/forskning/tverrfak/kultrans/aktuelt/konferanser/demarcations/.

39 N. Bateson (2010). *An Ecology of Mind. A Daughter's Portrait of Gregory Bateso*n anecologyofmind.com/

For Deacon, the inability to "*integrate the many species of absence-based causality into our scientific methodologies has not just seriously handicapped us, it has effectively left a vast fraction of the world orphaned from theories that are presumed to apply to everything.*" Deacon further speculates that "*the very care that has been necessary to systematically exclude these sorts of explanations from undermining our causal analyses of physical, chemical, and biological phenomena has also stymied our efforts to penetrate beyond the descriptive surface of the phenomena of life and mind.*" In the end, scientific rationalism and reductionism ring hollow.

Bateson, Deacon, and of course many Indigenous peoples, view the interrelationships and dynamics between things as—if not more—important and fundamental than what is connected or can be counted. As Sinding-Larsen reminds us, these "*perspectives are badly needed in an academic world that is increasingly becoming specialized and narrow.*" Acknowledging the paradoxes that Bateson and Deacon's perceptions of mind and nature reveal steer us toward a more nuanced and sophisticated understanding of the relationships between the parts and the wholes of ecological systems. However, not only are we not there yet, the empowered and privileged of this world continue to deny the utility, efficacy, and viability of the knowledge and management systems of those cultures who have come closest to this understanding.

Visualize, if you can, a world without numbers. Imagine that the only things that count in such a world are things that aren't and can't be counted. What is more important than developing and sharing knowledge about the myriad of ecological, social, and other relationships upon which your very survival and well-being, and those of your loved ones, depend?

Bateson, Deacon, and a few others have realized what most Indigenous cultures have known since time immemorial: Everything is one, everything is interconnected, and we haven't even scratched the surface of what we ought to know. In his book *Principles of Tsawalk*, hereditary chief of the Ahousaht Richard Atleo (Umeek) builds upon his previous work, *Tsawalk: A Nuu-chah-nulth Worldview*,[40] contrasting *Tsawalk* with the Cartesian view of nature where everything is separable and connections are unimportant. At the same time, Umeek argues that because every culture, indeed every being, has its own story or truth, "*one segment of humanity has no right or moral authority to suppress the stories of others.*" By weaving together Nuu-chah-nulth and Western worldviews, Umeek creates a philosophical foundation to confront many of the global crises we face today, while laying the groundwork for a more equitable, empathetic, and sustainable path to co-existence. As one conscientious reader of *Principles of Tsawalk* has grasped:

---

40 E. R. Atleo [Umeek] (2005). *Tsawalk: A Nuu-chah-nulth Worldview*, UBC Press. E. R. Atleo (2012). *Principles of Tsawalk: An Indigenous Approach to Global Crisis*, UBC Press.

> [Because] *humans know extremely little ... it is extremely dangerous for the story of one segment of humanity to dominate all other beings' stories. Colonization, however, has meant that one tradition of stories has become globally dominant, and it is from this ongoing process of domination that global crisis has resulted. Decolonization and social equality are, therefore, prerequisites to restoring any sort of ecological balance or justice to the world. This perspective is anti-dogmatic and anti-essentialist; it welcomes Western science as one vital source of useful stories, but opposes epistemological hegemony because of the suffering it brings.*[41]

The insights of Umeek, Bateson, and Deacon urge us toward a more enlightened understanding of the world around us, greater empathy toward others, and stronger connections with all life forms on this planet. Whether we get there or not depends on how (un)satisfied we are with the status quo and how (un)committed we are to changing our attitudes and institutions.

The promise of Indigenous ecological knowledge in environmental and *wildlife management* has not been met simply because we have not created, let alone envisioned, in partnership with our Indigenous hosts, the ethical space in our institutions and our approaches to nature for this to happen. We have not even given peripheral consideration to the concepts, values, understandings, and rights of Indigenous peoples in environmental decisions that directly affect them. Nor have we contemplated how damaging our singularly reductionistic materialistic view of the world has been on Indigenous peoples and their ways of relating to nature. We have lacked the understanding, courage, vision, and perseverance needed to change our attitudes and institutions. But change we must, a challenge that will not be undemanding, as Indigenous scholar Willie Ermine reminds us:

> *The dimension of the dialogue might seem overwhelming because it will involve and encompass issues like language, distinct histories, knowledge traditions, values, interests, and social, economic and political realities and how these impact and influence an agreement to interact. Even so ... the new partnership model of the ethical space, in a cooperative spirit between Indigenous peoples and Western institutions, will create new currents of thought that flow in different directions and overrun the old ways of thinking.*[42]

---

41 N. Theriault (2015). Comment on *Principles of Tsawalk: An Indigenous Approach to Global Crisis*, March 2. InhabitingtheAnthropocene.com

42 W. Ermine (2007). The Ethical Space of Engagement. *Indigenous Law Journal* 6(1):193-203.

The Sound of Silence

The *silence* we hear emanating from the contested spaces in which Indigenous ecological knowledge fights for its voice does not come from Indigenous peoples and their representatives and supporters gleefully championing an obstructionist, self-serving, fallaciously hollow agenda as Widdowson and Howard assert. Rather, the *silence* comes from the hubris, complacency, and intransigence of the privileged and disproportionately empowered guardians and colonial institutions of settler society. Until such time that we develop in partnership with our Indigenous hosts the ethical and institutional space for them and their knowledge in *environmental resource management*, rejecting the epistemology of the colonizers and/or affecting change from within when the odd decontextualized crumb of Indigenous knowledge passes the test, currently appear to be our only strategies. Not until we have co-created arrangements that temper and balance Western scientific knowledge with Indigenous knowledge in decisions that impact our First Peoples, their environments, and their futures will it be acceptable to *"keep the science clean."*

PART TWO

Land Rights and Title Wars

CHAPTER 7

"The Existing Aboriginal and Treaty Rights of the Aboriginal Peoples of Canada Are Hereby Recognized and Affirmed,"[43] Part One

> *When we talk about Nuu chah nulth cultural practices we are ... talking about responsibilities that have evolved over millennia into unwritten tribal laws. These reflect our relations to the natural world, and are the product of the slow integration, or co-evolution, of our culture within our environment. Thus, the environment is not a place of divisions but a place of relations, a place where cultural diversity and biodiversity are not separate, but are in fact interdependent. The most essential of these responsibilities are those that integrate people ... with the ecosystems found within their environment. ... These Nuu chah nulth practices maintained the balance within nature, the environment and the ecosystems of which our people, with all our cultural institutions and practices, are an integral part. This is bio-cultural diversity, a complex state of environmental relationships. These relationships have developed and been nurtured over millennia and determine our fundamental obligations and responsibilities to the ecosystems which sustain us.* (Tommy Mexsis Happynook)

DEVELOPING SUSTAINABLE RELATIONSHIPS WITH NATURE AND PASSING THIS KNOWLEDGE on is a responsibility and obligation found among virtually all Indigenous peoples worldwide. The fact that Indigenous ecological knowledge has more to do with maintaining relationships with and fulfilling responsibilities to that which sustains them, as opposed to *managing resources* from a position of detachment and dominance, is not overstated by Tommy Mexsis Happynook. For many Indigenous cultures, biological diversity and cultural diversity are so intertwined, so inseparable, that the loss of diversity in one sphere is recognized to result in a loss of diversity in the other. "*We are sick because the land is sick,*

---

43 *Section 35(1), Canadian Constitution Act, 1982.*

the land is sick because we are sick!" Pikangikum elder Mathew Strang shared with our small group of researchers as we stood on the edge of a Thunderbird nest near the periphery of the Whitefeather Forest in northwestern Ontario. Similarly, Dene Tha' First Nation elder Roy Salopree believes that, *"once we heal, the land will heal, the water will heal."*

Few would deny that the ecological knowledge of Indigenous peoples and the cultural values, beliefs, worldviews, languages, and traditions necessary to sustain their relationships and responsibilities to their lands are fundamental human rights. But when settler society expropriates Indigenous lands, resources, and knowledge, not only is it tantamount to cultural genocide, it deprives the world a critical voice in humanity's challenge to address some of the most pressing environmental, social, and economic crises humanity has ever faced.

Developing ethical approaches to incorporate Indigenous knowledge into *environmental resource management* must be as much about reconciling rights, responsibilities, and relationships as it is about reconciling knowledge claims. Specifically, responsibilities appropriated from Indigenous peoples' grasps to steward their lands and their relationships to them need to be restored. Rights and responsibilities are directly related. They are two sides of the same coin. You can't have one without the other, a fact that legal representatives for both sides often seem to lose sight of in debates and negotiations over Aboriginal rights and title.

We ignore at our own peril our ongoing failure to tackle head on the systemic barriers and power imbalances that permit colonial agents to dismiss the roles of Indigenous peoples and their knowledge in maintaining their traditional relationships with, and responsibilities to, their lands and resources. Until we design with our Indigenous peoples new approaches to incorporate them and their knowledge into decisions impacting their rights and responsibilities to their lands, Canada will remain in direct violation of the *United Nations Declaration on the Rights of Indigenous Peoples* and its treaties with Indigenous Canadians.

Broken Promises, Sharp Dealing, and Unfinished Business: Canada's Historic Numbered Treaties

Canada entered into seventy treaties with its original inhabitants between 1701 and 1923. Those with which I am most familiar, Treaties 1 to 11, cleared the way for the settlement and industrial exploitation of much of central and western Canada after Confederation. Most Canadians would not dispute that many First Nations have been adversely and permanently impacted by the onslaught of settlers that followed in the wake of these treaties. In almost every instance, current-day First Nation use and occupation of their lands are impoverished versions of their pre-colonial rights and livelihoods. This, in turn, has generated a host of destructive social, cultural, economic, environmental, and ecological impacts from which many First Nations have been unable to escape.

First Nation elders view their historic treaties with Canada as sacred. When their forefathers took *treaty*, they sought assurances that they would not be surrendering their lands or ways of life. Rather, they understood that they were agreeing to share their lands in peace and friendship with the newcomers. In exchange, they received guarantees from Treaty commissioners that their health and welfare would be taken care of and that their "*usual vocations and livelihoods of hunting, trapping and fishing*" *would be protected*. [Indeed] . . . *this was the sine qua non inducing First Nations chiefs to sign treaty*.[44]

Neither the federal nor the provincial Crown, however, share this interpretation. As Justice Binnie asserted in the 2005 Supreme Court of Canada decision in *Mikisew Cree v Canada*, the historic treaties were effectively "*land surrenders* [that] *gave the Crown right to take up lands*."[45] But the courts have also ruled that Canada must have a compelling legislative objective to do so, and must minimize infringements on the rights of those so dispossessed. In other words, "*no sharp dealing*."[46]

The Supreme Court of Canada has determined that the honour of the Crown requires the reconciliation of its rights with the pre-existence of Aboriginal societies. In *Mikisew*, Justice Binnie identified the need to reconcile ongoing tensions between the Crown's right to *take up land* and its solemn promises to protect and support First Nation use of "*lands not taken up for . . . their usual vocations of hunting, trapping, and fishing*." Consequently, "*the duty to consult and accommodate* [these rights] *is part of the process of fair dealing and reconciliation that . . . continues beyond formal claims resolution.*"[47]

In a thought-provoking paper on the Crown's unfulfilled Treaty 8 promises, Jim Webb highlights Justice Binnie's position in *Mikisew*: "*The negotiation of Treaty 8 was not expected to produce a future land-use blueprint for the territory, and negotiations were no more than a first step in a long process of reconciliation.*"[48] But that has not been the position of our federal or provincial governments. At virtually every opportunity, both levels of government obfuscate and limit the constitutionally protected treaty rights of First Nations—nothing but *sharp dealing*.

---

44   R. Fumoleau (1975). *So Long as This Land Shall Last*. McMilian and Stewart, Toronto.

45   *Mikisew Cree First Nation v. Canada*, 2005, SCC69.

46   "*Sharp dealing*" is a pejorative phrase often used in Canadian law to describe questionable behaviour that is technically within the rules of the law but borders on being unethical, and may include denial of previous commitments, threats, coercion, improper use of process, and so on.

47   *Haida Nation v British Columbia*, 2004, 3 SCC 511.

48   J. Webb (2010a). Unfinished Business: The Intent of the Crown to Protect Treaty 8 Livelihood Interests (1922-1939). In *Planning Co-Existence: Aboriginal Issues in Forest and Land Use Planning*, M. Stevenson and D. Natcher (eds.). CCI Press, pp. 61-79.

When Canada *made treaty* with its First Nations' peoples after Confederation, its intention to protect their traditional livelihoods was, for the most part, honourable, notwithstanding the occasional *sleight-of-hand trick* (e.g., faking the signatures of First Nation chiefs on some numbered treaties). However, Canada's implementation of its treaty commitments has been anything but honourable. Many First Nations have never received the level of agricultural support promised, resulting in a plethora of legal actions against the federal Crown known as *cows and ploughs* claims. Nor has the solemn promise of protecting the *"usual vocations and livelihoods of hunting, trapping and fishing of treaty Indians"* been kept.

After the signing of Treaty 11 in 1921, for example, the federal government endeavoured to create game preserves for treaty Indians in the western provinces and territories. Sixteen years later in Alberta negotiations broke down following the enactment of the *Natural Resources Transfer Agreements* of 1930, which transferred federal jurisdiction of natural resources to the western provinces. Alberta's NRTA states that the province *"will from time to time ... set aside ... unoccupied Crown lands ... to enable Canada to fulfil its obligations under the Treaties with the Indians of the province."* Initially, Alberta did not oppose the creation of game preserves for treaty Indians so long as they would be confined to such areas, that development would be allowed to proceed within game reserves, and that the federal government would assume responsibility for the Métis. But Canada refused on all counts. Subsequently, Alberta in 1938 created a dozen Métis settlements with a land base of 500,000 hectares for their exclusive use and a registered trapline system to protect fur-bearer populations from over-harvesting. Accommodating the rights of treaty Indians to trap and hunt on unoccupied Crown lands was a secondary consideration. Paradoxically, unable to comply fully with provincial fur trapping regulations, many First Nation trappers lost their traplines and livelihoods to white and Métis competitors.

To date, no game reserves have been created in the provinces to protect the livelihood rights of treaty Indians. Nor has the federal government revisited the issue. Webb argues that the abandonment of federal-provincial negotiations to establish First Nation game preserves is a fundamental breach of Crown treaty obligations, and remains *"unfinished business related to the reconciliation of Aboriginal-Crown relations."* Settlement and industrial resource extraction of treaty First Nation traditional lands in Alberta and other provinces and territories have continued virtually unabated for decades. Under increasing pressure from Indigenous groups and the courts, the provinces have developed consultation policies with respect to natural resource development on unoccupied Crown land. But these policies are based on narrow and prejudicial readings of the text of the treaties. They also flout Supreme Court rulings that the English text of the treaties do not constitute the full scope of the treaties, and that oral promises made by treaty commissioners to induce First

Nation chiefs to sign *treaty* must also be considered in order to fulfil the Crown's fiduciary obligations. More saliently, the Supreme Court has instructed that ambiguities in the text of treaties should be resolved in favour of Indigenous signatories. Sadly, these rulings have been largely eschewed by the provinces, who continue to view historic treaties as nothing more than English documents that can be interpreted in a straight forward manner. To date there is no shared interpretation of *treaty*, and *sharp dealing* abounds.

Contrary to what some leading agents of the colonial order assert,[49] the treaties do not "*mean what they say.*" English words and phrases found in the texts of the treaties such as *livelihood* and *usual vocations* fail to capture what First Nations' leaders agreed to and intended when they entered into treaty.[50] Indigenous legal scholars have long advocated for the reinterpretation of treaty rights in light of linguistic ambiguities associated with translating concepts from one language to another in order to arrive at a common understanding of the intent of the treaty parties.[51] Even "*hunting, trapping, and fishing*" fail to capture the full scope and meanings of what these activities did to sustain First Nation cultures, societies, and relationships to their lands. Rather, they are interpreted so narrowly that they ignore their overriding functions within wider social and cultural contexts, violations of which reverberate throughout Indigenous communities. Hunting, for example, continues to have social, cultural, ecological, economic, and other benefits beyond the simple, materialistic, decontextualized activity that most colonial agents associate with the word. Among other things, hunting involves planning, cooperation, and the sharing of knowledge, values, and products of the hunt. Above all, hunting reaffirms the cultural roles, identity, dignity, and purpose of providers while fulfilling socially sanctioned responsibilities, and relationships. In the Cree language, English words such as *hunting, vocation,* and *livelihood* are subsumed under the concept of *Pimachihowan*, the Cree way of being.[52]

Magnanimous as ever, Canada has tossed a bone to First Nations to mitigate the *sharp dealing*. Its called the Specific Claims Process. But there's not much meat on this bone for them to chew on, and they need not hold their breath for the justice they seek. In 2001, nearly 600 specific claims—mostly for breach of treaty obligations—had been filed nationally, 400 of which were backlogged. By 2008, more than 800 claims were outstanding, with

---

49 T. Flanagan (2008). *First Nations? Second Thoughts...* (2nd edition). McGill-Queen's University Press, Montreal.

50 J. Webb (2010b). On Vocation and Livelihood: Interpretive Principles and Guidelines for the Reconciliation of Treaty 8 Rights and Interests. In *Planning Co-existence: Aboriginal Issues in Forest and Land Use Planning*. M. Stevenson and D. Natcher (eds.), CCI Press, pp.81-96.

51 S.J. Henderson-Youngblood (1997). Interpreting *sui generis* treaties. *Alberta Law Review* 36(1):46-96.

52 Webb (2010b:87).

most taking an average of thirteen years to resolve—some apparently taking twice that.[53] If that were not vexing enough, a third of all specific claims are rejected.

Canada's approach to specific claims has been widely criticized as being unresponsive and unjust. Its most ardent critic, the Assembly of First Nations, has fought for years to establish an independent process for the adjudication of claims. Despite the creation of a Specific Claims Tribunal in 2007, and a slight but temporary reduction in the backlog, not much has changed in the years since. The Tribunal remains dependent on government funding and Canada's adversarial, time-consuming, and costly approach to resolving specific claims persists. Today, the AFN continues to advocate for a truly independent Specific Claims Process.[54] Meanwhile the expanding volume of First Nations' claims alleging breach of treaty underscores the salience of the growing tensions between Canada and its First Nations peoples.

Nothing to Look at Here: Treaty 8, Fiduciary Failure, and the Dene Tha'

The Supreme Court of Canada has ruled that the *honour of the Crown* is always at stake in dealings with its Indigenous peoples. Rarely, if ever, however, has Canada or its provinces achieved this benchmark. Case in point: the Dene Tha' First Nation.

Like many bands created under the *Indian Act*, citizens of the Dene Tha' First Nation are an amalgamation of two or more cultural groups—in this case, the South Slavey and Beaver Dene—that were forced into becoming a single political entity for administrative convenience. Inhabiting the upper Peace River and Hay River drainages of northeast BC, northwest Alberta, and southwest Northwest Territories, the ancestors of the Dene Tha' were known to early explorers as the Strongbow Indians. After signing treaty in 1900, federal administrators referred to them as the Hay Lakes, or Upper Hay Lakes, Indians. They have hence become known as the Dene Tha' First Nation.

For generations the Dene Tha' were free to travel, hunt, fish, trap, and gather pretty much anywhere they wanted, subject to relations with neighbouring groups. The arrival of the fur trade in the early nineteenth century did not so much disrupt their annual cycle as augment it, though some bands soon became attached to specific trading posts. Treaty 8 did little at first to undermine Dene Tha' relationships to their lands and resources. But over time, things began to change. More isolated from settler society than many First Nations,

---

53 Office of the Auditor General of Canada (2016). Report 6: First Nations Specific Claims. Indigenous and Northern Affairs Canada. oag-bvg.gc.ca

54 Assembly of First Nations (2019). *2019 Specific Claims Reform: Historical Review of Past Calls for an Independent Specific Claims Process.* afn.ca

Dene Tha' families were decimated by viral pandemics brought by outsiders in 1919, 1928, and again in 1940. In the mid-1920s, British Columbia instituted a registered trapline system assigning trapping areas to both native and non-native trappers. Subsequently, the RCMP ordered the expulsion of all Dene Tha' from northeast BC, even though they knew the area to be their primary *"hunting and trapping grounds"* and that they possessed a treaty right to hunt and trap in BC. In 1932, a game warden was dispatched by dog team to Hay Lakes (Habay), Alberta, to enforce compliance with the order. But upon his return he reported that:

> *There was nothing I could do . . . even if I had caught them on their lines, because these Indians are absolutely destitute and starving. . . . During the war I* [had] *seen lots of poor people in Germany and France, but I* [had] *never seen anything like what we have on the Boundary at Hay Lakes. I never had such a pitiful job in my life when I advised* [them] *. . . that only BC Indians are given trapping privileges in BC. The old people sat there and cried. They told me I could not find enough food in any one of their camps to feed one of my dogs for one night.*[55]

The game warden's report must have proved convincing; provincial authorities soon reversed their order, allowing the Dene Tha' to hold registered trapping areas in BC. But British Columbia's registered trapline system, and Alberta's a decade later, were a double-edged sword. Dene Tha' trappers now had to abide by provincial fur management regulations—open and closed seasons, bag limits, equipment specifications, etc.—violations of which, particularly in poor trapping years, often resulted in the confiscation of equipment and traplines and, in some cases, jail time.

In 1930 the responsibility for natural resources was transferred from Ottawa to the western provinces. Among other things, this resulted in an influx of white trappers and settlers into Dene Tha' traditional territory. As a consequence, Canada and both provinces endeavoured in 1934 to create a *"hunting ground exclusively for use of Treaty Indians at Hay Lakes and Upper Hay River."* Encompassing an area of 84,000 square kilometres in BC, Alberta, and the NWT, the initiative soon lost momentum owing to transboundary conflicts and the realization that registered trappers in BC could not be easily deprived of their traplines.

In the late 1930s Alberta created a registered trapline system for individual trappers, Native and otherwise. As trapping was a communal activity and fur-bearing species are subject to fluctuations, the RCMP recommended that registered traplines be allocated to whole bands rather than individual trappers. Nonetheless, for the sake of administrative convenience, the province assigned trapping areas to individual First Nation trappers,

---

55   R. Bouchard (2009). Dene Tha' Presence in Northeastern BC. Manuscript on file with the Dene Tha' First Nation.

introducing a major source of conflict among them while restricting their movements across the landscape by confining their land-use to specific areas. With respect to the Dene Tha':

> *These people in the olden days were free to move around from the Hay Lake to Fort Nelson in British Columbia, the Lower Hay River and Great Slave Lake. They would winter whenever winter caught up with them and they lived mainly off the country. Now we have registered traplines and* [they] *are compelled to remain at places like Hay Lake. They are fenced in and there just isn't enough fur and game left in that area to provide a living for them.*[56]

Within a few years after the NTRAs were enacted, provincial authorities took additional measures to end one of the principal means by which the Dene Tha' exercised their traditional rights and responsibilities to their lands. According to Jean Baptiste Talley and other Dene Tha' elders, provincial forestry and wildlife officers coerced the Dene Tha' in the mid-1930s to abandon their customary burning practices on the promise that, "*if they let the trees grow, they would be able to make lots money from logging in the future.*" For centuries, fires were set each spring along rivers, streams, and lake shores to facilitate travel by canoe, horse, wagon, and foot, and to create habitat favourable for moose, other big game species, berries, and medicines. Burning was so extensive in Dene Tha' traditional territory that the names of many rivers and lakes refer to the grasslands and prairies created by the *fires of spring*.[57] When Dene Tha' elders were young and camped at Moose Prairie on the western outskirts of what is now High Level, they could see Eleske on the Beaver First Nation reserve, some fifteen kilometres away—no trees anywhere. Over the course of a generation or so, prairies became forests, water courses became choked with deadfall, and traditional canoe routes and foot trails along river banks became impassable. As the Dene Tha' were a semi-nomadic people that moved across the landscape with the seasons, the cessation of traditional burning practices—like registered traplines—removed large portions of Dene Tha' territory from their use, paving the way for settler society to exploit and reap the benefits of their natural resources. Government promises to create a special hunting preserve for the Dene Tha' were never kept.

Federal government officials briefly contemplated the creation of *Indian reservations* for the Dene Tha' in the 1930s in order to better attend to their needs and entrench their dependency. The issue surfaced again in the late 1940s when a proposed road from central Alberta that would bring more settlement into northern Alberta pushed the initiative into high gear. Half a century after the Dene Tha' made treaty, federal Indian reserves were established at Hay Lakes (Habay), Meander River (Tache), and several other locations.

---

56 N. Walker, 3 December, 1948, NAC RG10, Vol.6734, File 420-2-2-1-1.

57 H.T. Lewis (1982). *A Time for Burning*. Occasional Publication No. 17. Boreal Institute of Northern Studies, University of Alberta, Edmonton.

Shortly thereafter, residential schools were built at Chateh (Assumption) and Tache.

Formerly, extended family groups travelled to their hunting and trapping grounds together, and remained there for the greater part of the year, securing resources at various locations across the landscape. With the advent of residential schools, they moved permanently to reservations. According to one official, the construction of a school on the Upper Hay River reserve (Habay) resulted in *"a flocking of the Indians from the neighbouring reserves so they could send their children to school and still have them living at home."*[58] Although men continued to spend the greater part of the year out on the land, women and children remained behind on reserve, initiating disruptions in familial social dynamics and relationships. With the creation of *Indian reservations* and the building of the Mackenzie highway in the late 1940s, Dene Tha' territory was opened up to agriculture, forestry, and oil/gas exploration. A cascade of adverse environmental and socio-cultural impacts soon followed.

Up until the mid-twentieth century the Dene Tha' were what some anthropologists would call *"foragers,"*[59] whereby small extended family groups would travel to various locations throughout the year to exploit seasonally available resources. In other words, people moved to resources. This was the way of life that the Dene Tha' thought they were protecting when they signed treaty in 1900. But now they were forced into becoming *"collectors,"* whereby seasonally available resources had to be routinely transported to specific locations where families were coerced to settle permanently. Not only was the Dene Tha' presence on their lands markedly reduced, but the transition from a semi-nomadic lifestyle to year-round residency in permanent settlements initiated fundamental changes in Dene Tha' social dynamics. No longer were the Dene Tha' able to exercise their traditional means of conflict resolution by voting with their feet. Alternative and culturally acceptable ways of resolving social tensions and conflict have proven elusive.

Meanwhile, agriculture and forestry in the 1950s and '60s *took up* large portions of Dene Tha' traditional territory destroying critical game and fur-bearer habitat, as well as Dene Tha' traditional land-use sites and centuries of evidence of their presence on the land. The oil and gas industry posed an even greater threat to local biodiversity and the Dene Tha' ability to live off their lands. Many of its impacts continue to this day. Seismic lines, service roads, pipelines, and transmission lines attract invasive species such as wolves and weekend hunters, reducing and displacing caribou, moose, and other species. Both operational and abandoned pipelines and well-sites release toxic chemicals into the environment, adversely impacting the health of fish, animals, and people. Compressor stations emit deadly carcinogens (e.g., benzopyrene), while flaring spews nitrous oxide and sulphur dioxide into

---

58   W. M. Schwartz to W. Lester, Director of Surveys, Department of Public Works, 13 November 1951. INAC File 775/30-3-212. Vol. 1.

59   L. Binford (1980). Willow Smoke and Dogs' Tails: Hunter-Gatherer Settlement Systems and Archaeological Site Formation. *American Antiquity* 45(1):4-20.

surrounding air sheds. Many Dene Tha' no longer hunt within ten to fifteen kilometres of these industrial sites, or anywhere else where gases can be detected. Those few that do are forced to wear gas masks. According to Dene Tha' elder James Metchooyeah, before the oil and gas industry arrived no one slept past 5 a.m. when out on the land from spring to fall; the cacophony of songbirds was that deafening. Today, when industrial activity dies down for the evening, only magpies and ravens break the silence of the forest. And gone are the days when James and other elders had to remind youth not to *"let the blanket be the boss of you."* As a consequence of these cumulative impacts, the Dene Tha' have had to travel much further than ever to hunt:

> *My family has been impacted by all the oil and gas and forestry that happened in our territory. We cannot go into areas that [we] once did and want to go. We cannot make a living as we once did from hunting, fishing, and trapping. There are less animals in the areas around the communities where we live as they have been covered by roads, pipelines, and cut blocks. . . . The animals are shifting and moving to places further away from us. As a result, younger men and families are starting to travel larger distances up to Bistcho, the areas west of Bistcho, Sulphur Lake near Manning and north of Indian Cabins. It is harder to find animals and people have to spend more money on gas to go out to these places.*[60]

The cumulative environmental impacts of industry on the Dene Tha' heartland have increased the costs of hunting exponentially, while taking those who can no longer afford to hunt off the land entirely. The social and cultural impacts have been profound and threaten the very fabric of Dene Tha' society.

Today, a minority of Dene Tha' still conduct traditional land-use activities within their ancestral territory. However, their ability to do so has been severely compromised. Most must now travel to the very margins of their lands and beyond to have a reasonable chance of a successful hunt, bringing them into conflict with other land-users, Indigenous and otherwise. This tangle of industrial impacts continues to sabotage the ability of the Dene Tha' to exercise their treaty rights and fulfill their responsibilities to their lands and future generations.

A not-often-recognized collateral impact of forcing Indigenous peoples off their traditional territories is the subversion of their ability to develop new experiential ecological and cultural knowledge about their lands and resources. Subsequently, contemporary ecological knowledge and expertise has come to be vested in foreign actors who fill the void. The Dene Tha' experienced this phenomena recently with respect to woodland caribou. Hunters and

---

60   Erwin Eth-Chillay Interview, Survey of Dene Tha' First Nation Traditional and Current Land and Resources Uses in Areas that may be Affected by the Mackenzie Gas Project. Dene Tha' First Nation (2006) ab 1, p. 3-4. Manuscript on file with the Dene Tha' First Nation.

elders know a lot about caribou distributions, movements, and behaviours such as they were decades ago, but have comparably less present-day knowledge of caribou. Current expertise, and thus management authority, about this animal now resides with government, industry, the academy, and others who have an interest in their lands.

As painful as the Dene Tha' First Nations' relationship with industry has been, the true extent of their suffering will be incomprehensible to many. Some band members contend that the petroleum industry is responsible for the death of hundreds of family members and friends during the oil boom of the 1960s, 70s, and 80s. With the traditional trapping economy in a tailspin, the Dene Tha' were not prepared for the onslaught of oil field workers that descended upon them, or the infusion of cash that came with casual work in the oil fields. Years of unrestrained substance abuse and domestic violence followed in their wake. For many years, it was common for women to be absent from their family homes for extended periods as oil field workers would pick-up them up in bars and the streets of High Level, dropping them off, sometimes days later, to find their way back to their reserves. During this period, hundreds of Dene Tha' died unnatural deaths—as many as 500 according to two of my informants—to alcohol-/drug-fuelled domestic violence and accidents. But authorities turned a blind eye to the chaos and carnage. The unchecked violence, loss of life, and social upheaval destroyed many Dene Tha' families.

It was during this time that former priest-turned-anthropologist, Jean-Guy Goulet, lived among the Dene Tha', documenting century-old values, beliefs, and traditions that allowed them to survive this horrific chapter in their lives.[61] The emotional and psychological scars from this period, nevertheless, still persist today among survivors and healing has not come easy. Dene Tha' rarely, if ever, disclose such unspeakable details of their pasts, even amongst themselves. It was not until I had spent several years working with Dene Tha' elders and hunter/trappers to document the environmental, cultural, and social impacts of resource extraction that they felt comfortable enough with me to share this grave injustice. It was their hope that, in so doing, its victims and their families would eventually find some solace and restitution. To my knowledge, there has been no official investigation of this egregious tragedy by any government authority. Maybe they just thought—and still think—that the carnage was just normal?

Given all that has happened to the Dene Tha', it is inconceivable how they could possibly exercise their constitutionally protected treaty rights. If their story was unique, perhaps reparations might be possible. But tragically, their experiences have been repeated many times across this country in areas where natural resources are up for grabs to the highest bidder. Historic treaties are considered sacrosanct by many First Nations. Yet Canada has

---

61   J. G. Goulet (1998). *Ways of Knowing: Experience, Knowledge, and Power Among the Dene Tha'*. UBC Press.

done all it can to dodge its treaty and fiduciary obligations to its founding peoples. In the final analysis, Canada's historic treaties have failed the Dene Tha' and scores of other First Nation signatories, including the Beaver Lake Cree Nation.

What Cumulative Impacts? The Beaver Lake Cree

Each year between 2008 and 2016, Tribal Chiefs Ventures—a Treaty 6 tribal council with whom I worked—held an environmental workshop for its five northeastern Alberta member nations. As the co-coordinator of this annual event, I had been looking forward to the 2013 meeting for weeks for it promised to be more informative than most. You see, the former chief of the Beaver Lake Cree Nation Alphonse Lameman had been invited to provide an update on his nation's claim against Alberta and Canada. I was not disappointed.

As I sat listening to Al describe how his nation's ancestral territory had been carved up and destroyed by industry, I wondered how his people could even remotely exercise their treaty rights, let alone their traditional relationships and responsibilities to their lands. I learned that over the past four decades, the oil and gas industry had significantly degraded 90 percent of the Beaver Lake Cree once pristine traditional land base. As a consequence of 35,000 oil and gas sites, 22,000 kilometres of seismic lines, 4,000 kilometres of pipeline, and related infrastructure and activities, most of their water sources were now polluted, toxins had accumulated in fish, boiled water advisories were the norm, and ungulate populations were on the verge of extirpation throughout their territory. As Al continued, his words reminded me of what Algina Monias, an esteemed elder from the neighbouring Heart Lake First Nation, once shared with me: *"There are no song birds anymore because there are no berries, and there are no berries or fish because there is no water, and what little there is, you can't even drink."*

The constitutionally protected treaty rights of the Beaver Lake Cree and other northeast Alberta First Nations to live off the land much as their ancestors did have been irrevocably impacted. While the effects of any one of the 19,000+ oil/gas authorizations in Beaver Lake's traditional territory might have been manageable, considered together, they threaten to destroy forever the Beaver Lake Cree's way of life and relationship to lands that have sustained them for thousands of years. This was the basis of their claim against Canada and Alberta.

Launched in 2008, the Beaver Lake claim was the first ever to challenge and be granted a trial on the cumulative impacts of industrial development. But for over a decade Canada and Alberta fought to dismiss the claim asserting it was *"unmanageable, overwhelming, frivolous, improper, and an abuse of process."* In April 2013 the Alberta Court of Appeal sided with Beaver Lake, telling Canada and the province that it had had enough of their "*bickering and stonewalling, that their actions were inconsistent with Supreme Court of Canada decisions, and to get back to court.*" The significance of this judgment is such that Beaver Lake's claim is the first time Canada's legal system has been forced to consider the cumulative impacts of the tar sands on a First Nation's ability to exercise its treaty rights. On a national scale, the Beaver Lake case potentially represents the most consequential case on treaty and environmental rights and jurisprudence in Canada.

But, as unwilling fiduciaries, and knowing full well that the band's pockets are not deep, the defendants and their lawyers continued their mischief and antipathy, delaying court proceedings for another five years. In April 2018 the Beaver Lake Cree filed a motion asking the court to award them a portion of the anticipated trial costs based on the significance of the case. In October 2019 Judge Beverley Browne of the Alberta Court of Queen's Bench sided with Beaver Lake ordering Canada and Alberta to pay in advance the legal costs of the BLFN, stating that "*it would be manifestly unjust to either compel Beaver Lake to abandon its claim or to force it into destitution in order to bring the claim forward.*" After a decade of fundraising and wresting funds from critical community services, Beaver Lake now had the financial resources to proceed with its legal action until resolved. While the award of legal costs in advance of judicial review and judgement is precedent-setting, we should not anticipate a conclusion to the matter anytime soon.

In June 2020 the Alberta Court of Appeals granted the province's request to have the order set side to allow it to admit new evidence demonstrating that Beaver Lake has sufficient resources to fund its litigation. Further, the court ruled that "*if the Beaver Lake Cree Nation* [still feels] ... *entitled to advance costs, it is incumbent on it to reapply.*"[62]

Canada and Alberta have continually eschewed their fiduciary obligations to protect First Nation treaty rights, and to retroactively, let alone proactively, manage the cumulative environmental impacts of tars sands operations. Planting grass and bison atop desolate, sterile landscapes and other government sanctioned reclamation programs are absurd, and could never replace the complex ecological systems that once thrived in their place. At the same time, both governments have downplayed the significance of any research addressing cumulative impacts. Moreover, gag orders have even been placed on federal scientists to prevent them from discussing their findings with the media.[63] Overall, both governments have been complicit in keeping the accelerating cumulative environmental effects of tar sands production unreported and under wraps, to say nothing of the harmful social and cultural impacts.

---

62 *Anderson v Alberta (Attorney General)*, 2020 ABCA 238.

63 C. Linnitt (2012). Stephen Harper Hates Science: Federal Scientists Muzzled to Protect Tar Sands Reputation. (November 8) desmogblog.com

But after all this time, the Beaver Lake Cree and their lawyers and supporters remain steadfast that justice will eventually prevail. According to Jack Woodward:

> *The Beaver Lake case will define the point where industrial development must be curtailed to preserve treaty rights. . . . At issue is the cumulative impact of industry, not each individual project. The court will be asked to say if the level of industrial activity in* [their] *hunting grounds has now crossed the line to make it impossible to reasonably exercise* [their treaty] *rights. If the Beaver Lake* [Cree] *are successful, there will be constitutional controls on development to allow the land to recover and to prevent any further encroachments that might disturb wildlife populations. . . . This would be the most powerful ecological precedent ever set in a Canadian court . . . because it* [will] *protect the entire biological system with a view to preserving its sustainable productivity. . . . It will be the first time a court is asked to draw the line defining too much industrial development in the face of constitutionally protected treaty rights.*[64]

Perhaps the most jaw-dropping thing about the Beaver Lake claim is not the amount of time it has taken to get to this point, or the perseverance of the Beaver Lake Cree, but that it even exists at all. Who among federal and provincial politicians and high-ranking government officials thought it was a good idea to allow the adverse impacts of thousands of industrial authorizations pile up to the point of ecological collapse? Who among them spoke up and said that the ability of First Nations to exercise their treaty rights under such circumstances would be severely compromised, and that, as a consequence, they may be in breach of their treaty obligations. Who among them thought that the day would never come where they would have to *pay what's owed*? All they needed to do to see the future was to look at the Mikisew Cree, the Dene Tha', and other First Nations whose lands have been destroyed, and treaty and Indigenous rights violated, by unbridled, government-sanctioned industrial resource extraction.

It is not so much the adverse environmental impacts of individual industrial resource extraction projects that threaten First Nation treaty rights and bio-cultural diversity, but the multiple and cumulative effects of many projects. At the same time, the cumulative environmental and ecological impacts of resource development are the tip of the iceberg. The resultant inability of First Nations to access and use their traditional lands is not only a violation of treaty rights as currently defined and understood by the Crown and the courts, it creates a cascade of adverse economic, social, and cultural impacts that wreak havoc on First Nation communities. Yet these too have been largely ignored or downplayed by government and industry.

---

64 C. Linnitt (2013). The Beaver Lake Cree Judgment: The Most Important Tar Sands Case You've Never Heard Of. (May 24) thenarwhal.ca

In February 2018, the federal government introduced the *Impact Assessment Act*, a bill to replace the woefully inadequate 2012 *Canadian Environmental Assessment Act*, while doing away with the beleaguered National Energy Board.[65] *Bill C-69* was developed to restore public trust in cumulative impacts management, and to ensure that the *"rights and traditional knowledge of Indigenous peoples are considered in assessments."* The act ensures that assessments would also examine health, social, and economic impacts of proposed projects, including mandatory consideration of potential impacts on Indigenous peoples, rights, and cultures.

As of February 2019, the Senate Energy Committee was reviewing *Bill C-69* against a backdrop of rotating protests by supporters and beneficiaries of Canada's oil and gas industry. I guess they didn't read the proposed bill. It fails to make significant changes to Canada's approach to environmental impact assessment. When you put lipstick on a pig, it's still a pig. While the bill contains more provisions for strategic and regional assessments, there are no mandatory requirements for assessing impacts beyond a project-by-project basis. Moreover, the vast majority of existing projects currently contributing to regional cumulative impacts are exempted from review, and Canada's obligations to achieving its international commitments under the *Paris Accord* and *United Nations Declaration on the Rights of Indigenous Peoples* are effectively ignored. *Bill C-69*, in essence, allows the federal government to offload assessments onto the provinces, and provides virtually no guidance to federal officials to fulfill the government's constitutional duty to consult and accommodate the rights of Indigenous peoples. On June 21, 2019, *Bill C-69* received royal assent.

Oink!

Like other provinces, Alberta has no specific legislation to address the cumulative impacts of resource development on its citizens, Indigenous or otherwise. Alberta's *Land Use Stewardship Act* creates regional land-use planning and environmental management frameworks intended to create *"regional plans . . . using a cumulative effects management approach . . . [including] defining threshold values for identifying adverse impacts on the land base to determine appropriate management actions."*[66] But there is no policy or department to oversee the mitigation of existing or future cumulative impacts, just more clichés *"to manage the cumulative effects of development on air, water, land, and biodiversity at the regional level."* Rather than accepting its fiduciary responsibility for managing the cumulative impacts of resource development subsequent to authorizing such activities, the province off-loads this responsibility on other stakeholders with such wonderfully worded platitudes as *"cumulative effects management focuses on achievement of outcomes, understanding the effects of multiple*

---

65   *Bill C-69. An Act to Enact the Impact Assessment Act and the Canadian Energy Regulator Act to Amend the Navigation Protection Act and to Make Consequential Amendments to Other Acts.* First Reading, 8 February 2018. Parliament of Canada.

66   *Cumulative Effects Management.* landuse.alberta.ca

development pressures, assessment of risk, collaborative work with shared responsibility for action and improved integration of economic, environmental and social considerations." Right!

Cue Charlie Brown, Lucy, and the football!

The cumulative impacts of multiple industrial resource extraction projects are the elephant in the room for which neither Canada nor the provinces accept responsibility. In exchange for some of the lowest resource royalties in the industrialized world, our governments have allowed the cumulative environmental, ecological, social, cultural, and other impacts of resource development to pile up virtually unchecked, destroying the lands and ways of life of many Indigenous communities in the process.

Modern Day Treaties: Restitution or Colonial Hammer?

Comprehensive land claims agreements remain one of the most common colonial institutions Indigenous Canadians are forced to access to protect their rights and interests. Sharing in the economic benefits of resource extraction, protecting the environment, preserving culture, and gaining greater control over their lives and futures provide the incentives for Indigenous peoples to enter into modern day treaties with the federal Crown. Creating certainty for government, industry, and the general public with respect to the ownership of contested lands and resources provide the impetus for the colonial governments. Yet it often takes years, even decades, of protracted and costly negotiations for Indigenous parties, Canada, and the provinces/territories to find common ground. The stonewalling and chicanery by federal and provincial government officials approach infamy. Indeed, some BC First Nations are nearing their fourth decade of negotiations. As Jack Woodward shared with me, Clem Paul, and Bob Turner of the North Slave Métis Alliance years ago, *"the basic provisions of comprehensive land claims agreements should take no more a day to negotiate—it's that simple."*

In exchange for ceding title to the lion's share of their traditional lands, Indigenous parties obtain legal ownership to a fraction of their original land base and cash settlements to address pressing social, cultural, housing, health, education, and other needs. Shared management authority over both Indigenous and Crown-owned lands is sometimes accomplished by the creation of cooperative environmental management boards, whereby decision-making is shared—supposedly—between representatives of the state and Indigenous signatories.

But Indigenous Canadians enter into comprehensive land claims negotiations at great cost and disadvantage to themselves and their descendants. While modern day treaties are usually translated into Indigenous languages, only the English and French versions have any legal currency when disagreements over provisions arise. You see, the goal of Canada's federal government has never been the reconciliation of the rights and title of its founding peoples with those of other Canadians. Rather, the federal Crown's objective all along has been the extinguishment of Aboriginal rights in order to create greater certainty for settler society in the process of expropriating Indigenous lands for settlement and development. In exchange, Indigenous Canadians get cash and legal *ownership* to a snippet of their original land base.

Don't get me wrong. I do not mean to offend those Indigenous parties who fought tooth and nail, and made tremendous concessions, to obtain the few crumbs the federal government reluctantly tossed their way. Indigenous signatories were and continue to be between a rock and hard place. And we put them there!

Canada's ongoing opposition to revamping its approach to comprehensive land claims deeply troubles many in this country. Some feel that Canada has given up—and back—too much ground to its original inhabitants. Yet, for most Indigenous signatories, the promise of modern-day treaties, like their historic antecedents, has not been met.

I first became familiar with Canada's comprehensive land claims policy in the 1980s and '90s when the Nunavut Land Claims Agreement was being negotiated. The NLCA—still the largest land claim settlement in Canadian history—was signed in 1993 and paved the way for the creation of the new territory and government of Nunavut six years later. The 42 articles of the NLCA address a wide range of subject matters from ownership of land and resources to economic development, employment, environmental protection, *wildlife management*, social issues, and cultural affairs, as well as political development. Among other things, Inuit beneficiaries got:

- The rights to *"harvest wildlife"* throughout the Nunavut settlement area (which they had already in the vernacular of *Qallunnatitut*) subject to government regulation;

- Equal representation with federal and territorial authorities on a new set of resource management and environmental boards with no consideration to the power and capacity imbalances created;

- A share of federal government royalties from oil, gas, and mineral development on Crown lands;

- The right to negotiate with industry for economic and social benefits from the development of non-renewable resources on Inuit-owned lands; and

- Capital transfer payments of $1.9 billion over fifteen years.

All Inuit gave up was the right to govern themselves on their own terms as they had done for millennia, surface rights to 90 percent of Nunavut, and mineral rights to 99 percent of the territory's subsurface. Had legal advisors on both sides obtained a thorough education and training in *Inuit qaujimaijatungit* (Inuit history, knowledge, values, traditions, etc.) and/or the social sciences and humanities, I cannot help but think that the NLCA would look very different.

Not surprisingly, the implementation of the agreement has not gone well, particularly in achieving levels of Inuit participation in government operations and contracting. Essentially, Nunavut's government is structured after existing territorial models—not an Inuit style of governance in sight. With a mix of Inuit and non-Inuit workers whereby Inuit generally occupy the lowest-paid (manual labourers) and highest-paid (ministers and deputy ministers) positions in government, most day-to-day decision-making remains in the hands of non-Inuit middle managers who know how to get things done within such colonial governance structures. The same holds true for government contracting—non-Inuit remain the beneficiaries of most government contracts.

In 2006, after talks with federal negotiators and lawyers to rectify the injustice broke down, Nunavut Tungavik Incorporated on behalf of Nunavut's Inuit beneficiaries commenced legal action against Canada. Before NTI filed its lawsuit seeking over $1 billion in damages, Canada had vetoed seventeen of its attempts to resolve the impasse through arbitration. After years of negotiation, an out-of-court settlement was finally reached in 2015 awarding Nunavut's Inuit $255 million in damages and costs, additional funding for new training initiatives, and new dispute resolution processes for implementation of the NCLA.

More recent land claims agreements appear to be no more than a perfunctory improvement over previous ones. The 2010 *Maa-nulth First Nations Final Agreement* constitutes the full and final settlement in respect of the Aboriginal rights and title of the five Maa-nulth First Nation signatories. What the Maa-nulth nations got was the right to levy direct taxes on their citizens, fee simple ownership to five percent (24,550 hectares) of their original land base, the right to oversee use of these lands, and transfers of $80 million for programming and service delivery to be distributed over twenty-five years. That's about as much as a CEO of a large Canadian corporation makes over the same period. All each First Nation had to give up was its:

- Aboriginal title and rights to the rest of its traditional territory, including the subordination of Maa-nulth First Nation law and codes of conduct to federal and provincial legislation;

- *Section 87* Tax exempt status; and

- Right to challenge any provision of the agreement.

After I completed a draft of this chapter, I sent it to Tom Mexsis Happynook for his comment. He reminded me that, *"although they didn't get their whole territory back, they have developed other strategies to build up their land base over time . . . like purchasing lands that come up for sale in the Bamfield Inlet, fifty hectares so far."* They have also purchased most of the businesses in Bamfield and acquired majority ownership of Western Forest Products, which holds timber harvesting rights over much of Maa-nulth traditional territory. They can now support elders as well as First Nation members wishing to pursue a career in the trades, and no citizen makes less than $17.22 per hour. Perhaps most significantly from Tom's perspective the *Huu ay aht Constitution*

> *. . . means we are now a third order of government under the Canadian Constitution. Our Hereditary chiefs now have a governance role to play in leading our Nation into the future through our Constitution. . . . The Maa nulth Treaty has been a blessing . . . we can truly plan for seven generations, and are governed by several ancient principles that direct our government's decision-making: Hish uk Tsawalk (everything is one–everything is connected), Iisaak (greater respect), and Uu a thluk (taking care of). . . . The lives of our people have changed dramatically and our communities are thriving. We would never have been able to do any of this under that archaic Indian Act. Negotiating a new relationship with Canada and BC was the best thing we have ever done.*

Imagine what could have been accomplished had they obtained legal title to even 10 percent of their traditional land base. Nevertheless, for First Nations wishing to enter into comprehensive land claims negotiations they could do worse—and likely will— than the Ma-nulth treaty.

Currently, there are about seventy Indigenous rights and self-determination discussion tables across the country. According to the government of Canada, *"the goals of these discussions are to bring greater flexibility to negotiations, jointly develop NEW ways to recognize rights and title in agreements, and explore NEW ideas and ways for Indigenous groups to advance their vision of self-determination for the benefit of their communities and all Canadians* (emphasis added)."[67] Nice, but empty words. Do not expect Canada to reform its approaches to divesting Indigenous Canadians their traditional lands and resources any time soon. Until it does, wait for it . . .

Cue Charlie Brown, Lucy, and the football!

---

67 *Exploring New Ways of Working Together.* https://www.rcaanc-cirnac.gc.ca/eng/1511969222951/1529103469169#chp1

CHAPTER 8

"The Existing Aboriginal and Treaty Rights of the Aboriginal Peoples of Canada Are Hereby Recognized and Affirmed," Part Two

The Tail That Wags the Rez Dog

I AM NOT A LAWYER. ANY LAWYER COULD TELL YOU THAT. I HAVE BEEN CALLED MANY things—some not fit for print—but never a lawyer. Nonetheless, much of my work over the years has in one way or another brought me into direct contact, and sometimes conflict, with lawyers. Case in point: the Mikisew Cree.

University of Saskatchewan anthropologist David Natcher and I were confounded. We had just finished the first draft of our social and cultural impact assessment for the Mikisew Cree First Nation, and its lawyers were questioning our methodology and findings. Funded through an agreement with Shell Oil, the study attempted to assess the social and cultural impacts of oil sands and hydroelectric development on the Mikisew Cree.[68]

Back in the early 1980s when Doug Proch and I were digging holes in Wood Buffalo National Park, we came to know a few people in Fort Chipewyan, the home community of the Mikisew Cree. Foremost among them were respected Mikisew elders and traditional land-users Snowbird Marten and Lawrence Courtoreille. Fort Chip was a vibrant community during the early 1980s. People were generally healthy, much of the local diet was composed of traditional foods, and muskrat trapping and commercial fishing were mainstays of the local economy.

But in the intervening thirty-five years between then and 2015 things had changed dramatically. Water levels in the Peace-Athabasca Delta had fallen precipitously, muskrats

---

68   M. Stevenson and D. Natcher (2015). *Our Graveyard Would Not be Full: Impacts of Industry's Environmental Footprint on Mikisew Cree Social and Cultural Values,* Manuscript on file with the Mikisew Cree Industrial Relations Corporation.

were all but extirpated from the region, and local fisherman were pulling deformed fish out of Lake Athabasca. Significantly fewer people participated in traditional use activities, relying principally on nutritionally deficient, exorbitantly expensive store-bought foods to survive—two-week old, green pork chops were selling locally for $45.00 a kilogram. Obesity, Type 2 diabetes, and cancer were widespread, including a rare form of bile duct cancer, which prematurely took the lives of several Fort Chip residents including my mentor, consultation partner, and former Athabasca Chipewyan Chief and Treaty 8 Grand Chief, Tony Mercredi. Not unexpectedly, Fort Chip's cancer outbreak attracted considerable national and international attention. Meanwhile, Alberta's governing and petroleum elites embarked on a campaign to belittle the concerns of community members and local whistleblower Dr. John O'Connor. By 2015, five out of six Mikisew Cree no longer lived in Fort Chip or elsewhere within their traditional territory.

Against this background, Dave and I felt that a comparison of traditional food-sharing practices with a nearby First Nation community where the impacts of resource extraction were less, was in order. The North Tall Cree First Nation settlement of Fox Lake, some 200 kilometres upstream on the Peace River, proved to be an ideal candidate as Dave had recently completed a study of this community's food-sharing network. We both thought that as a measure of each community's social capital an inter-settlement comparison of traditional food sharing practices might be revealing. It was.

Compared to the Mikisew Cree, the Cree community of Fox Lake not only shared traditional *country foods* more widely, the number of people involved in local food exchanges was far greater. In other words, less country food per capita was being shared overall in Fort Chip. Generally, when traditional foods are shared among First Nation members, traditional values and ecological knowledge are exchanged, while cultural identity and socially sanctioned relationships are reaffirmed. The social and cultural values of exchanging traditional foods in Fox Lake were clearly just as important as their nutritional value. This led us to conclude that the *binding* social capital of Fox Lake was greater than that of the Mikisew Cree—a finding that we should have anticipated by the latter's ongoing diaspora out of Fort Chip. A combination of resource development impacts had contributed to a significant reduction in local sharing practices, displacement of most band members from their homeland, and the declining health and well-being of those community members left behind.

We thought that this information might be of some interest and value to the Mikisew Cree. But for some reason the nation's legal advisors recommended that this chapter be expunged from the report. While neither Dave nor I could fathom why, after considerable persuasion and elaboration of our rationale on our part, we were able to convince our client and its lawyers to retain this chapter in the final report. This was not the first time I had been instructed by lawyers to alter my interpretations and conclusions to suit, presumably, what they perceived to be their client's best interests. Regrettably, and against my better judgement, I have entertained similar requests while undertaking traditional land-use studies for other Indigenous clients.

Lawyers working for First Nations deal almost exclusively with elected chiefs and councils created under the *Indian Act*. Rarely do they engage with or get to know intimately elders, hereditary chiefs, spiritual leaders, traditional healers, artisans, hunters, and other land-users and keepers of traditional values, culture, and knowledge. And they certainly do not get to know them in the same way an anthropologist or any social scientist would. In other words, they remain sequestered from the custodians of those cultures whom they were supposedly hired to protect and represent.

Bruce McIvor of *First Peoples Law* has remarked that, if anyone is unsure who represents First Nation peoples in legal proceedings with the Crown, *"they need only consult the first page of the Supreme Court of Canada's Delgamuukw decision—it was the hereditary chiefs of the Gitxsan and Wet'suwet'en—not an Indian Act chief and council to be seen."*[69] For some First Nations who do not recognize hereditary chiefs (e.g., Pikangikum), elder advisory councils have been created to which *Indian Act* chiefs and councils must answer. But I suspect that such First Nations are in the minority.

A few legal scholars have pushed Aboriginal jurisprudence in directions where most fear to tread. For example, the evidentiary power of Indigenous oral history is now recognized by Canada's supreme court. For the most part, professional lawyers working for and on behalf of Canada's Indigenous peoples are well-meaning and well-educated in Canadian law. But, while they might be empathetic to the plight of Indigenous Canadians—some may even be Indigenous themselves—they sometimes lack the acumen and skill sets needed to best represent the rights and interests of their clients. Some never acquire the acuity or develop the tools, either through their formal education or practice, to become intimately familiar with Indigenous cultures and the tangle of colonial events, processes, and institutions that have led to their current circumstances. Subsequently, the narratives they create and the solutions they seek are framed narrowly within established precedent under current Aboriginal jurisprudence. At the same time, like most anthropologists (including this one), many *Indian Act* chiefs often possess only passing familiarity with the latter, and must rely heavily on the advice of legal advisors. This is not to suggest that there are no exceptional lawyers out there. I have had the good fortune to know and/or to work with Jack Woodward, Carolyn Buffalo, Ken Staroszik, Monique Ross, Bill Wilson, Ovide Mercredi, and Brian Slattery, to name a few. I have no doubt that these individuals have transcended

---

69   B. McIvor (2019). Why Canadian Law Should be on the Side of the Wet'suwet'en in the Pipeline Confrontation. 10 January, firstpeopleslaw.com

the limitations of their legal educations and remain committed to pushing Canada in a more just, ethical, and equitable direction in its engagement with Indigenous peoples.

Irrespective of their credentials, lawyers working for Indigenous parties frequently develop positions and arguments on behalf of their clients on the basis of limited information. Not only may existing data sets be outdated or incompatible with contemporary reality and recent research findings—our knowledge is changing that fast—the acquisition of new knowledge is an expensive proposition likely to incur additional costly consulting and legal fees. Subsequently, any amendment to the established narrative, especially if it has become part of legal proceedings, requires an *act of God*. In retrospect, I suspect that this was the hurdle that Dave and I had to clear with the Mikisew. Some of our findings clearly did not agree with the conclusions of previous researchers—who were not anthropologists—which had already been incorporated into its lawyers' storyline.

Who Talks Like That? Part 3

Many lawyers working on behalf of Indigenous Canadians continue unwittingly to use language and concepts that undermine their clients' rights and interests. This is especially so in venues where federal government officials endeavour to reconcile the rights and title of Indigenous peoples with those of other Canadians. Rupert Ross, in *Dancing With a Ghost: Exploring Indian Reality*,[70] points out that in comprehensive land claims and other negotiations controlled by Euro-Canadian governments Indigenous claimants must translate their values, priorities, and understandings into:

> *. . . the language of the dominant discourse, with the associated risk of misrepresenting the true aspirations of the Aboriginal community.* [Thus] *in order to protect their rights and adjust to the government's negotiation strategy, First Nations must be as technical, adversarial and legalistic as governments. As a result, First Nations become more dependent upon legal consultants and technical experts.*

Chief John Snow of the Wesley First Nation in Alberta does not overstate the pitfalls of Indigenous peoples expressing their rights in a language that exacts violence on their rights and cultures:

> *Today we are being asked to spell out our Indian rights in a foreign language— the English language—in constitutional form. We are accustomed to talking about our rights in our own languages with our elders. Because of problems of*

---

70   R. Ross (1992). *Dancing with a Ghost: Exploring Indian Reality*. Octopus Publishing, Markham, Ontario.

interpretation we have always been in a weak position in our dealings with government. We have experienced an additional disadvantage because we have had to pursue our rights through the English legal and legislative systems. Explaining our rights in a foreign language is almost impossible, because sometimes we cannot find English words equivalent to our Indian words.

Echoing Ross's main thesis that Indigenous and non-Indigenous peoples are "*. . . separated by an immense gulf, one which the Euro-Canadian culture has never recognized, much less tried to explore and accommodate,*" Chief Snow provides useful instructions to Indigenous Canadians when dealing with agents of the colonial order:

We interpret what we see and hear through our own cultural eyes and ears. When we deal with people from another culture, our interpretations of their acts and words will very frequently be wrong. It follows that when we respond to their acts and words, relying upon our interpretations of them, we will respond by doing and saying things which we would never consider appropriate had we known the truth. We have not understood the degree to which the rules of their culture differ from ours. We must learn to expect such difference, be ever wary of our own cultural assumptions in interpreting their acts and words, and do our best to discover their realities and truths.[71]

It seems to me that the legal profession upon which Indigenous peoples have been forced to rely produces two types of lawyers: those who work exclusively within and are confined by existing legal doctrine and precedent, and those who push the envelope. It is with the latter where hope for reconciliation and co-existence may most profitably be directed. Maintaining or operating within the status quo, irrespective of the financial and other rewards of doing so, will not get us where we need to go.

Even then we should not anticipate real justice anytime soon. While Indigenous Canadians have been forced to rely on court injunctions to protect their rights to lands and resources, over 80 percent of injunctions filed by First Nations against industry corporations and provincial governments have been denied. Conversely, 76 percent of the injunctions filed against First Nations by corporations have been granted.[72]

---

[71] J. Snow (1985). Identification and Definition of Our Treaty and Aboriginal Rights. In *The Quest for Justice: Aboriginal Peoples and Aboriginal Rights*, M. Boldt, et al. (eds.). University of Toronto Press, pp. 41-46.

[72] *Land Back*. A Yellowhead Institute Red Paper (2019) redpaper.yellowheadinstitute.org

Reflections on Aboriginal Title

Lost in Translation

The Supreme Court of Canada has defined an Aboriginal right as *"an element of a practice, custom, or tradition integral to the distinctive culture of the Aboriginal group claiming the right,"* of which Aboriginal title—*"the right to the land itself"*—is paramount. At least since the *Royal Proclamation of 1763*, First Nations living under the protection of the Crown have had the exclusive right to their territories, providing that their lands had not been previously surrendered to the Crown. As Brian Slattery observes in his seminal analysis,[73] Aboriginal title was viewed at *"common law as co-existing with the ultimate underlying title of the Crown, and could not be transferred or sold to private interests, but only to the Crown by way of treaty."* Such groups were entitled to use their lands to whatever purposes they saw fit, including non-traditional uses as new circumstances presented themselves. In other words, the Crown recognized Aboriginal title lands to be reserved for the exclusive use of Indigenous groups occupying their traditional territories. It was not necessary for Aboriginal title, whatever its expression—there may be as many forms of Aboriginal title as there are Indigenous legal systems—to conform to the requirements of English property law. Of course, from the perspective of most First Nations they, not the Crown, hold the ultimate underlying rights and responsibilities to their lands.

With the relentless expropriation of Indigenous lands by settler society over the centuries, this conception of Aboriginal title at common law became more problematic and difficult to sustain, especially in British Columbia and other areas of Canada where Indigenous groups had not *ceded*—in the eyes of colonial governments—title to their traditional territories. In Slattery's opinion, while dispossession did not extinguish Aboriginal title, *"the scope and practical effects of dispossession were so significant that as time passed the situation became increasingly difficult to reverse without severely affecting the interests of innocent third parties and the public at large."*

So, as Slattery notes, for the better part of three centuries our judiciary has tried to balance the desire to correct great historical wrongs against their resultant impacts on society at large. But the facade came crashing down in 2005 with the Supreme Court of Canada decision in *R v. Marshall* and *R. v. Bernard*.[74] Having had its thumb on the scale of justice all along, the court sought to convert the concept of Aboriginal title into rights compatible with English property law.

What are the implications of *Marshall* and *Bernard*? For one, no consideration was given to the fact that the translation of Indigenous customary law into English common

---

73 B. Slattery (2006). "The Metamorphosis of Aboriginal Title." *Canadian Bar Review* 85(2): 255-286.

74 *R v. Marshall; R v. Bernard* [2005] 2 SCR 220.

law cannot be accomplished without doing grave injustice to Indigenous sociopolitical arrangements and institutions. Regardless of what form of Aboriginal title may take, or have taken, collective rights cannot be converted into individual rights. Even in more settled, complex, and socially stratified Indigenous societies, individual rights were sanctioned only so long as they did not derogate the collective rights of the group. In a recent study of traditional Secewpmec (Shuswap) land tenure systems commissioned by the *First Nation Tax Commission*, Bjorn Simonsen and I were surprised to find a greater diversity in Secewpemec tenure arrangements and attachments to their lands than expected.[75] Some historic Secewpmec groups were predominantly nomadic and egalitarian. More settled groups, however, possessed land tenure systems such that the most valued locations (e.g., eagle cliffs, deer fences, fishing stations, etc.) were inherited and held by chiefly clans on behalf of the group wherein rents were charged to commoners and outsiders wishing to access and use these places. While such a relationship to the land is not easily reconcilable with the notion that First Nation peoples in Canada did not own the land, the late-nineteenth-century ethnographer James Teit was emphatic that "*personal ownership in land did not exist*" among the Secewepmec.[76]

In the *Marshall/Bernard* decisions the Supreme Court transformed Aboriginal title from a *specific right* shaped by the customary laws of particular Indigenous groups to a *generic right*—i.e., rights that apply across the board regardless of the laws of the Indigenous groups in question, and answerable only to the rules and standards of English property law (e.g., fee simple estates, profit à prendre, easements, etc.). However, as Slattery asserts:

> *There is the danger that, in translating Indigenous practices into English legal categories, something important will be lost in translation. English property law is an intricate and artificial system, which evolved in a particular historical context and reflects distinctive social values, arrangements, and institutions. In applying English rules, courts may unconsciously misconstrue and devalue the outlook and practices of Indigenous societies, especially those whose modes of life are foreign to European agricultural economies. . . . At the extreme, this approach may lead courts to favour European over Indigenous perspectives, forcing Indigenous practices into the procrustean bed of English legal categories and rejecting modes of use and occupation that do not 'fit'.*

---

75   Manny Jules, Chief Commissioner, wanted this information in order to consider changes to federal legislation that would entertain fee-simple property ownership on reserve lands.

76   J. Teit (1909). *The Shuswap, Report of the The Jesup North Pacific Expedition, Volume II, Part VII*. Memoir of the American Museum of Natural History. E. J. Brill Ltd. (Leiden) and G. E. Stechert and Co., New York.

Slattery's solution to this dilemma was to view Aboriginal title as based in neither English common law nor Indigenous law, but on a distinctive form of title—a *sui generis* right—that developed from relations with the British Crown during the early centuries of colonization. This right reflects the exclusive right of Indigenous groups to possess and use their traditional lands for such purposes as they see fit, subject to the following caveats:

- the lands cannot be transferred to anyone other than the Crown, which holds the underlying title to the land.

- the lands cannot be used for purposes that are incompatible with the nature of the group's basic attachment to the land, and

- that Aboriginal title remains a collective right held and governed by all members of a nation.

From the perspective of the outsider, Aboriginal title is a uniform right, which does not differ from one group to another. Viewed from within, Slattery suggests that it:

> . . . *delimits a sphere within which the customary legal system of each group continues to operate, regulating the manner in which the lands are used by group members and evolving to take account of new needs and circumstances. In this respect, the sui generis conception of aboriginal title represents a blend of the diversity envisaged by the custom-based conception and the uniformity contemplated by the English-based conception. . . . In effect, this approach does not attempt to describe the detailed features of Indigenous land regimes, much less to translate them into categories of English. Aboriginal title does not result from the translation of Indigenous customary practices into non-Indigenous legal categories. Rather, Aboriginal title is a distinctive inter-societal right that bridges the gap between Indigenous and European-based land systems and regulates their interaction. No translation needed.*

In the 2014 Supreme Court of Canada decision in *Tsilhqot'in vs. British Columbia*,[77] the court appears to have adopted a view of Aboriginal title more in line with Slattery's. No longer did Aboriginal title have to *"comport"* with English property law to be recognized in law. Reversing her position in *Marshall/Bernard*, Chief Justice Beverley McLachlin agreed that forcing *"ancestral practices . . . into the square boxes of common law concepts"* should be avoided. No longer did Indigenous groups need to rely on sustained and intensive occupation of small geographic areas to prove title in the eyes of the court, rendering the *postage stamp* view of Aboriginal title adopted in previous lower and Supreme Court rulings obsolete. Rather, regular and exclusive use of large swaths of land for traditional

---

77   *Tsilhqot'in Nation v. British Columbia* 2014 SCC 44 [2014] 2 SCR 257 34986.

practices and activities (e.g., hunting, fishing, trapping, and gathering in legal terms)—even if the area claimed was used only some of the time—were now sufficient to ground a claim of Aboriginal title. While Indigenous groups may now be able to enjoy the rights and privileges to use and occupy their traditional lands much as their ancestors did, this does not mean that Aboriginal title is absolute and not subject to justifiable infringements. Economic development can still proceed on Aboriginal title lands if there is a *"compelling legislative objective"* (in the colonial narrative). In the end, Canada's top court decided that the Tsilhqot'in had proven Aboriginal title to 40 percent (1,750 square kilometres) of their traditional territory.

The implications of the *Tsilhqot'in* decision are far-reaching. The court has placed a greater burden on the Crown to obtain consent, justify infringements, and meaningfully consult and accommodate Indigenous groups prior to court recognition of Aboriginal title. Failure to do so may expose government and industry to damages and cancelled authorizations. But it is hard to fathom why Indigenous groups yet to enter into comprehensive land claims negotiations would want to attach themselves to a process that requires them to *"cede, release, and surrender"* title to their traditional lands. Indigenous peoples whose ancestors signed historic treaties with the Crown have widely maintained that the numbered treaties were not about surrendering their lands to the Crown, but establishing respectful and mutually beneficial relationships with settler society—in other words, co-existence. The Supreme Court's endorsement of a more liberal test for Aboriginal title in *Tsilhqot'in* may embolden Treaty First Nations to reject the old rules and revisit the question of what they gave up.

But let me be clear. The *Tsilhqot'in* decision creates no panacea for Canada's Indigenous peoples. The failure to address issues of governance and sovereignty undermines the nation-to-nation relationship envisioned by Indigenous parties. Likewise, the significance of overlapping and/or competing claims of Aboriginal title to the same territory remains unresolved. Following *Delgamuukw*, *Tsilhqot'in* sets out a three-part test for a claim of Aboriginal title:

(i) *the land must have been occupied prior to sovereignty,*

(ii) *there must be a continuity between present and pre-sovereignty occupation of the land, and*

(iii) *that occupation, at sovereignty, must have been exclusive.*

Although neither the *continuity* nor the *exclusivity* condition was a contentious issue in *Tsilhqot'in*, many First Nations find these requirements stacked in favour of the Crown. Both the *Delgamuukw* and *Tsilhqot'in rulings* necessitate an unbroken continuity—or relationship between present and pre-sovereignty occupations if the former is presented as proof of Aboriginal title of the latter. In many cases, this requirement—squarely grounded as it is English common law—has not and cannot be met.

The *exclusivity* of use and occupation condition since the claim of sovereignty by the Crown is just as problematic. Many Indigenous groups did not have "*the intent or capacity to retain 'exclusive' control over the land,*" as the SCC said they must. Rather, they worked out arrangements with others to use and share their lands that were more nuanced and adaptable to changing circumstances. Given the traditional governance and land-use systems of many Indigenous groups, it is impossible to conceive how they could possibly meet the Supreme Court's *continuity* and *exclusivity* of use and occupation requirements to prove Aboriginal title. Until our courts reconcile in common law these and other fundamental cultural differences that connect us and Indigenous peoples to our planet, we will remain "*lost in translation.*"

We Do Not Own the Land, the Land Owns Us!

Let me repeat: I am not a lawyer. But I do suspect that Canada's Supreme Court has not made its final decision with respect to Aboriginal title. The *exclusivity* and *continuity of use* conditions for grounding a claim of Aboriginal title does nothing to move the yardsticks toward a more ethical and accurate understanding of how rights to land and resources were traditionally conceived by, and apportioned among, Indigenous groups. Many, if not most, First Nation traditional territories overlap—sometimes significantly—with those of neighbouring groups. This has given rise to the popular platitude heard in many circles across the country that "*the natives have claimed title to 200 percent* [or some other such percentage] *of Canada.*" Exclusive use, occupation, and defence of land by First Nations was relatively rare—though not unheard of—and usually occurred between temporarily warring factions. Even among some settled groups of Nuu-chal-nuth and Secewpmec, neighbouring groups established peaceful relations and arrangements allowing them to share, use, and frequently occupy the territory of the other. Despite the progress made in the *Tsilhqot'in* decision, the *exclusive use* condition is embedded deeply in English property law—even profit à prendre does not adequately describe the land-use arrangements of Indigenous groups—and arguably infringes the rights of Canada's First Peoples to their lands and to govern themselves consistent with the *law of the land.*

On numerous occasions when discussing Aboriginal title and land ownership with First Nations elders, they have corrected me employing the epithet: "*We do not own the land, the land owns us.*" Perhaps more than any other, this characterization captures the true nature of Aboriginal title and the right to sovereignty over their lands. When Indigenous elders use this expression I sense they are talking about a deep feeling of respect for, and responsibility to, the lands and resources that have sustained them and their peoples for generations. And I suspect there is not a word or turn of phrase in English that can better describe the true nature of the relationship that many Indigenous peoples have with their lands.

A right to sell land, or do with it as one pleases subject to regulation, is not equivalent to the right bestowed upon one who is *owned by*, has duties to, and *belongs to the land*. The latter is an earned right that transcends monetary and materialistic considerations. When an individual *belongs to the land*, it can neither be bought nor sold as one inherits the responsibility to care for it on behalf of present and future generations. It is a moral imperative that entails not just environmental and ecological obligations, but social and cultural ones as well. It is a relationship to land that is more sacred, more ethical, and more ecologically grounded than that granted by fee simple ownership, which seems overwhelmingly profane in comparison. Although this concept may be hard to grasp for many Canadians, it may resonate with small-scale farming families who have toiled their plot of land for generations. It is apparent to me that, from a social and cultural perspective, *the right to belong to the land* is a form of title or an attachment to the land that is of a higher order than any category of land ownership that evolved under English common law. In the end, however, Indigenous Canadians have been forced to defend their rights and title to their lands by translating them into concepts that obscure and diminish the very rights and attachments they are trying to protect.

There are few, if any, jurisdictions in Canada where Indigenous peoples are able to fulfil their responsibilities to their lands and resources, and to steward them sustainably. Federal and provincial legislation has made sure of that. The *continuity* and *exclusivity* requirements to establish Aboriginal title continue to hamstring Indigenous peoples in their efforts to defend their rights to their lands and resources, and to sustain their cultures, societies, and the environments upon which they depend. Even so, I do not see a stampede of lawyers rushing to assist Indigenous peoples to challenge the courts on this matter, or other unjust aspects of Aboriginal jurisprudence—e.g., Canada's shallow interpretation of so-called *hunting, trapping, and fishing* treaty rights—to right these wrongs.

Canada's approach to Aboriginal title has been shaped by the *doctrine of discovery* and the concept of *terra nullius* (Latin for land belonging to nobody). Employed by colonial powers worldwide as legal and moral justification for the colonial dispossession of Indigenous lands, these doctrines have been resoundingly rejected by Canada's Royal Commission on Aboriginal Peoples and United Nations' Declaration of the Rights of Indigenous Peoples as racist, scientifically false, legally invalid, morally condemnable, and socially unjust. Yet Canada's courts continue to view Aboriginal title as *"a burden on the Crown's underlying title."* But it seems to me that things have gotten turned around. The Crown's claim of sovereignty places a burden on the true nature of Indigenous peoples' underlying title, *the right to belong to the land*. The future of who we become in this country and the place of Indigenous peoples in it may just turn on this fact.

PART THREE

Cultural Wars

CHAPTER 9

Trust Us Again, Just One More Time: Adventures in Land-Use Planning

THE TRADITIONAL KNOWLEDGE AND LAND-USE RIGHTS OF INDIGENOUS CANADIANS ARE AS intertwined as they are integral to their cultures and futures. Yet both continue to be eviscerated by our country's governing and corporate elites and institutions. Whether a result of ignorance, hubris, some mix of the two, and/or other factors is a matter of debate. The war is being waged on multiple fronts. Two that continue to resonate with me are being led by government agents of the colonial order. The first involves provincial land-use planning—in this case, by the province of Alberta—the second, Indigenous cultural heritage preservation by federal, provincial, and territorial agencies.

What Are You Talking About? Most of You People Hunt at the IGA!

Roy (Vermillion) and I could not believe our ears. Did he just say that? The owner of this racial slur was an industry representative on the Regional Advisory Council for the Lower Athabasca Regional Plan. Roy was the executive director of the Athabasca Tribal Council and Treaty 8's representative on the RAC. I was the Treaty 6 appointee. Roy had just finished a passionate monologue about why animals, hunting, and his peoples' connection to the land were critically important to them, now more so than ever. Both of us were stunned by this xenophobic remark as were several others on our fifteen-member regional land-use planning committee.

Formed in 2009, the RAC for the LARP was charged with developing a vision and framework for a fifty-year land-use plan that would oversee Canada's largest industrial and controversial gamble, the Alberta's tar sands. The Lower Athabasca Regional Plan has been embroiled in controversy ever since.

It all began several years earlier with the development of Alberta's Land Use Framework, which provides the legislative authority to create and implement seven regional land-use plans across the province. In order to ensure consistency with *Alberta's Land Stewardship Act*, dozens of provincial acts were amended. In addition, multi-stakeholder regional advisory councils were (or would be) created along with a land-use secretariat to oversee the development and implementation of regional land-use plans.

Alberta began the long process of overhauling its antiquated land management regime in 2007 using all the right words and platitudes. Large conservation and recreation areas would be created side-by-side with industrial development zones. Every 10 years regional land-use plans would be reviewed and amended where necessary. Consultation with the general public and Aboriginal communities would be extensive, and all major stakeholders would be represented on the Regional Advisory Councils. Eventually, the Lower Athabasca Regional Advisory Council—the first RAC in the province—would include appointees from municipal governments, environmental organizations, tribal councils, and the petroleum, forestry, and agricultural sectors.

Fighting hard to keep his blood pressure in check, Roy calmly rebuked our fellow committee member, citing the high cost of food in his community and the need to conserve First Nations' land not *taken-up* by industry for nutritional, cultural, and environmental reasons. After the meeting, the industry executive apologized and the two reconciled, more or less. Our small disparate group never again experienced a similar transgression. Nonetheless, a residual tension hung over many of our deliberations as we set about to produce the framework of a regional land-use plan that would balance the needs, rights, and interests of Indigenous and non-Indigenous Albertans.

Among other things, our diverse cohort was asked to assess the viability of three bitumen production scenarios (up to a peak of six million barrels per day), and to select 20 percent or more of the region for conservation.[78] Such areas had to support Aboriginal traditional use, exclude industrial activity, and be of sufficient size (4,000-5,000 square kilometres) and landscape connectivity to preserve regional biodiversity. We were also asked to consider options for community development, physical and social infrastructure needs, recreation and tourism development, population growth and labour needs, and impacts to local and Aboriginal communities. Our advice to the Alberta government would set a clear vision with specific outcomes, objectives, and strategies for the final LARP as well as establish a variety of land-use classifications and management frameworks.

To some extent, and in retrospect, we achieved our mandate. Sure, Roy and I were often challenged to defend the rights of our respective tribal councils' First Nation members.

---

78 *Terms of Reference for Developing the Lower Athabasca Regional Plan* (2008). <u>landuse.alberta.ca</u>

And yes, we knew the process might be rigged from the start.[79] It was. For example, despite repeated requests to consider the value of ecosystem services (carbon sequestration, water filtration, etc.) to arrive at a true cost-accounting of the three bitumen production scenarios, we never did receive and were not allowed to consider this information. Yet the total non-market value of ecosystem services in Canada's boreal forest ($93.2 billion) is estimated to be 2.5 times that of the combined net market value of forestry, mining, the oil and gas industry, and hydroelectricity ($37.8 billion).[80] Carbon sequestration alone accounts for $1.85 billion per annum, while the value of subsistence services to Indigenous peoples is estimated to be as high as $575 million. Right from the start we had anticipated that things might occasionally go off the rails. They did. Perhaps the most contentious issue we debated was whether non-Indigenous Albertans would be allowed to hunt and fish in conservation areas. They were.

Throughout the process, Roy and I reported back to our tribal chiefs and councils. We did not get all that they wanted in the plan. But for an advisory committee composed of members with radically different views on how the world ought to work, we were able to find consensus on most issues. After fifteen months of soul-searching and handwringing, we produced a vision and framework that would guide land-use planning in the lower Athabasca region for the next half century. The fact that such a diverse cross-section of the Canadian mosaic could reach agreement on such a complex set of competing interests and issues was perhaps our most notable achievement.

What We Advised

Our vision statement stressed the need to balance *"sustainable economic, social, and environmental outcomes . . . through the use of aboriginal, traditional and community knowledge, sound science, innovative thinking, and accommodation of rights and interests of all Albertans."*[81] Thirty-six specific strategies within six of the plan's eight key outcomes addressed Aboriginal issues, including building Aboriginal capacity to participate in the regional economy, ensuring meaningful consultations with Aboriginal communities, identifying Aboriginal stewardship responsibilities, documenting traditional knowledge, and including Aboriginal peoples in land-use planning.

---

79   This may explain why the Métis appointee on our committee never attended any meetings, after his first.

80   National Aboriginal Forestry Association (2006). *First Nations Boreal Forest Issues Workshop*, February 24, Ottawa. www.nafaforestry.org

81   Lower Athabasca Regional Advisory Council (2010). *Advice to the Government of Alberta Regarding a Vision for the Lower Athabasca Region*. https://www.landuse.alberta.ca/LandUse Documents

Outcome 7 ("*Aboriginal Peoples' Rights, Traditional Uses, and Values are Respected and Reflected in Land Use Planning*") was particularly hard fought, and won, sort of. Roy and I disagreed with the wording of the second objective of this outcome, which sought to balance the "*constitutionally protected rights of Aboriginal peoples and the interests of all Albertans*" in land-use planning. How can the constitutional rights of one group be balanced by the interests of the other, we wondered? How are these equivalent? Although we were unsuccessful in changing this wording, our committee identified numerous roles and responsibilities for Aboriginal peoples in land-use planning and environmental assessment/monitoring intended to generate options for the "*mitigation, accommodation, and reconciliation of Indigenous rights.*"

Achieving sustainable development objectives was dependent upon documenting Indigenous knowledge to assess environmental changes through time, to enhance understanding of cumulative environmental impacts, and to develop performance measures and roles for Aboriginal peoples in planning and environmental impact mitigation (including the role of traditional burning in maintaining ecosystem biodiversity). It was particularly important to undertake traditional subsistence needs assessments to improve land-use decision-making and maintain populations of game species to support traditional use and the exercise of treaty rights.

As per our terms of reference, conservation areas had to be of sufficient size, representative of the region's biodiversity, supportive of traditional use, and demonstrate landscape connectivity. As six percent of the region was already protected by various means, we recommended that an additional 14 percent be set aside as new conservation areas, with another 12 percent proposed for conservation purposes in other areas, making clear distinctions between land developed by industry and land allocated for conservation and traditional use. Thus, 32 percent of the region, mostly north of the mineable tar sands, was selected to achieve conservation objectives by maintaining biodiversity and creating benchmark areas of adequate size for assessing environmental impacts.

Soon after our advice was submitted to the Land Use Secretariat, Alberta shopped it around the region inviting First Nations and Métis community feedback. Although no funding was initially available to support this initiative, $100k was eventually offered to each First Nation to participate on the condition that the funding also be used for consultations in other planning regions where they possess treaty rights. But some affected First Nations chose not to participate. Not only had Alberta's treaty chiefs rejected the province's Land Use and Aboriginal Consultation policies, First Nation funding for LARP was woefully inadequate to undertake the mountain of work required to adequately defend their rights and to engage with the province. In the end, participating First Nations recommended that 40 percent of the region be set aside as conservation areas where they could exercise their treaty and Aboriginal rights.

What Albertans Got

To the surprise of only a few, the final plan approved by cabinet and released to the public in 2012 bore little resemblance to what the RAC recommended or what First Nations wanted.[82] It was as if cabinet had conducted a word search of our draft framework, deleting words and phrases that might conceivably unnerve supporters and beneficiaries of Alberta's petroleum economy.

The final vision statement for the LARP makes no reference to Aboriginal peoples at all. Of the seven cabinet-approved outcomes, only one—*The Inclusion of Aboriginal Peoples in Land-Use Planning*—addresses Indigenous issues in any detail. Anything *Aboriginal* is siloed into a single outcome with a lone objective that *"encourages the participation of Aboriginal peoples in land use planning."* No meaningful roles for Indigenous peoples in planning, or the identification and management of individual and cumulative impacts, are identified. Rather, Aboriginal involvement is relegated to the development of a few recreational trails and cultural tourism attractions, including the *"Richardson Backcountry Stewardship Initiative . . . should they chose to participate."* Alberta nevertheless committed to *"considering how the constitutionally protected rights of First Nations to hunt, fish, and trap for food"* can be maintained near main population centres, and to *"engage Aboriginal communities in the development of a water quantity management framework for the Lower Athabasca River."*

Perhaps the most disturbing aspect of the plan was that only 16 percent of the region—half of that recommended by our RAC—was set aside for conservation, with only one area satisfying the size and connectivity terms of reference. The final LARP also offered little protection for *endangered* woodland caribou. In the end, the province committed to consulting with Aboriginal peoples only *"when government decisions may adversely affect the continued exercise of their constitutionally protected rights."* Encouraging Aboriginal participation? Including Aboriginal people in land-use planning? You guessed it . . . ,

Cue Charlie Brown, Lucy, and the football!

First Nations Response

Critics blasted the plan for pandering to industry without doing anything meaningful to address conservation and the rights and interests of Aboriginal communities. First Nation leaders were particularly outraged:

> *They already felt their voices were not given enough precedence in the stakeholder groups, but they had agreed and compromised with the other players at*

---

82   *Lower Athabasca Regional Plan 2012-2022.* landuse.alberta.ca/LandUseDocuments

the table. But the government pushed ahead. They took the draft plan around the region, holding community consultations nearly everywhere. Then they came back with a final draft, with nary a mention of the problems the plan posed for First Nations.[83]

Athabasca Chipewyan Chief Allan Adam asserted that *"the land use plan [had] been watered down to cater to industry,* [and] *if it keeps going in that direction, there will be nowhere left to exercise our treaty rights."* Mikisew Cree Industry Relations director Melody Lepine remarked, *"the consultation process for them was just going through the motions."* Both First Nations (and several others in the Treaty 6 and 8 areas) had acted in good faith, providing extensive materials to the Land-Use Secretariat, in addition to participating in RAC meetings and provincial consultations.

The development of LARP began with promise, ended in controversy, was opposed by many parties, and passed without any sort of consensus. Litigation by First Nations and environmental groups to protect endangered woodland caribou soon followed. Applications from six directly affected First Nations for an independent review of the plan came next. Subsequently, a panel was convened to address their grievances. The size of conservation areas, cumulative effects management, and the roles of First Nations in implementing the LARP were particularly contentious. After careful scrutiny, the review panel rejected the provincial Crown's position that the *"LARP does not affect Aboriginal rights and interests."*[84] Among other things, it agreed with First Nation applicants that the plan:

- *did not protect Aboriginal culture,*

- *gave businesses priority over the constitutional rights of Aboriginal groups,*

- *created new conservation areas without reference to traditional use,*

- *had few environmental protection measures and no thresholds for action,*

- *had no measures to manage traditional land-use, and*

- *eroded existing traditional use rights, blocking the creation of new areas for such use.*

The review panel also recommended that Alberta conduct a health study on contaminants in the Athabasca River and to replace *"project-by-project assessments with a framework to address the overall proliferation of resource-development project impacts . . . on people living in* [the] *area."* In order to achieve the purposes described in *ALSA*, the province was directed to institute:

---

83   S. Bell (2012). LARP Further Divides First Nations, Industry. 10 January, *Northern Journal*.

84   *Review Panel Report 2015, Lower Athabasca Regional Plan.* https://open.alberta.ca

> *. . . a Traditional Land Use Management Framework . . .* [to] *be developed and included as an important component of the LARP. This will recognize and honour the constitutionally-protected rights of the First Nation communities residing in the Lower Athabasca Region. Such a framework would assist all stakeholders, operators, regulators, governments, and Aboriginal peoples in land use planning for the region in the foreseeable future.*

As 2019 gave way to 2020 water-quantity and air-quality management frameworks as well as a few *wildland* parks had been established. To date, no management frameworks or tools—including the identification of indicators and thresholds—to assess multiple and cumulative impacts on biodiversity or Indigenous rights and cultures in the region have been developed.

In retrospect, the province's effort to solicit advice from a small representative cross-section of northeastern Albertans, and a handful of First Nations and Métis communities, was a sham from the start. The ultimate authority for the scope, content, and implementation of the LARP—indeed all regional land-use plans—rests with the provincial cabinet. The roles of RACs are purely consultative. At the same time, most of the goals and policies under ALUF relating to Indigenous peoples are nothing more than platitudes. The *terms of reference* for the LARP specified that "*land-use must be managed to include Aboriginal traditional use activities,*" and take "*into account Aboriginal issues with respect to Aboriginal consultation, environmental protection and human development.*" The discretionary nature of the enabling legislation, however, makes it clear that the participation of Indigenous peoples in the development of regional plans is limited. There is no mechanism with any teeth to challenge or enforce changes in the content of regional land-use plans.

In the end, the development of the Lower Athabasca Regional Plan was all *smoke and mirrors*, a parlour trick of unfathomable proportions, even for the government of Alberta.

Map or be Mapped: The Paradox of Traditional Land-Use Mapping

> *More Indigenous territory has been claimed by maps than by guns*
> (Bernard Nietschmann, geographer)

Settler society's control over Indigenous territories is expanding in inverse relation to its connection to the natural world. An ancillary factor in dispossessing Indigenous peoples of their lands and resources worldwide is modern society's reliance on maps. Maps are not necessarily a bad thing; Indigenous peoples across the globe have been forced to depend on maps to defend their land-use rights. Indeed, Nietschmann believes that "*more Indigenous land can be reclaimed and defended by maps than by guns.*" Nevertheless, the way that traditional land-use mapping is conducted sabotages this outcome—a conclusion I came to only after years of conducting traditional-use studies with scores of Inuit, First Nations, and Métis elders and land-users.

Indigenous peoples have been forced to portray their connections to their lands in ways that further the interests of the dominant culture, while undermining theirs. As some researchers have argued, the mapping of Indigenous territories is linked to a broader history of *"cartographic colonialism that forces Indigenous peoples to subject themselves to western systems of geographic knowledge."*[85] As these authors assert, *"mapmaking is an art, not a science,"* and the rigid international standardization applied to the mapping of Indigenous territories stifles cultural expression and subverts Indigenous peoples relationships to their lands. In the words of Yves Lacoste, *"the map is, and has been, fundamentally an instrument of power . . . an abstraction of concrete reality . . . a way of representing space which facilitates its domination and control."*[86]

In Canada, governments and industry frequently provide funding to Indigenous groups to map their traditional land-use activities in the contexts of assessing the impacts of resource development or negotiating land claims and impact benefit agreements. For many Indigenous peoples, mapping current and historic use and occupation of their territories is seen as the first line of defence to protect their rights and connections to their lands. Although cartographers are taught that *"the map is not the territory,"* for many Indigenous communities forced to defend their lands *"it has become the territory."*[87] Subsequently, the dots, lines, and polygons digitized on two-dimensional maps become the iconic representations of Indigenous land-use, and the authoritative reference upon which land-use decisions and actions are taken. In turn, Indigenous peoples are effectively excluded from management decisions. Sound familiar? At the same time, Indigenous peoples' *"perceptions of themselves and their territories, their resources, and their histories are transformed,"* and relationships to their cultural landscapes are sabotaged.[88] The end result is that the playing field of resource politics is tilted in favour of those who benefit most by divesting Indigenous peoples of their lands and resources.

The interpretation of traditional land-use maps by government and industry rarely supports Indigenous interests. Large polygons of traditional use areas are not considered

---

85 T. L. Joly et al. (2018). Ethnographic Refusal in Traditional Land Use Mapping: Consultation, Impact Assessment, and Sovereignty in the Athabasca Oil Sands Region. *Elsevier* 5(2):335-343.

86 Y. Lascoste (1973). An Illustration of Geographical Warfare: Bombing of the Dikes on the Red River, North Vietnam. *Antipode* 5(2):1-13. https://doi.org/10.1111/j.1467-8330.1973.tb00502.x

87 M. Stone (1998). Map or be Mapped. *Whole Earth* (fall) Vol. 94. questia.com/magazine/1G1-21260280/map-or-be-mapped

88 J. Engel (2015). Decolonial Mapmaking, Reclaiming Indigenous Places and Knowledge. *Landscape Magazine*, 4(2), Winter. https://medium.com/langscape-magazine/decolonial-mapmaking-reclaiming-indigenous-places-and-knowledge-4779b7f8b81c

specific enough and do not contain enough information to be reliable, or so the reasoning goes. Moreover, they are often viewed as land grabs. Conversely, too much information—e.g., exact locations of kill sites across wide geographic areas—can be used against Indigenous land-users. Lawyers for mineable tar sands companies, for example, have asserted that their clients' projects will not impact the constitutionally protected rights of Indigenous peoples because they hunt everywhere else:

> *You obviously hunt in many other areas of your traditional territory where there is no industrial activity. Consequently, our project will not impact your ability to hunt.*[89]

At the same time, in heavily developed areas such as Dene Tha' territory, industry representatives often challenge traditional land-use studies and have been heard to remark, *"We never see any First Nations people out here. If their lands are so important to them, where are they?"*

Overlapping Indigenous territories are almost always looked upon with suspicion. They do not conform with society's conception of *property ownership*, and thus diminish the credibility of First Nation claims. Lastly, while developers will often propose buffers of various size around campsites and cabins (typically 50-100 metres), the remaining land base—the raison d'être for Indigenous use and occupation of specific locales in the first place—is open to exploitation. Although this *dots-on-a-map* approach has been effectively rejected by the Supreme Court in the *Tsilhqot'in* decision, it continues to be *de rigueur* for government and industry proponents. All things considered, Indigenous groups may be forgiven for refusing access to their members' traditional land-use information. For many Indigenous Canadians, traditional land-use mapping has become a *Catch 22*.

New and better ways of traditional land-use mapmaking need to be found. Recording oral histories and place names in the local Indigenous language should be mandatory. Indigenous land-uses around intensively and seasonally exploited and/or occupied sites (e.g., specific resource use locations, campsites, cabins, trails, etc.) almost always exhibit a pattern that can be modelled by a series of concentric rings of decreasing intensity up to dozens, if not hundreds, of kilometres away. Such approaches also have the potential to record important social, ecological, and other information. A more culturally appropriate picture of Indigenous land-use may be obtained by mapping individual land-use histories, or map biographies, without reference to the standard—and distorted—two-dimensional geographic representations of space found on topographic maps. Encouraging Indigenous elders, hunters, and other land-users to draw their own maps on blank pieces may provide critical information about the importance and cultural value of specific locations and resource use areas relative to others.

---

89   Paraphrased from an oil sands company's legal counsel's remark to Melody Lepine, Director of Government and Industry Relations, Mikisew Cree First Nation.

Indigenous Land-Use Planning

Traditional land-use mapping will likely always be a key component of Indigenous land-use planning. But it is by no means the only one. All sorts of needs assessments must be considered, from economic to sociocultural to environmental. Interestingly, the courts have said that Indigenous peoples have a right to develop resources on their lands—even if such activities were not part of their ancestral way of life—so long as they do not abrogate the constitutionally protected rights of present and future generations. Few Indigenous groups, however, have had the resources to reach consensus on how they wish their lands to be used, and by whom. Nor have they had access to resources to build the capacity needed to implement their land-use plans. Apart from documenting traditional land-use, there is usually no government funding available for such initiatives. Consequently, they are at a distinct disadvantage when engaging with other stakeholders in regional land-use planning processes.

In contrast, most municipal governments and industry stakeholders come to the table with concrete blueprints for lands under their jurisdiction, as well as the capacity, resources, and institutional support to implement them. In the absence of well-formulated land-use plans constructed by Indigenous peoples, the prospects of achieving sustainable social, cultural, economic, and environmental outcomes within larger provincial land-use planning processes remain remote. And, as experience has shown, if Indigenous peoples do not have the opportunity to develop their own land-use plans, someone else will do that for them.

Postscript: Where'd He Go?

Within minutes my pilot and I were enveloped in a yellowish-brown haze as the sun fell toward the horizon. We had just left Fort Chipewyan on our flight to Fort McMurray, 220 kilometres away. With Lake Athabasca slowly disappearing behind us, I could not shake the shame I felt.

Several hours earlier, Mikisew Cree elder Archie Antoine, his grandson Robert, and I had just returned from a short trip to Peace Point and back. We had spent the better part of the last two days in Archie's boat dodging gravel bars on the lower Peace River in Wood Buffalo National Park. Water levels on the Peace River were near record lows, and I was amazed at Robert's ability to skillfully pilot his grandfather's boat around dozens of submerged and unseen water hazards—not to mention the trust that his grandfather placed in him to do so. You see, Robert was no ordinary twelve-year-old from Fort Chip.

Earlier that summer at the 2015 Treaty Days celebrations in Fort Chipewyan, I had spoken with Mikisew chief Steve Courtoreille about the possibility of assessing the condition of Peace Point's archaeological sites. I was in Fort Chip undertaking a social and cultural impact assessment of large scale resource development projects—principally the Alberta tar sands and BC Hydro's Bennett dam—on the Mikisew Cree, and had not been back to Peace Point since 1982. Two months later, with the chief's blessing, the three of us set off for Peace Point. In addition to Robert's intimate knowledge of the river, I was impressed with his thirst to know more about his people's history as we inspected Peace Point's cliff face for exposed hearths, bones, and chert artifacts.

Robert, I soon learned, had been encouraged by his mom to live with his grandfather, an esteemed Mikisew Cree elder/hunter/trapper, thus side-stepping much of the mischief other kids his age often get into around Fort Chip. But just as soon as we tied up to the dock, Robert vanished, leaving Archie and me with the thankless job of offloading and dragging our gear up the boat ramp to Archie's truck. The boarding time for my flight to Fort McMurray was fast approaching, and I was both frustrated and disappointed. Maybe I had been wrong about Robert all along. Agitated, I turned to Archie, "*Where the hell did he go?*" Archie returned my outburst with a smile.

Twenty minutes later, Robert reappeared with a sheepish grin on his face. He had been dying to show me his most recent and prized possession, a brand new eighteen-foot aluminum boat and motor. I finally understood. The boat was Robert's rite of passage into adulthood, one which declared to the world that he had become a hunter. Like his grandfather and generations before him, he now *belonged to the land*. It would only be a matter of time before Robert assumed his grandfather's mantle.

As we continued on our journey through the thickening haze, the humiliation of my indiscretion was replaced by a deeper sense of shame. There below us, hundreds of square kilometres of once-pristine boreal forest had been transformed into a desiccated industrial wasteland dominated by open-pit mines, tailings ponds, dust clouds, pipelines, smoke stacks, and giant processing plants. Flying low over the Athabasca River on our approach to Fort McMurray, my thoughts turned to Robert and what the future held for him, his family, and his people.

CHAPTER 10

Divided No More: Adventures in Indigenous Cultural Preservation and Resurgence

Celebrating the Great Peace

IT WAS ONE OF THE LARGEST CELEBRATORY GATHERINGS OF PEOPLE EVER ON THE PEACE River. On the occasion of Canada's 150th birthday as a country, upwards of 1,200 people from all over western Canada gathered at Peace Point on the north bank of the great river that took its name. They had come to celebrate the monumental peace that was forged here between Canada's two founding First Nation peoples—the Algonquin-speaking Cree/Ojibwe and Athabascan-speaking Dene—a century before Confederation and decades before any European ever set eyes on the Peace River.

The history of the Peace Point treaty is not well known; a comprehensive oral history and archival search of the treaty has yet to be undertaken. In 1792 Alexander Mackenzie was told that after the peace was established, Peace Point (formerly known as Prairie Point) became the boundary between the Cree and Dene peoples.[90] As a young fur trader in Canada's north during the early twentieth century, Phillip Godsell met an elderly Denesuline (Chipewyan) chief who recalled in impressive detail the events leading up to the treaty.[91] Though undoubtedly one-sided and clearly a casualty of artistic license, Godsell's retelling of Chief Montaignais's recollections underscores the historical significance of the treaty, which he assigned to around 1760:

> *Old Montaignais's story of the last great battle, which had taken place on the Peace River when the Cree and their Saulteaux allies had threatened the existence of the Beavers by massing their resources in an attempt to drive them out*

---

[90] A. Mackenzie (2001). *The Journals of Alexander Mackenzie: Exploring Across Canada in 1789 & 1793.* Narrative Press.

[91] P. Godsell (1939). *Red Hunters of the Snows.* The Ryerson Press, pp.203-07.

of the valley of the Peace, corresponded in many points with incidents related by Sir Alexander Mackenzie and no doubt have a strong foundation in fact. . . . This fight probably occurred in the vicinity of the stream they called the Battle River—Notinigao Sipi—which empties into the Peace about forty miles westward of Fort Vermillion. . . . Prior to 1782, the Beavers had very few fire-arms, and these had been obtained from the English traders of Hudson Bay through Chipewyan middlemen. . . . Consequently, when the advance guard of the Crees, armed with English muskets, met the southernmost bands of Beavers near the head-waters of the Churchill River and along the Athabasca, they were able to do considerable havoc among them and eventually succeeded in driving them to the north shore of the Peace [formerly the Beaver River]. *But, according to my friend Montaignais, the fiery Tennesaw* [Dene Tsa] *would go no further. Once and for all they decided to make the Peace River the permanent southern frontier of their hunting-grounds.*

Then the moccasin telegraph brought rumours of hordes of Crees and allied tribesmen gathering on the shores of Lesser Slave Lake. So numerous were the conical buffalo-hide lodges of these enemies, said the rumours, that the very sky was stained with the smoke of their fires. Then, one by one, . . . [Dene Tsa] *spies emerged from the shadowy forests with word that the Crees were dancing at night round huge camp-fires with vermillion and yellow ochre—the paint of war—daubed upon their bodies. Through the forested aisles sped the swiftest runners of the Beavers, carrying word to the fierce tribesmen of the Salt Plains, to the Slaves of Great Slave Lake, and to the Land of the Little Sticks wherein dwelt the Yellow Knives and Dog-Ribs, of the impending onslaught of the Crees. A flotilla of bark canoes, manned by a half dozen tawny ambassadors, also slipped down the Peace, bound for the Chipewyans of Athabasca Lake to exchange lynx and beaver skins for muskets, lead, and powder. Slowly but surely these warriors answered the call and converged upon the north shore of the Peace.*

Already Cree warriors could be seen flitting from tree-trunk to tree-trunk on the south side of the river, their eagle feathers fluttering a taunting invitation to their enemies to cross and come to grips. Soon seven hundred grease-daubed warriors of the combined Athapascan tribes were yelling and howling defiance from the north side of the river at the five hundred whooping blood-crazed Crees and Saulteaux on the other.

The tall and fierce Frozen Foot led the Chipewyans, Barren Bear headed the tawny Yellow Knives, while Sunrise remained behind—imbued, perhaps, as much by fear as patriotism—to defend the squaws and papooses and camp equipment in the forest in the rear. . . . For three days the warriors yelled and howled defiance at each other, brandished their weapons in the air and fired arrows at each other, only to see the winged missiles fall into the water, for the river here is very wide. It was the kind of battle . . . with much noise and few casualties . . . that almost every warrior would live to talk and boast about around the lodge fires in after years.

But the fight seemed in danger of being prolonged indefinitely, or until one side ran short of dried meat and provisions, when a nondescript and ragged Slavey hunter brought himself to a ruse. Taking a flint and steel, and tying them in his long hair, he crawled through the underbrush until he reached a bend in the river out of sight of the contending factions. Slipping into the water, he swam stealthily across, and, reaching the southern shore unseen, clambered out among the willows. Cautiously he made his way toward the battleground occupied by the invading Crees. Reaching an area covered with brule and deadfall to the west of the enemy, he struck his steel against the flint until a shower of sparks caused the punkwood beneath to smolder and redden. Blowing upon this, and nursing the small flame, he ignited some shreds of resinous birch-bark and tossed them into a mass of dried wood he had hurriedly gathered together. Fanned by the wind, the flames soon leapt to the overhanging boughs, and within an hour a terrific holocaust was raging through the woods, driving the terror-stricken Crees and their Saulteaux allies before it. Vainly they sought to outdistance the Great Destroyer, but the smoke and flames bore swiftly down upon them, urged forward by the fierce wind generated by the fire itself. All about them frightened forest animals plunged through the underbrush with shrill cries of terror while thick white coils of suffocating smoke rose even higher in the sky. Now and then some fleeing warrior would trip and stumble over a spreading vine or the contorted carcass of a tree, only to be swallowed in the roaring inferno that followed at his heels.

. . . Many Crees died that day . . . [and] for many weeks the place was alive with feasting crows and wolves. . . . It was enough! The Crees had learned to fear the Tenne-saw. Shortly afterward, the Crees sent ambassadors to the Beavers and the Chipewyans, suggesting that all should bury the hatchet and enjoy together the friendly consolation of the calumet of peace.

> *At Peace Point, where the mile-wide Peace River casts its mighty flood into the waters of the Slave, the head-men of the warring tribes assembled in a panoply of paint, porcupine quills, eagle feathers, and their barbaric finery. Presents were exchanged, and long harangues were made, first to each other and then to the Great Spirit to witness the solemn compact* [that] *was about to be enacted. The peace pipe was passed from hand to hand, its friendly incense mingling with the fragrance of the balsams. Then, at the foot of a tall sentinel pine, the hatchet was forever buried and the tree denuded of its lower branches to form a lobstick in honour of the day. Thus the Beaver River received a new name—the Peace River—which will continue to perpetuate the compact that was made upon its bank long after the Beaver tribe has crumbled into dust.*

Indigenous Canadians were in no mood to celebrate in the months leading up to Canada's 150th anniversary as a country. A century and a half of cultural genocide was nothing to commemorate.[92] More Indigenous groups across the country were planning protests than celebrations. However, meetings I had with Mikisew Cree chief Steve Courtoreille and Athabasca Chipewyan chief Allan Adam in 2016 confirmed that they viewed the Peace Point treaty as something to celebrate in Canada's 150th year. They saw the celebration as an opportunity to commemorate the sovereign nature of First Nations' peoples in the face colonial oppression, and maybe even educate fellow Canadians about their history. That representatives of this country's two founding First Nations' peoples concluded, after an epic battle, a peace among themselves well before any colonial agent *discovered* the region was something that the chiefs wanted to share with the rest of the country, especially in 2017. They wanted Canadians to know that a century or so before Confederation, two self-governing peoples forged a monumental peace treaty that was to govern relations between them "*as long as the sun shines, the rivers flow, and the grass grows.*"

Everybody who was anybody was there. Dene and Cree leaders from all over the western provinces and the Northwest Territories converged on Peace Point. The prime minister of Canada and his family were there, as was the premier of the province and other provincial dignitaries and politicians. Three days of treaty celebrations attracted extensive regional and national media attention. It might have been the largest and grandest celebration ever witnessed on the Peace River, since perhaps the historic treaty itself.

Within months after the celebrations, First Nations across the county began to develop consensus on a host of issues affecting their rights and interests—particularly on matters related to land-use, environment, economic development, health, and education—striking fear into the hearts of Canada's governing and corporate elites. There was

---

92 P. Palmater (2017). *Canada 150 is a Celebration of Indigenous Genocide.* March 29, https://nowtoronto.com/news/canada-s-150th-a-celebration-of-indigenous-genocide

strength in numbers, and things began to change for the better. Youth—Indigenous and non-Indigenous—across the country were learning about Cree and Dene cultures, history, and prehistory. The vision of the chiefs was on the way to being realized.

It Never Happened

The only problem with this description is that it never happened—merely a product of an overactive imagination. The celebrations never took place!

Follow-up efforts to obtain political and financial support for the celebrations fell flat on their face. The chiefs sent a co-authored letter to the prime minister's office informing him of the proposed festivities, inviting him and his family to the event, and requesting financial support to hold it. You see, a federal deadline for *Canada 150* proposal celebrations had just passed, and there were few other options available to access funding to plan and hold the celebrations. The PMO response: Radio silence! Months went by. Crickets!

A letter sent to the federal member of parliament for MacMurray-Cold Lake met with the same response. Indian and Northern Affairs personnel in Edmonton were eventually contacted, and although receptive to the proposal, the end result was the same. Some funding for celebration planning and archaeological assessment was obtained from the province of Alberta. But far greater support was needed to hold the main event.

Meanwhile, Parks Canada's lack of cooperation and stonewalling, already legendary in my mind, reached new heights. Peace Point's archaeological sites are located in two-metre river deposited sediments atop a limestone escarpment on both Mikisew Cree Reserve and Wood Buffalo National Park lands. Anything the chiefs wanted to do at Peace Point had to be done with the blessing and support of Parks Canada.

With Chief Courtoreille's permission, I contacted the Parks office in Fort Smith about the possibility of assessing the condition of Peace Point's archaeological deposits. Few archaeological sites in western Canada, maybe the entire country, demonstrate the degree of cultural stratification and preservation found at Peace Point—each cultural layer a chapter out of a historical novel spanning 2,400 years. As early as 1980 I had expressed my concerns about the vulnerability of Peace Point's archaeological sites. Cultural levels near the cliff face were particularly susceptible to ice scouring events during spring floods and erosional processes caused by humans. The fact that Peace Point's treaty occupies a distinctive place in the history of this country's two founding First Nations peoples alone should have qualified its inclusion on the Historic Sites and Monuments Board list of nationally significant historic sites. It's equally remarkable and unique archaeological record should have been a slam dunk.

However, Parks Canada's obstinance vis-à-vis Peace Point was on full display in 2015. I was directed to a particularly officious Parks employee who told me I would have to obtain an archaeological permit. I responded that I was not going to collect any artifacts or disturb any cultural deposits, merely observe the extent of erosion along Peace Point's cliff face, and maybe take a picture or two. It didn't matter. What I couldn't comprehend was how my intentions were any different than any other park visitor wanting to experience and photograph the magnificence of the park. Subsequently, I proposed that she accompany me, Archie Antoine, and his grandson Robert during our visit. She reluctantly agreed.

What we found was a mixed surprise. The archaeological deposits along Peace Point's cliff face had not been as severely impacted as I had anticipated. No more than a foot or so had been lost in the vicinity of the twenty-four cubic metre excavation unit that I, Doug (Proch), and several Mikisew Cree youth dug in 1981. What I did not expect to find 100 metres or so upstream was a large shed and set of iron stairs carved into limestone bedrock and descending to the beach below. Apparently, some sort of environmental (water?) monitoring station had been excavated into the river bank just metres outside the Mikisew Cree Reserve. In the process of construction, approximately 80 cubic metres of Indigenous prehistory as well as its underlying limestone bedrock had been destroyed.

When I queried the Parks employee as to who was responsible, when this occurred, whether an archaeological permit had been approved, and if mitigation had taken place prior to construction, I did not receive a coherent reply. Back home, online searches and phone calls revealed that no archaeological permit had been issued prior to authorization of this facility's construction—no assessment, no mitigation, whatsoever.

How was this possible? Parks Canada had known about Peace Point's historical and archeological significance for decades. I had even written a book about it in Parks Canada's signature monograph series. The sanctimony intensified months later when I was forced to jump through hoops to obtain an archaeological permit to hold the treaty celebrations in the event that some of the proposed facilities on national park lands might impact Peace Point's archaeological sites. For the enlightenment of celebration participants we had also planned to expose the walls of the 1981 excavation unit. This too necessitated a permit. Despite repeated efforts to submit acceptable drafts, permits were never issued.

Almost too much to comprehend already, Parks Canada's hypocrisy reached a crescendo when I learned that the federal government had recently spent millions of dollars on the search for the Sir John Franklin Arctic expedition ships, and then lied about it. Apparently, all it needed to do to find these ships was to speak with local Inuit, which it eventually did. Parks Canada, in partnership with other government departments and private-sector partners, had been looking for Franklin's ships for years, surveying hundreds of square kilometres of Arctic seabed. In 2014 and 2016, with information provided by Louie

Kamookak, the ill-fated *HMS Erebus* and *HMS Terror* were finally located. The Harper government initially reported that the search for Franklin's ill-fated Arctic expedition cost Canadian taxpayers $1.1 million. But this sum did not include the $1.7 million that the Department of National Defence contributed to the search, or the millions in corporate and private donations. The Arctic Research Foundation, a registered charity authorized to issue tax receipts established by *BlackBerry* co-founder Jim Balsillie, played a key role in outfitting the expedition by donating $3.4 million to the cause. The federal government's report also does not include the $7.2 million ad campaign the Harper government launched to promote the role of the Franklin expedition in Canada's history. While Canada was cutting budgets for defence and veterans affairs, and laying off national park employees across the country, it was pouring money into finding and promoting the Franklin expedition discoveries. And then it tried to cover it up.[93]

Sure, most Canadians support this country's claims to sovereignty over its Arctic waters and islands, especially with the reality of an ice-free, year-round Northwest Passage just around the corner. But at what cost? If Canada was really serious about establishing jurisdiction over its Arctic, it would invest heavily in enhancing food security and employment opportunities in Inuit communities. It would assist Inuit to strengthen their connections to their lands through expanded hunter support and Canadian Ranger programs. It would subsidize the development of industries based on local resources, and support the preservation, research, and development of Inuit cultural heritage resources. But that would take real commitment. The low-hanging fruit presented by the discovery and promotion of an inept British explorer and his unremarkable ships—not to mention their roles in advancing the colonial agenda—was too attractive for the Harper government to ignore.

Under Chief Courtoreille's leadership, there was substantial support and interest in involving youth and elders in the planning and preparations leading up to the Peace Point treaty celebrations. The Lake Athabasca Youth Council was keen to have its students participate with elders and archaeologists prior to and during the celebrations. Plans to create a local steering committee were in the works. But things changed quickly after Chief Courtoreille lost his reelection bid. The new chief and council members had different priorities. Multiple phone calls and emails to the new Mikisew chief and CEO were never returned. The initiative died an agonizing and perplexing death.

I had not expected this outcome. Was it the result of a lingering despondency and anomie that might be expected in any First Nation community undergoing the magnitude of the diaspora experienced by Fort Chip's Cree and Dene resident families? Perhaps it was because the community had just been devastated by the tragic deaths of four hunters in late

---

93 Paragraph content paraphrased and summarized from E. Thompson's *'Franklin Expedition Search Cost Twice as Much as Harper Government Claims'*. 14 August 2015, ipolitics.ca

April of 2017? Maybe it was because of the fact that during the social and cultural impact assessment I undertook with Dave Natcher two years earlier, I was forced to terminate a local assistant who eventually assumed the position of Mikisew's CEO? Or perhaps it was the Mikisew Cree's loss in Canada's Supreme court decision in *Mikisew v Canada* (2005), which held that there was no constitutional requirement to consult prior to passing legislation impacting *Aboriginal rights*. Or was it a combination of all these and/or perhaps other factors? I didn't know. And maybe it didn't matter. I could not stop thinking about Robert and his family.

Nothing to Look At Here, Part 2: Mismanaging Alberta's Cultural Heritage

I couldn't figure out what he was doing. William Yatchotay is a revered Dene Tha' elder and spiritual leader. I had grown to profoundly respect and admire this man over the previous few years while conducting traditional land-use interviews for the Dene Tha' First Nation. His humility and willingness to share with me his knowledge of his people's culture and history were remarkable.

Our small team of Dene Tha' First Nation elders and lands department personnel had just landed our helicopter on a gravel bar below a heavily wooded bank on the Petitot River (M'becholeha). Northwest Alberta and northeast BC constitute the heart of Dene Tha' traditional territory and we were convinced that this location would yield evidence of Dene Tha' use and occupation. No sooner after we landed, Baptiste Metchooyeah, Matt Munson, and I were madly scouring the exposed river bank for ancient Dene Tha' artifacts. William was looking up in the trees.

You see, William knew that wherever Dene Tha' traditional use sites are located, earlier and often repeated evidence of Dene occupation will be found. He was looking high up in the trees above the river bank for cut marks and rope fibres that would reveal the presence of former food and equipment caches. William soon found what he was looking for. Minutes later, Baptiste and Matt found butchered caribou bone and other evidence of early historic/prehistoric Dene Tha' settlement. Looking in trees for archaeological sites? Who knew that was a thing?

The archaeological potential of the region came swiftly into focus for all of us. Soon thereafter, the Dene Tha' hired Grezgorz (Gregory) Kwiecien of Taiga Heritage Consulting to record historic and prehistoric evidence of Dene Tha' use and occupation throughout their traditional territory. Meanwhile, I had been retained to work with Dene Tha' elders and hunter/trappers to document their traditional land-use activities in areas of ongoing and proposed oil/gas development. But it was clear that the nation needed a real archaeologist, or at least a practising one.

Gregory is an archaeologist the likes of whom I have never met. Polish by birth and spirit, this ex-punk rocker's love for boreal forest archaeology was as baffling as it was unmatched. Most archaeologists studiously avoid working in the boreal forest. Digging through roots is wrist-spraining, back-breaking, and any evidence of human use and occupation is usually covered by a riotous growth of trauma-inducing understory and a thicker layer of biting insects. As a consequence, few areas of Canada are less known archaeologically than Dene Tha' traditional territory. After five years of undertaking archaeological impact assessments of forestry cut blocks in northwestern Alberta, Gregory and his team found nothing, nada. Without the advantage of *Lidar* technology, tens of thousands of shovel tests in locations considered suitable for the recovery of archaeological sites produced nothing more than advanced cases of arthritis and temporary psychological disorders requiring multiple forms of medication. Subsequently, no archaeologist alive has more knowledge about where *not to find* archaeological sites in Canada's western boreal forest than Grezgorz Kwiecien. The corollary of this, of course, is that no archaeologist has more knowledge about where to find prehistoric archaeological sites in the boreal forest.

Alberta's sixth-largest lake, Bistcho Lake (M'becho), and surrounding areas of Alberta, BC, and Northwest Territories, played key roles in the history and cultural development of the Dene Tha'. Yet archaeologists have deliberately avoided the region for decades. There was nothing to be found here! At least that was the opinion of a provincial archaeologist, the first and only of his kind ever to have visited Bistcho Lake prior to Gregory's explorations. It was not until Dene Tha' education director Perry Moulton organized a retreat of multi-disciplinary researchers (including Stan Boutin) at Tapawingo Lodge that the true archaeological potential of Bistcho Lake was revealed. In a matter of a few days, Gregory found sites all over the lake, including the region's first projectile point—a 2,000-year-old stemmed early Taltheilei tradition (Dene) dart point made of Peace Point chert.

In the intervening years, Gregory and his team discovered dozens of prehistoric and early historic sites around the lake and scores more throughout Dene Tha' traditional territory. Many locations revealed evidence of repeated pre-contact use, occupation, and long-distance trade and movement. And virtually all of them doubled as Dene Tha' traditional land-use sites. Gregory and his team not only looked in the most obvious places—high terraces, lake-shore promontories, the intersection of water courses, etc.—but in low-lying shorelines, muskeg, and other areas where many traditional use sites are located and where most archeologists fear to tread.

In the summer of 2019, William, several Dene Tha' students, and Gregory and his team unearthed from a two-by-two-metre-square excavation unit near the lake's fishing lodge half-a-dozen projectile points—an unheard of occurrence in Canada's boreal forest—some made of exotic stone from hundreds of kilometres away. Repeatedly occupied, culturally-stratified archaeological sites have been found at Bistcho, Meander River (Tache), and elsewhere throughout Dene Tha' traditional territory. Nothing to look at here? Evidence of prehistoric and historic Dene use and occupation was everywhere. You just have to have the knowledge and patience of William Yatchotay and the tenacity of Grezgorz Kwiecien to find it.

In Gregory's opinion, hundreds—possibly thousands—of sites of contemporary, historic, and pre-contact Indigenous occupation have been destroyed by government-approved industrial activities in northwest Alberta alone. As a consequence, irreplaceable evidence supporting Dene Tha' connections (and claims) to their lands has been erased forever. For decades the government of Alberta has given free rein to oil/gas companies to carve up northwestern Alberta's boreal forest without undertaking historic resource impact assessments. Other than the most obvious locations—places where millennial backpackers might camp overnight—there were no *triggers* to warrant such investigations. Thanks to William Yatchotay and a dedicated and unstoppable archaeologist these now abound, and gone are the days when Alberta can grant resource development authorizations with impunity.

William Yatchotay (left) and Gregory Kwiecien measuring the depth of pre-contact Dene artifacts at an archaeological site overlooking Bistcho Lake, Alberta

For decades our governments have attempted to conserve, interpret, celebrate, and promote colonial history while suppressing Indigenous history. Whether out of ignorance or wilful intent, again is a matter of conjecture. Of the nearly 1,000 nationally historic sites in Canada, only a handful commemorate Indigenous pre-colonial history. Even then, the complexities and nuances of Indigenous prehistory and culture are often trivialized. Most Canadians do not even realize that the biological diversity of this continent prior to colonization was as much a product of Indigenous activity as nature. At the same time, Indigenous place names have been quickly erased from the colonial mindset, only to be replaced by those of settler society. Few Canadians can recall even a single historical event involving our First Peoples or name a heroic Indigenous personality. And while our governments stand idly by as Indigenous prehistory is destroyed, the blame is not wholly theirs alone.

The hands of government archaeologists are tied in more ways than one. Unless there is a compelling legislative reason to hold up projects, such as the wholesale destruction of a provincially or nationally significant archaeological site, governments allow them to proceed. But what constitutes a significant site? Pre-contact sites in Canada are not considered worth saving unless they yield well-formed tools, are very very old, and/or exhibit a combination of unique characteristics such as Peace Point. Even then there is no guarantee that such sites will be preserved. At the same time, an almost cartoonish and antiquated reliance on projectile point typologies and older is better presumptions consume Canadian archaeology. In turn, the discipline stagnates, and the preservation of pre-colonial Indigenous cultural heritage winds up in the trash heap of history. *Terra nullius*, here we come!

Nunavut (Our Land) or *Pitagangit* (None-of-it)?

Most Inuit I have come to know have told me that their lives have not improved since the creation of the Nunavut government and territory. Sure, some Inuit occupy high-level government positions. But the majority are employed in menial and entry-level positions. Meanwhile, much of the real work and decision-making gets done by a transient flock of non-Inuit middle-managers and private contractors who will eventually fly south clutching their nest eggs 'neath their wings. Combined with Nunavut's colonial government structure, an almost insurmountable barrier to accommodating the needs, rights, and aspirations of Inuit communities into government policy and practice is created. Subsequently, many Inuit have had enough and grassroots movements to reclaim their culture, history, and jurisdiction over their lands and resources are beginning to emerge.

One area of resistance involves the rejection of the prevailing academic narrative about the peopling of the Arctic. In particular, many Inuit eschew claims by archaeologists that the *Tunnit* (Paleo-Eskimos, aka as the pre-Dorset and Dorset cultures) were unrelated to the Inuit (Neo-Eskimos, aka Thule culture) who displaced the *Tunnit* some 800 years ago. Sure, differences in material culture are obvious. But we also know that in some locations the two co-existed for many decades, and exchanged certain stylistic traits and adaptive strategies. Moreover, recent genetic analyses indicate that Paleo-Eskimos were "*closely related* [but not identical] *to the founding population of Neo-Eskimos.*"[94] Inuit lore suggests that *Tunnit* were an unusually shy, large, and strong people. But no one really knows what happened to them. Were they absorbed by the Inuit? Did disease or warfare wipe them out? Whatever the case, many Inuit insist that the *Tunnit* are part of their lineage and culture, and reject academic claims that they are unrelated to the former and merely a recent occupant of their homeland.

Resistance to prevailing archaeological orthodoxy and government regulation recently manifested itself in an effort by Iqaluit's Inuit to reconstruct a 400-year-old Thule Inuit whalebone, rock, and sod house (*qammaq*) at Qaummaarviit Historic Park, twelve kilometres southwest of the territory's capital. Years ago, this small island was developed as a territorial park to showcase traditional Inuit culture to local visitors. The only problem was that Inuit were not directly involved in the interpretation of the site's history. I know this because I was the archaeological consultant who developed the interpretive products for the park. Little reference was made to recent Inuit use and occupation of Qaummaarviit—surely another egregious oversight on my part.

Led by 100-year-old Inukie Adamie and his son Naulaq, a group of Iqaluit's elders have recently reclaimed Qaummaarviit. For generations the Adamie family has called Qaummaarviit home, and wanted to reassert jurisdiction over the island and its history. In particular, they wanted to showcase the integrity of their enduring connection to the island by re-constructing an ancient Thule Inuit house excavated by Dr. Doug Stenton in the early 1980s directly over its ruins.

The territory's archaeologist and Nunavut's department of Cultural and Heritage went ballistic. Disturbing an archaeological site—even if it is one of thousands of its type found across the territory—is strictly prohibited by law. Inuit Heritage Trust subsequently intervened. It was determined that the feature had to be excavated in its entirety before the *qammaq* could be reconstructed and reused for interpretive purposes. I thought that my days of Arctic archaeology were long over, but in August 2018 I found myself overseeing a crew of a dozen professional archaeologists led by Gregory unearth 15,000 artifacts

---

94   P. Flegontov et al. (2017). *Paleo-Eskimo Genetic Legacy Across North America.* https://doi.org/10.1101/203018

spanning 4,000 years of Inuit history.

While I was at Qaummaarviit, two noteworthy events occurred: the arrival of an Aboriginal Peoples Television Network film crew and the capture of a bowhead whale under Naulaq's co-captaincy. It was serendipity. While much of the meat and *maqtaaq* would be shared among Iqaluit's Inuit community, the ribs and baleen were destined for the reconstruction. The first bowhead hunt in years just happened to coincide with *Wild Archaeology*'s first foray into Arctic Canada. The last two episodes of the show's second season did an adequate job describing what it called *cultural revitalization*. After all, this is the major theme of the series. Yet the show missed the opportunity to illuminate what was really going on.

Cultural resurgence is a messy business and not accomplished without sacrifice, principled resistance, and collateral damage. The show's producers could not have known *a priori* that they would be caught up in a grassroots movement to resist government intervention in Inuit lives. "*What's the matter with these people?*" they phoned to ask me, referring to the lack of Inuit interest in and compliance with *Wild Archaeology*'s priorities and timelines. Even after the rationale was explained to them, real-world cultural resistance and the assertion of Inuit rights—including the hunting and butchering of a non-endangered bowhead whale—were not considered good TV, even for APTN, and *pitagangit* made it to air.

A few years ago, Meeka Mike and her associate Jacaposie Peter had seen and heard enough. The Nunavut government had become an impediment to the preservation and resurgence of Inuit culture. Subsequently, they embarked on a crusade to institute a more ethically and culturally grounded lexicon of Inuktitut words and concepts into Nunavut's educational curriculum and government practice. The *Tusaqtut* project was first and foremost an act of resistance against a colonial bureaucracy that was exercising increasing control over Inuit lives. Though the project began with promise, found enthusiastic local support, it ended in failure.

Over the course of several years, Meeka and Jacaposie worked diligently with Inuit elders to document and record *Inuit qaujimajatuqungit*. While the Department of Education and the Qikiqtani Inuit Association contributed modest sums to the initiative, nearly a million dollars in funding and in-kind support was raised from private sources.[95] Meeka estimates that she and Jacaposie's volunteer time alone far exceeds this amount. In due course, they produced a lexicon of traditional Okomiut (south Baffin Inuit) words relating to Inuit cultural practices, landscapes, and codes of conduct. In addition, they documented historic Inuit knowledge specific to Arctic animals, seasonal weather patterns, and global warming, while identifying behavioural and biophysical indicators and thresholds of environmental

---

95   Walter and Duncan Gordon Foundation, Kaplan Foundation, Oak Foundation, Small Change Fund. and First Air, among others.

and ecological change. Binders containing written documentation of this knowledge, however, currently collect dust somewhere on some government bookshelf in Iqaluit. To date, *pitagangit* has been introduced into educational curricula or government practice.

Meeka Mike and the author, August 2018, Iqaluit Harbour, Baffin Island, Nunavut

PART FOUR

Agents of the Colonial Order or Post-Colonial Allies?

CHAPTER 11

Capacity for What? Capacity for Whom?

The process of colonization required the complete subjugation of our minds and spirits, in addition to our physical subjugation, so that our lands and resources could be robbed from underneath our bodies. [It was] a cultural bomb, [intended] to annihilate a people's belief in their names, in their languages, in their environment, in their heritage of struggle, in their unity, in their capacities and ultimately in themselves. Indeed, through the combined efforts of government institutions and Christian workers, [we] faced severe persecution for practicing our spirituality, for speaking our languages, and for attempting to live the way our ancestors before us had lived. The federal boarding and residential schools continued this tradition, aiming their most concerted and brutal assaults on our most vulnerable and precious populations: the children. While the devastation wrought from these assaults was not totally complete, it has been sufficiently thorough to severely disrupt our ways of living and to cause us to question the usefulness and importance of the ways of life given to us.

We were taught that the conquest and "civilizing" of our people [were] inevitable; that we too must give way to "progress." It was hammered into our heads that our Indigenous cultural traditions were inferior ... that there was nothing of value in our old ways, and that those ways were incompatible with modernity and civilization. . . . In order for the colonizers to complete their colonizing mission, they were required to not only make themselves believe these ideas, they were also required to make us—the colonized—believe them.

In one way they were correct; within the confines of colonialism our ways were irrelevant and incompatible. Indigenous traditions are of little value in a world based on the oppression of whole nations of people and the destructive exploitation of natural resources. Our values and lifeways are inconsistent with the materialism and militarism characteristic of today's world powers. In this world that colonialism has created, there is no place for Indigenous knowledge. When Indigenous Peoples were taught the worthlessness of our traditions and knowledge, it was designed to perpetuate the colonial machine. . . . Unless they were willing to complete a project of complete extermination, their sense of peace required the muting of Indigenous voices, the blinding of Indigenous worldview, and the repression of Indigenous resistance.

However . . . we know these ideas about Indigenous ways of life to be false. At any point in history, we could have worked jointly towards conditions that would facilitate the return of Indigenous ways of being while appreciating the knowledge that supported those ways. Even now this is not an impossible task. The same human beings who created the conditions of this world also have the capacity to change it. In telling us we must change and adapt, they really meant that the old ways must end because they were unwilling to change their colonizing ways. They were unwilling to end their occupation of our homelands; they were unwilling to foster the restoration of the plants and animals indigenous to our homelands; they were unwilling to discontinue their exploitation and destruction of all that we cherished; and they were unwilling to let us retain the knowledge of alternative ways of being. Because the colonizers wanted to continue colonizing, we had to change and our way of life had to be destroyed.

. . . Fortunately there have always been those among us who understood the political motivations behind [colonial] *thinking, who held fast to the original directions given specifically to our ancestors, and who resisted colonization by carrying that knowledge into the present. There is a growing number of Indigenous people and non-Indigenous allies who have seen the fallacy of* [the colonizer's] *self-purported superiority and who have complete faith in the ways of life that sustained us for thousands of years. In fact, many of us even go so far as to suggest that eventually these ways may resolve some of the global crises facing all populations today.*[96]

Some will be quick to dismiss the words of University of Victoria professor Waziyatawin, and other Indigenous scholars and leaders who have expressed similar sentiments. They will believe that whatever value Indigenous ways of knowing and being may have once had, they are irrelevant in today's modern world. They will see that Indigenous people live like they do and assume that assimilation has been so complete as to render any effort to preserve and reclaim traditional ways and knowledge as mischievous and detrimental to

---

96   Waziyatawin (2010). *Indigenous Knowledge, Anti-Colonialism and Empowerment.* Federation for the Humanities and Social Sciences. April 30, <u>ideas-ideas.ca</u>

society. But for Waziyatawin and many Indigenous scholars, elders, and leaders, the revaluing and resurgence of Indigenous knowledge and cultural practices are deeply intertwined with the processes of decolonization and reconciliation. And while such a project must begin in Indigenous communities, this alone may not be sufficient. We must be committed to working with our First Peoples to dismantle and reconfigure colonial attitudes and institutions that oppress their cultures and ways. The stakes are too great to do otherwise.

Reconciliation and co-existence are not just about reforming unjust laws and institutions, but reforming ourselves. As Stefanie Irlbacher-Fox observes, resistance to injustice and developing an ethic of *allyship* must form the basis of our relationship with Indigenous peoples in order to achieve co-existence. But it will not be easy:

> *Co-resistance requires compassion. Compassion for oneself, as an ally attempting to decolonize oneself, and compassion for Indigenous peoples. No one is perfect. An ally's compass in their conduct and personal decolonization journey should include a combination of conscience, values, and a commitment to staying open to constant self-evaluation and self-correction, without ego. Decolonization is not an act of isolated self-creation. It is a messy process of relational in-the-world becoming and, as such, is often a difficult task. [But by] reaching a place of potentially transformative discomfort ... an often completely new and deeper understanding of Indigenous peoples' cultural practices begins to fill what was once a space of ignorance and privilege, replacing erroneous beliefs with appreciation and understanding. Unsettling thus becomes a basis for transforming settler's self-understanding, and also the understanding of Indigenous peoples and the injustice and privilege shaping Indigenous-settler power dynamics.*[97]

Unsettling Pedagogy: One Step Back, Two Steps Forward

Decolonizing one's self cannot be accomplished without a critical examination of the myths and assumptions that underpin and privilege settler society. Through thoughtful self-reflection and critique of societal norms, values, and institutions, and how they marginalize and silence Indigenous peoples, reconciliation may become possible, even unavoidable. And perhaps one of our best hopes for rapprochement on a societal scale lies in transforming our educational institutions. Continuing to churn out unwitting followers and compliant soldiers of the colonial order will not achieve reconciliation. Our universities and colleges fail all of us if they do not instill in their graduates, regardless of chosen field,

---

[97] S. Irlbacher-Fox (2014). Traditional Knowledge, Co-existence and Co-resistance. In *Decolonization: Indigeneity, Education & Society* 3(3):145-158.

the wherewithal to challenge the stories they have been told. We need to ensure that those students who go on to occupy spaces where our country's Indigenous peoples fight for their rights and futures possess the acumen to question and reconfigure settler institutions while joining our Indigenous hosts in their resistance, resurgence, and quest for justice.

Yep, the very folks about whom I have been most critical may yet become the greatest allies of Indigenous peoples and true co-architects of co-existence. But we must get them early before they do real damage. In partnership with Indigenous educators, we must provide them with learning opportunities to develop the courage, confidence, and skill sets to challenge and deconstruct the colonial mindset, to reconfigure colonial institutions, and to rewrite colonial histories. Only then will they be able to stand side-by-side with our Indigenous hosts to confront the systemic barriers that render them bit players in shaping their futures. In the meantime, some of these colonial agents need to take a step back.

Until *Science* reconciles general relativity with quantum mechanics, until the paradoxes revealed by the *double-slit* and *delayed choice quantum eraser* experiments are resolved—you know, like how the act of observation can affect the behaviour of matter or how future events can affect what happens in the present—its disciples who engage with Indigenous peoples need to fall back. This is especially so for conservation bureaucrats, biologists (except Tim), captains of industry, engineers, and other devotees of positivism and scientific reductionism. Objectivity and reality are not the same thing. The quantum world—you know, the stuff everything is made of—has clearly demonstrated that objective reality is an illusion. There are different ways of experiencing, knowing, and describing our world that have allowed Indigenous peoples to develop sustainable relationships with their environments for millennia. For the sake of everyone and our collective future, we need to hear their voices, in their own words, before we can't.

Lawyers and other legal professionals who make their living working at the Indigenous-settler rights interface also need to take a step back. No longer is it acceptable for legal advisors to Indigenous peoples to remain sequestered from the custodians of those cultures whom they represent. They need to *culture up*! They need to really get to know and understand their clients, and how seemingly minor infringements of Indigenous rights can have catastrophic social, cultural, and ecological consequences. They need to understand the connections that bind their clients to their lands and to each other, and how easily they can be severed by the ignorance, hubris, entitlement, complacency, and actions of colonial agents. Like their colleagues in the natural and technical sciences, law students must include a healthy dose of social and critical theory during their formal education. This goes double for trial court judges, and triple for lawyers representing settler governments and big corporations who have perfected every trick, stalling tactic, and obfuscation in the book in order to best advance the interests of their clients while limiting the rights of our founding peoples.

We can no longer pardon such practices. Students of law must graduate with the ability to challenge Canadian laws and policies that dispossess Indigenous peoples of their lands and resources. In particular, we must acknowledge that the *doctrine of discovery* has had devastating impacts on Indigenous peoples, reinterpret Canadian law in a manner consistent with the *UNDRIP*, ensure that violations of Indigenous rights to their lands are redressed, and resolve that this doctrine never again be invoked in contemporary court cases or negotiations.[98]

I hold out little hope that the mindsets of our federal and provincial politicians will be reformed any time soon. I have met and known many politicians and leaders with integrity—James Ahnassay, Ovide Mercedi, Aqqaluk Lynge, Conroy Sewpegaham, Johnsen Sewepagaham, Phil Fontaine, Terry Teegee, Tom (Mexis) Happynook, Morris Monias, Charlie Watt, Dwayne (Sonny) Nest, Bill Wilson, Tony Mercredi, Rosemary Kuptana, Andrew Weaver, Jean-Paul Gladu, Kim Darwin, Steve Courtoreille, Paul Quassa, Paul Okalik, Allan Adam, Clem Paul, Jack Anawak, and Bill Erasmus to name a few. And most of them just happen to be Indigenous. But their first priority is with their constituents, not other Canadians. That said, few federal and provincial politicians have an enviable track record in either sphere. Short of electing them out of office only to be replaced by other clones, a little cultural sensitivity training might go a long way. The same holds true for high-ranking government bureaucrats, captains of industry, and other devotees and beneficiaries of the colonial mindset. Even then, such measures have proven to be ineffective pathways to reconciliation over the long term as the institutional inertia of the status quo soon takes over. Perhaps somehow, some way, the thinking of our governing and corporate elites can be overturned. Maybe convincing them that the resurgence of our Indigenous peoples is in their financial best interests may bear fruit? In the meantime, a more promising avenue for change may be found in the early education of our youth.

All students, regardless of cultural background, must start learning about the historical and contemporary realities of our Indigenous peoples as part of the school curriculum. I am not talking about the John A. Macdonald *architect of Confederation* versions of history that we slept through in grade school. I am talking about the revisionist histories of University of Saskatchewan professor James Daschuk's *Clearing the Plains*,[99] among others. Indigenous languages should be taught at an early age in all of our schools with the goals of instilling in learners how important language is in framing their views of the world, while broadening their appreciation of Indigenous and alternative worldviews.

---

98   Assembly of First Nations (2018). *Dismantling the Doctrine of Discovery.*

99   J. Daschuk (2013). *Clearing the Plains: Disease, Politics of Starvation and the Loss of Indigenous Life.* University of Regina Press.

Post-secondary institutions must re-examine, acknowledge, and apologize for their long-established roles in perpetuating unjust Indigenous-settler relations. For too long bean-counters, big corporations, and politicians have pushed our universities in directions that favour their interests, the status quo, the bottom line. As a former associate of the Canadian Circumpolar Institute, I find it reprehensible that the University of Alberta, the largest post-secondary institution in one of Canada's largest cities, no longer has a world-class department dedicated to Arctic and northern studies. We must reverse this trend before it's too late.

Academics who hide behind the curtain of objectivity, of being neutral and detached from their research, need to step up. Any research that even remotely impacts the rights and interests of Indigenous Canadians needs to be vetted by the same, elaborated upon, and shared widely with the lay public and translated into words that everyone can understand.

Our universities need to reconfigure their curricula and provide all graduates with tools to critically examine the cultural assumptions, biases, and myths behind what they have been taught. This is especially true of graduates in the hard sciences, and will assist them to filter out the Eurocentric baggage that forms the basis of their supposed *objectivity* and blinds them to Indigenous experience and realities. All university graduates, not just those in the social sciences, should be required to pass courses in Indigenous studies. Specialized knowledge in their respective disciplines will still be needed for their careers, but it must be tempered with a broader, more contextual, and balanced understanding of our Indigenous hosts and of the world around us. We must shift focus from reducing things down to their constituent parts to discovering the connections that hold things together. We must allow our university students to see how deeply interconnected the environmental, economic, social, and political crises that we face today are, and encourage them to pursue ways of resolving them.

I do not mean to denigrate the good work already done by Indigenous peoples, grassroots organizations, NGOs, church groups, and even some universities to educate Canadians about our colonial history and the contemporary realities of our First Peoples. Decolonizing ourselves "*has complex layers that must be engaged in order to disrupt the settler colonial status quo . . .* [and to discover] *what kinds of spaces and pedagogies lead to the most substantial shifts in settler consciousness, and how to effectively generate conversations that centre Indigenous lands, sovereignties and resurgence.*"[100]

---

[100] L. Davis at al. (2016). Complicated Pathways: Settler Canadians Learning to Re/frame Themselves and Their Relationships with Indigenous Peoples. *Settler Colonial Studies*, 21 October. https://doi.org/10.1080/2201473X.2016.1243086

Capacity-Building from the Ground Up

Building a land and resource base that will create sustainable economies for First Nations . . . [that's] *what I would call real capacity-building.*
(Matthew Coon Come)

We Got a Program for That!

I had never met a federal minister before. As the turn of the millennium approached, I found myself in downtown Ottawa sitting across the table from Indian and Northern Affairs minister, Jane Stewart, and her advisor. Flanked by Chief Frank Meneen of the Tall Cree First Nation and Chief Johnsen Sewepegaham of the Little Red River Cree First Nation, and their advisors (Bernie Meneen, Jim Webb, and Mike Stern), I was marginally hopeful that our meeting would amount to something. With unemployment rates hovering around 80-90 percent, both First Nations were experiencing tough economic times. Meanwhile, forest companies *"were raping their lands while getting rich on their resources"* as the chiefs put it. Previous attempts to create forestry jobs and assume greater control over forestry management had failed owing largely to a lack of funding and provincial cooperation. Having recently secured timber rights to a large portion of their traditional territories, the chiefs were asking for a modest 10 percent of a well-designed $10 million capacity-building initiative. If successful, the two First Nations would leverage the remaining funds from financial institutions, creating hundreds of long-term sustainable forestry jobs.

After thirty minutes or so of listening to the chiefs and their advisors, the minister told us, *"I'm sorry, we don't have any funding for things like that,"* after which she turned to Chief Meneen, saying with a straight face, *"Now, Frank, I understand you have some serious social problems in your community. Maybe we can do something about that?"* The response she received from Bernie Meneen floored both her and her assistant. Not one to beat around the bush, Bernie laid into the minister:

> *For over a decade now we have told our young people that there will be good jobs for them. Stay in school, be patient, have faith, we told them. I must now go back and tell them that we failed them once again. Our youth are tired of broken promises. The more militant ones will rise up and start burning the forests, and then, after that, they will come after you.*

Oblivious or insensitive to the fact that social conditions on most First Nation reserves are in large measure a function of economic conditions, the minister gathered herself together requesting that the chiefs get back to their federal member of parliament with more information about the social conditions in each community. I am pretty sure they never did.

For years, *capacity-building* has been a catch phrase in government and industry circles when referring to the high rates of unemployment in Indigenous communities. Education, training, and employment in mining, forestry, oil/gas, hydro development, and other resource extraction industries are seen as the best way to combat poverty and reduce welfare dependency in rural Indigenous communities. Although this approach continues to drive virtually all government and industry—and even some Indigenous—approaches to capacity-building, it has generally failed to improve the lives of most Indigenous Canadians. Capacity-building initiatives aimed exclusively at increasing Indigenous participation in natural resource extraction may, in fact, be a setup for disappointment and greater dependency.

Over a decade ago, Garden River First Nation PhD candidate Pamela Perrault and I explored the issue of capacity-building in the forestry and resource extraction sectors.[101] Many of our paper's discussion points had been previously raised by former Assembly of First Nations grand chief, Matthew Coon Come:

> *Capacity-building refers to the need for First Nations People and First Nations organizations to gain the competence and ability to do various things. In Burnt Church it was a term used by the government to say that the Burnt Church people were not ready to fish for lobster, nor ready to manage the fishery in a responsible way, or to engage in business and economic development. Capacity-building has become a polite and politically correct way for governments and others to say to the First Nations: You are not ready to do this yet. But if you wait, if you are patient, if you get more training, if you make the arrangements we suggest, if you just do this our way, sooner or later you will have the capacity to do what we do. And when you accomplish this, when you have qualified for our programmes, when you have slowly managed to gain the qualifications we require, then we will consider some kind of partnership with you.*[102]

The words of Matthew Coon Come speak eloquently to the thinking behind most government and industry-driven Indigenous capacity-building initiatives in natural resource development. In order for Indigenous peoples to capture jobs and business opportunities, they must develop the skills and capacities needed, championed, and exploited by this cohort while subordinating those of their communities. This is not to suggest that some capacity-building initiatives have not benefited Indigenous peoples economically,

---

101 M. Stevenson and P. Perreault (2008). *Capacity For What? Capacity For Whom? Aboriginal Capacity and Canada's Forest Sector.* Sustainable Forest Management Network, Edmonton, Alberta.

102 M. Coon Come (2001) Capacity Building in First Nations. In *Aboriginal Forestry 2001: Capacity Building, Partnerships, Business Development, and Opportunities for Aboriginal Youth.* Proceedings of the Conference of the First Nations Forest Program, Saskatoon, January 21-24.

personally, and in other ways. However, existing approaches to building the capacity of Indigenous peoples to participate in resource extraction constitute only a fraction of the capacity requirements of Indigenous peoples and communities. With a focus on enhancing capacities to capture existing employment opportunities in this sector, we reduce the complex world in which many Indigenous peoples live to a tractable problem that can be solved by our intervention, by our remedies. By ignoring the contemporary realities of our founding peoples and decoupling relationships among otherwise interdependent variables, we assume that Indigenous workers will have a greater chance of being rewarded by a system that benefits most by their participation.

The myths that underpin this approach are many. Myths are the folk tales we tell ourselves about how the world ought to be, and translate easily into metaphors. In the realm of Indigenous capacity-building in the natural resource development sector, these can be translated into the following sound bites:

- We're not all that different!

- What's good for us, is good for you!

- To be successful, you need to become more like us!

- But you're not ready, you need training, you need patience!

- Once you think and act like us, and value what we value, we will hire you!

- If we build it, you will come, but if you don't, it's not our fault, it's yours!

Current government and industry-sponsored approaches to Indigenous capacity-building in natural resource extraction and other sectors have become stuck in their own unexamined myths, metaphors, and sound bites. Consequently, their effectiveness and our collective ability to address the real challenges at hand are derailed. Integral to this project is the conversion of Indigenous workers to the colonial mindset and capitalist concepts of work.

Lazy Man's Work

The spread of capitalist values at the expense of traditional Indigenous values remains one of the more insidious impacts of resource extraction. In most Indigenous communities, wage labour encourages a shift from *"task-oriented forms of production governed by social relationships to a labour orientation governed by the clock."*[103] Even so, traditional concepts of

---

103 K. Pickering (2004). Decolonizing Time Regimes: Lakota Conceptions of Work, Economy, and Society. *American Anthropologist* 106(1):85-97.

work and time have not been completely erased in many Indigenous communities. This was clearly demonstrated to me one summer many years ago in Pangnirtung.

A small cohort of local men with carpentry skills had been hired to build a bridge across a small river running through the hamlet in order to relocate its garbage dump. However, with the traditional economy in deadfall and steady paycheques every two weeks, the men spent most of their time over the next few months hunting for their families, much to the chagrin of territorial planners and bureaucrats. As the date for the official opening of the bridge approached, the men laid down their harpoons and rifles, picked up their tape measures and saws, and got to work. Within six weeks, the bridge was finished, three days before the governor general of the Northwest Territories was due to arrive for the official opening. The only fly in the ointment in this otherwise momentous occasion was the Inuktitut text on the commemorative cairn. Upon its unveiling, "*the place where you go to wipe your ass*" bronze plaque was met with uproarious laughter by Inuit onlookers and puzzled looks by the governor general and his entourage.

As with the Lakota Sioux and many Indigenous peoples, the Pangnirtarmiut flouted time-values that interfered "*with the task-oriented demands of more materially certain, socially [and culturally] embedded economic activities.*" Still, many Indigenous peoples in remote communities are confronted and conflicted by the dilemma of balancing task-oriented, socially sanctioned, and culturally appropriate means of production with nine-to-five wage labour, or "*lazy man's work,*" as Lakota elders call it.

I Guess that Moose Didn't Have Any Ribs!

Joseph Martel, Dene Tha' hunter and band councillor, nearly fell off his chair. After an exhausting fall moose hunting trip to the southern edges of Dene Tha' traditional territory, after days of trekking through muskeg, transporting, preparing, and delivering meat to community members, this is the response he received from a fellow band member.

Canada's governing and corporate elites are rarely willing to acknowledge or take any responsibility for the collateral damage and adverse impacts of resource extraction on Indigenous peoples and communities. The extinguishment of the extended family as the basic unit of Indigenous social order, production, and reproduction, and its replacement by the nuclear family, may be one of the most pernicious social engineering experiments ever inflicted on Indigenous Canadians. Meanwhile, cracks are beginning to emerge in their resolve to resist the tsunami of colonial forces and agents with whom they are compelled to engage. Increased social isolation and decreased cultural interaction are the result, and the traditional values and practices of many Indigenous groups risk being replaced by capitalistic values of individual wealth accumulation and profit.

In this respect, I find it all the more remarkable that this is not always the case. Assembled to discuss the multiple, integrated, and cumulative environmental, social, and cultural impacts of the oil/gas industry on the Dene Tha', a large group of hunter/trappers collectively informed me that their traditional sharing practices were under threat. Yet they also stressed that, *"If we ever sold moose meat to each other, we would cease to be Dene Tha'."* However, the Dene Tha' sharing ethic is not indestructible and fissures are beginning to appear. As Joseph Martel lamented, some people no longer express gratitude commensurate with the gift of meat: *"I guess you don't know how to make drymeat", "I guess that moose didn't have any ribs,"* and similar quips are becoming more and more common.

Dreaming of Capacity in the Natural Resource Sector

Shovel Work

The economic benefits of large-scale resource development for Indigenous communities are lauded by government and industry to the virtual exclusion of their negative cultural, social, and other impacts. Increased access to jobs and money has the potential to lift Indigenous peoples out of poverty and despair, or so the reasoning goes. The negative effects of Indigenous employment in this sector—if they are perceived at all—are swept under the rug. Government approvals of mining and other resource extraction projects in *Indian country* are often contingent upon meeting Indigenous hiring quotas. Most jobs available to Indigenous workers, however, are unskilled and at the bottom of the wage scale. *Shovel work* as the Métis of the North Slave region in the NWT put it. Consequently, they do little to curtail the ethnic stereotyping (aka racism) and high rates of Indigenous turnover in most industrial construction sites and camps.

The North Slave Métis, with whom I worked to document the anticipated environmental, social, and cultural impacts of the proposed Diavik diamond mine, understood that a mountain of misery awaited them if this mine was approved. The mine's proposed twelve-hour-a-day, two weeks on-two weeks off shift-rotation schedule was considered particularly corrosive. Long-term absences of family heads (especially women) combined with the inability to fulfil social responsibilities and obligations back home were anticipated to wreak havoc on domestic relationships. Diavik, on the other hand, argued that this shift routine would give Indigenous workers plenty of time to hunt on their days off. Besides, it worked well with non-Indigenous workers and would provide much needed income to upgrade their hunting outfits. But the Métis knew that they would need at least a week to recover and reintegrate back into the social and cultural life of their families and communities. Subsequently, they and other Indigenous groups proposed a more appropriate work schedule and the construction of a camp near the mine site so workers could be closer to their families. In the end, they got neither, and they and their families were left to cope as best they could.

Nearly three decades ago, the Little Red River Cree and Tallcree First Nations made a strategic decision to engage the Alberta government to regain influence over natural resource extraction on their traditional lands. After lengthy discussions, a cooperative agreement grounded in the award of an annual 750,000 cubic metre forest-tenure was produced. But the nations' approach to forestry was different. In addition to identifying employment and training opportunities for band members, the cooperative planning board sought to establish resource-use priorities and guidelines compatible with the principles of traditional and sustainable use. As conditions of their forest tenures, the nations signed timber supply agreements with two local forestry companies, both of whom agreed to transfer woodlands management responsibility to the bands and institute capacity-building initiatives in woodland-based employment and business opportunities. Up to 300 long-term jobs operating under a sustainable-use framework were just around the corner.

Initially, the Little Red River Cree were trained in fire-fighting and silvicultural operations. Up to thirty members worked four to six months each year fighting fires, while sixty or so were engaged in seasonal tree planting. Another thirty band members trained as log-haul truckers for winter logging operations, while a handful of band members were employed as forest technicians. For ten years the woodlands division derived revenues of $2-2.5 million annually from forestry operations against a $1-million dollar payroll, most of which went back into band coffers to fund essential programs and services.

But the successes were short-lived. The province walked away from the planning table owing to objections raised by non-Indigenous business interests. A decline in the softwood lumber market and changes in the nation's leadership forced the nation to scale down forestry operations, laying-off half the forestry division. Only a handful of band members continued to find employment as truck drivers and heavy equipment operators. Notwithstanding a promising beginning and a considerable legacy of research with the Sustainable Forest Management Network, Little Red's forestry operations have not delivered the benefits anticipated by its forest tenures and supply agreements.

Farther north in Nunavut, mining has failed to produce anything close to the `level of economic prosperity promised by the Nunavut Agreement. In fact, Inuit employment in the mining industry peaked decades before the creation of the territory. By 2016, only 20 percent of the employees working in Nunavut's two operating mines were Inuit, 97 percent of whom occupied unskilled positions. Virtually all technical, managerial, and skilled jobs were filled by non-Inuit.[104] To complicate matters, 99 percent of Nunavut's mineral rights

---

104 W. Bernauer (2019). The Limits to Extraction: Mining and Colonialism in Nunavut. *Canadian Journal of Development Studies/Revue canadienne d'études du développement* 40(3):404-422.

are owned by the federal Crown, which distributes a pittance of resource royalties—50 percent of the first $2 million and five percent thereafter—to Inuit organizations. At the same time, Canada's federal government has streamlined environmental assessment regulations in Nunavut. Despite longstanding opposition from Nunavut's hunters and trappers organizations, the territorial government and Nunavut Tunngavik Inc.—which is supposed to represent Inuit beneficiaries of the agreement—continue to grease the wheels for mineral extraction projects that threaten Nunavut's *umaijuit* and subsistence economy. The social, cultural, economic, and other implications of this support appear of little interest or concern to territorial and federal government authorities.

The resource extraction sector is infamous for its instability. Booms in wage labour opportunities are almost always followed by busts once infrastructure is in place or when market demand for natural resources fall. Economic hardship and the loss of community social and cultural capital inevitably follow. Driven more by the short-term interests of natural resource developers than the long-term needs of impacted communities, capacity-building initiatives in this sector operate under the assumption that Indigenous peoples generally lack the skills to take advantage of its job and contracting opportunities. Any capacities that benefit the long-term needs of Indigenous peoples and their communities are purely coincidental.

This notion needs to be turned on its head. Indigenous communities may, in fact, possess considerable strengths required for their economic empowerment and long-term sustainability. Collectively, we need to reframe the issue, and ask: What are the existing capacity needs and strengths of Indigenous communities and individuals to, not just participate in the resource extraction sector over the short-term, but to implement their own aspirations for their lands over the long term? Through implementation of such approaches, the real capacity needs of Indigenous peoples and communities have a greater chance of being identified and realized.

Indigenous communities must also have the opportunity and resources to prioritize and build consensus about how their lands should be used, and by whom. Too often they are forced into reactionary mode. In order to realize sustainable economic development and land-use management outcomes commensurate with their desired relationship with their lands and resources, we need to support their efforts to conduct and implement traditional land-use studies, resource valuations, economic assessments, trade-off analyses, and other land-use planning initiatives.

Personal and community empowerment may be the reward for those individuals who develop skills to *engage* government and industry actors, and to *represent* themselves and their communities in these engagements. But it is a tall order. Elders and traditional land-users with a lifetime worth of experience on the land, for example, may be well positioned to represent the cultural values and needs of their communities, but possess less capacity to engage effectively with government and industry. Conversely, younger people who have obtained formal training in careers esteemed by settler society may lack the experience and acumen to effectively represent community aspirations. Many Indigenous groups have created opportunities for youth-elder interaction and traditional knowledge transfer, but more opportunities of this nature need to be developed and made more relevant to community needs, rights, and interests.

Robert Antoine, Where are You?

Encouraging Indigenous youth to stay in school—not only to obtain skills to participate in resource extraction, but other employment and business opportunities rewarded by settler society—has the potential to provide long-term positive outcomes for Indigenous peoples and communities. Sure, we need more Indigenous lawyers, doctors, scientists, entrepreneurs, and dozens of other vocations valued by the dominant culture. But, perhaps more than anything else, we need more Robert Antoines.

Increasingly, fewer and fewer Indigenous youth are developing the required skills and knowledge base needed to maintain their relationships with and responsibilities to their lands and resources. The inability to derive an economically viable livelihood from traditional land-use activities, combined with an expanding industrial footprint across their territories, forces many Indigenous people off their lands. Not coincidentally, some industrial developers continue to assert that First Nations' claims of treaty and Aboriginal rights infringements are spurious and obstructive. *"We never see anybody out here"* is a common refrain heard by Dene Tha' leaders from industrial workers. Traditional land-use studies have heretofore done little to convince government and industry otherwise. As we have seen, the more specific or comprehensive a traditional land-use map is, the greater the chance that it will be spun in favour of industry interests. For the Dene Tha', and many other First Nations, lands and resources not heavily impacted by resource development have increasingly been hard to find and access. With each passing year, natural resource extraction separates more and more Indigenous peoples from their lands and resources.

The decline in traditional land-use is often met by the attraction of off-reserve employment opportunities. As a consequence, the social and cultural capitals of Indigenous communities are undermined. This push-pull effect continues to challenge many First Nations as they attempt to balance economic opportunity with cultural traditions and responsibilities to their lands and communities. In the process, Indigenous knowledge is threatened as others have noted:

> *A critical analysis of why Indigenous knowledge . . . is becoming "lost" rarely moves beyond the rather simplistic assertion that the "elders are dying," or the*

> *assumption that* [Indigenous knowledge] *systems are more vulnerable than Western systems simply because they are oral in nature. This kind of Eurocentric analysis is unfortunate because it fails to recognize how and why traditional Indigenous knowledge systems became threatened in the first place.*[105]

If Canada is serious about accommodating the constitutionally protected rights of Indigenous Canadians, and preserving this country's biological and cultural diversity, traditional Indigenous economies must be heavily subsidized, just like Canada's farming sector and other vocations in the national interest. The same holds true for the preservation and teaching of Indigenous knowledge and languages. The two cannot be separated. In a wonderfully insightful exchange with educator Derek Rasmussen, Tommy Akulukjuq of Pangnirtung questions whether English (*Qallunnatitut*) can be translated into Inuktitut:

> *... We can use the workings of English and have them translated into Inuktitut, but are they really Inuktitut words, or are they just a transfer of English into Inuktitut phrases and sounds? ... Do they really capture the language and the feeling of what is being said?*[106]

In response, Rasmussen recalls anthropologist Norman Hallenday's conversation with Kenojoak Ashevak, the great printmaker from Kinngait (Cape Dorset):

> *After a long chat he asked her to write the Inuktitut word for 'art' in syllabics. She said she couldn't, because there was "no word for 'art' in Inuktitut." Admitting to some frustration, he then asked "what was it that we've been talking about?" Kenojoak answered (through translation), "that which takes something real and makes it more real than it was before." Isn't that beautiful and clear? I've mentioned that phrase to art teachers at several universities and they all think it is one of the most succinct definitions they've ever heard in any language.*

Both co-authors understood that "*Culture is the canvas, language is the paintbrush.*" Indigenous knowledge cannot be separated from the languages in which it is expressed. Nor can the survival of Indigenous languages be divorced from the survival of Indigenous cultures. And cultural diversity cannot be separated from biological diversity. For too long, we have ignored or not understood the connections.

Finally, key roles for Indigenous land-users and traditional knowledge holders must be found in environmental assessment, monitoring, reporting, and remediation. Few

---

105 L. Simpson (2004.) Anti-colonial Strategies for the Recovery and Maintenance of Indigenous Knowledge. *The American Indian Quarterly* 28(3&4):373-384.

106 D. Rasmussen and T. Akulukjuk (2009). My Father Told Me to Talk to the Environment Before Anything Else: Arctic Environmental Education in the Language of the Land. In *Fields of Green: Restoring Culture, Environment, and Education*. M. McKenzie et al (eds.), Hampton Press, pp.279-292.

individuals are better qualified to monitor the environmental and ecological impacts of industrial authorizations than Indigenous peoples grounded in their cultures. Whereas the cost of maintaining the status quo is unsustainable and places undue financial burdens on all Canadians, the long-term benefits of these projects far outweigh their short-term costs.

A Two-Way Street

Capacity-building in the resource extraction sector goes both ways. Industry must also acquire the capacities to engage Indigenous peoples and develop sustainable relationships with Indigenous lands expropriated by settler governments. Current education and training initiatives have failed to provide government and industry actors with the necessary professional competencies to recognize and mitigate the impacts of their decisions and actions on Indigenous peoples and communities. A broader, long-term project of educational reform to develop these capacities in this cohort was considered above. But industry and government also need to assess their short-term capacities to uphold their fiduciary obligations to, and accommodate the constitutionally protected rights of, Indigenous peoples and, where appropriate, undertake measures to address capacity deficiencies.

We need to develop innovative capacity-building strategies and programs that are driven from the ground up, yet articulate with the more positive aspects of conventional top-down approaches. Recognizing the strengths and weaknesses of each will lead to the creation of arrangements wherein multiple voices, and multiple ways of knowing and doing, are valued and considered.[107] Initiatives that set the stage for effective dialogue among different cultures and knowledge systems maximize opportunities for the development of more nuanced and comprehensive understandings of the problems we face, and the solutions needed to resolve them.

---

107 K. M. Wilkinson et al. (2007). *Other Voices, Other Ways, Better Practices: Bridging Local and Professional Environmental Knowledge.* Yale University of Forestry and Environmental Studies Bulletin 14.

CHAPTER 12
Stumbling Toward Reconciliation

IS CANADA'S CLANDESTINE WAR TO DIVEST INDIGENOUS CANADIANS OF THEIR LANDS AND resources really a thing? Or is it just another *trumped-up* conspiracy theory by a slightly unhinged anthropologist? Was, and is, this country's treatment of our First Peoples really that egregious? Aren't Indigenous peoples at least partially responsible for their own circumstances? Why should they be given special rights that other Canadians don't have? Aren't we all equal? Why should we be held accountable for the wrongs of past generations? Why can't we just move on? Why can't we just get along? These are the kind of questions that might linger with some readers.

A war does not have to be intentional or calculated to inflict casualties and serious collateral damage. The motivations, ignorance, hubris, and entitlement of our governing and corporate elites is not a historical accident; they are baked into the Canadian mind-set at an early age. And they have had dire consequences, intended or not, for Indigenous Canadians. One need only look at the high rates of unemployment, poverty, homelessness, suicide, and other pathologies found in Indigenous communities across this country to see that this is war. Sure, we no longer take Indigenous lands by force. We have invented more mendacious and insidious means to accomplish this objective (see chapters above). The unspoken purpose and ultimate result is cultural genocide. And cultural genocide is war.

The war is unfolding on multiple fronts, and being fought most bitterly in arenas where Indigenous rights and interests to lands and resources are vigorously contested. But first and foremost, the war is being waged in the minds of Canadians whose collective fears and paralysis keeps us from finding any real justice for our founding peoples.

Canada's economy was built on the dispossession of Indigenous lands and resources. Thus, it is ironic that, after 500 years of colonization, Indigenous peoples have turned the table on their oppressors and are threatening to bring down the Canadian economy. I am, of course, referring to the 2019-20 Canada-wide Wet'suwet'en protests and blockades, and the many acts of civil disobedience that will inevitably follow if we do not confront the hard truth.

There are those who will assert that I need to take off my rose-coloured glasses. That I am biased and naive. I would only disagree with the latter. I harbour no illusions of objectivity. Indeed, I have had many negative encounters with Indigenous peoples that could have permanently stained my perceptions of them. Chiefs have asked me to pad my reports to favour their financial interests. Indigenous assistants whom I trusted left me hanging. Some even submitted fraudulent invoices for work that was never done. But these experiences pale in comparison with the acrimonious run-ins I have had with members of my own culture. Am I apt to give Indigenous peoples the benefit of the doubt? You bet! If you have to ask why, you need to reread the foregoing chapters.

The societal transformations and mind-shifts that we all know must come will not happen any time soon. This country's first-past-the-post electoral system allows political parties with a minority of the popular vote to govern the majority. Political contributions from big corporations and big unions influence government decision-making and spending. This is not the stuff of free and democratic societies, but oligarchies in the grips of *savage capitalism*, like our neighbours to the South. Transitioning to a system of proportional representation—just as 90 percent of European countries have done—may move our country in the right direction. Until we undertake the necessary political reforms, our governments and their corporate masters will continue to be unrelenting and complicit architects of unsustainable economic growth, environmental degradation, and cultural genocide.

The need to transform our relationship with our Indigenous hosts through broad educational reforms consumed much of the space in the last chapter. It is critical that we educate our youth, particularly those who will pursue careers that directly engage and impact Indigenous Canadians. We need to develop the skill sets of both Indigenous and non-Indigenous actors to achieve reconciliation in the spirit of cooperation and mutual respect. We need to subsidize the resurgence of traditional economies, the connection of Indigenous peoples to their lands, and Indigenous languages and knowledge. But we also need to be pragmatic. The institutional reforms we seek will require many more allies and much more time than we think. Meanwhile, as momentum builds, we have an opportunity to address some of our blind spots and prejudices.

Blind Spot Removal

Behind almost every conservation initiative in modern society, every effort to develop or maintain a sustainable relationship with nature, *Science* pulls the strings. As a consequence of its preconceived objectivity, and historical accident and precedent, *Science* occupies a uniquely privileged position in Canadian society and has become a driving force in environmental policy, legislation, and practice.

Apart from its analytical reductionism to the virtual exclusion of the connections that hold the world together, there is nothing inherently wrong with the scientific method. Like most knowledge systems, it, in the absence of political interference and cultural bias, is self-correcting. It is a voice that has a right to be heard. Yet those who worship at its altar generally dismiss the knowledge of others. Sometimes this is done unintentionally, even subconsciously, by well-meaning professionals. Arguably, most of the time, it is not. The supposed supremacy of *Science* is reinforced by beliefs that humans are external to natural systems, we can control nature, we have the sufficient means and knowledge to do so, and that ecological disorder is something to be corrected in order to achieve some preconceived level of ecological stasis or certainty. However, those who champion the scientific method in their interactions with Indigenous peoples ought to remember that ecological systems are always in a state of flux and that all knowledge is culturally constructed. Western science is just one of many ways to organize experience and create understanding. No knowledge system has a monopoly on the truth. All voices need to be heard, especially now as we confront some of the greatest challenges the world has ever faced.

The culture and language of *Science* has strongly influenced the design of comprehensive land claims, *wildlife co-management*, environmental assessment, and other agreements and arrangements with Canada's Indigenous peoples. As such, they remain formidable barriers to the inclusion of Indigenous peoples and their knowledge and practices in these institutions. Every time a conservation bureaucrat, wildlife manager, environmentalist, researcher, or representative of Indigenous interests uncritically employs language and concepts born in the hegemony of the conservation bureaucracy, s/he favours the interests of the prevailing social, political, and economic order, while robbing Indigenous Canadians of their rights, connections, and responsibilities to their lands.

Canada has failed to design policies and institutions that meaningfully accommodate the rights of Indigenous Canadians into government practice. Somehow in discussions leading to *Section 35 of the Canadian Constitution Act of 1982*—a process heavily dominated by scientific and legalistic jargon—the concept of *responsibilities* fell off the table. What is needed is an informed and focused dialogue about the responsibilities that attend the rights of Indigenous Canadians. What are the responsibilities of Indigenous peoples to take care of their lands? How are they realized on the ground? What capacities are needed to fulfil these responsibilities and maintain sustainable relationships to their environments? How can we accommodate them into policy and legislation? Continued assertion of Aboriginal rights in the absence of accommodating Indigenous responsibilities to their lands and resources will not achieve reconciliation. Alternatively, a focused conversation of these issues has the potential to foster a mutually cooperative and respectful exploration of strategies and institutions that will allow the rights and responsibilities of both to be realized.

On Knowledge Validation

One of the most common blind spots preventing the application of Indigenous knowledge in *wildlife co-management* and environmental impact assessment involves its validation by scientific standards. Time and again, I have been reminded of the pervasiveness of this roadblock, perhaps no more so than during a traditional knowledge conference I attended in Girdwood, Alaska, some twenty or so years ago. At the beginning of our session participants had to remind conference organizers that *"Validating Traditional Knowledge"*—as if it needed to be validated by scientific authorities—was an inappropriate title. As one participant (whom I know well) observed: *"The fact that Indigenous peoples have been around for thousands of years, and are here today, is validation enough that their traditional knowledge systems work?"*

Indigenous ecological knowledge is almost without exception subjected to Western scientific methods of validation to be accepted or given any credibility in environmental decision-making. *Science*, of course, is not the ultimate arbitrator of truth and knowledge, and it is certainly not imbued with the authority to authenticate or invalidate the knowledge of others. Nonetheless, its disciples sure act like it is. While anything to do with numbers usually passes the test, non-quantitative or subjective aspects of Indigenous knowledge—anything that has cultural, spiritual, or non-materialistic dimensions or content—are dismissed. Yet it is the social and cultural contexts in which Indigenous ecological knowledge resides where it achieves its full meaning, efficacy, and value. Clearly, different approaches to knowledge creation necessitate different methods of validation. Mohawk scholar Marlene Brant-Castellano is unequivocal about this:

> *Culturally different approaches to knowledge creation imply the need for different methods of gathering and validating information. In many Aboriginal communities . . . individual perceptions* [have] *to be validated by community dialogue and reflection before they became collective knowledge, the basis of collective action. Because the integrity and validity of research cannot be assured by Western methodologies alone, they must be tempered by methodologies that are compatible with Aboriginal methods of investigation and validation.*[108]

At the same time, the knowledge claims of environmental resource managers, *wildlife* biologists (except Tim), and the like are often viewed as childish or with suspicion by Indigenous peoples. Not only may the latter harbour misgivings about the political motivations of the former, scientific methodologies and knowledge claims are rarely vetted by community members before being transformed into regulation. Nor have scientific claims

---

108 M. Brant Castellano (2004). Ethics of Aboriginal Research. *Journal of Aboriginal Health* (January): 98-114.

withstood the test of time. Because each system of knowledge has its own methods of construction and processes of validation, the acceptance of knowledge claims by the practitioners of one system need not be contingent upon validation by the other. Standards of validation acceptable to Western science are not only inappropriate when applied to Indigenous knowledge, but may reject outright valuable information, knowledge, and wisdom held by Indigenous peoples necessary to sustain their cultures, and the species and habitats upon which they depend. Indigenous systems of knowledge that have proven viable over the millennia deserve our full attention in humankind's quest to achieve sustainable environmental outcomes and conservation objectives with our world. Thus, there is an ethical obligation on the part of those mandated to incorporate Indigenous knowledge into their decisions to ensure that its authenticity is assessed by locally approved and culturally appropriate means and sources of validation.

Decolonizing Environmental Management and Assessment

The Wet'suwet'en: Shades of Things to Come

Canada-wide protests. Blockades of major rail systems, shipping ports, and government offices. Dozens of arrests. Acts and threats of violence against Indigenous protesters. Not since the Oka stand-off of 1990 have Canadians been so deeply divided over the rights of its Indigenous peoples. Years in the making, the Wet'suwet'en crisis of 2020 could have been avoided.

At the centre of the conflict is Coastal GasLink's proposed $6-billion 670-kilometre pipeline in northern BC, a key component of LNG Canada's $40-billion gamble to move natural gas from Dawson Creek through Wet'suwet'en traditional territory to Kitimat. Touted as the largest private-sector investment in Canadian history, LNG Canada obtained the necessary government approvals in October 2018. Six months later, it received a massive tax break from the province. Based upon impact benefit agreements signed with twenty First Nations along the proposed route (including several Wet'suwet'en bands), a BC Supreme Court injunction in late December 2019 ordered removal of the Wet'suwet'en blockades allowing GasLink to proceed with construction. Multiple skirmishes and arrests at blockades followed. At every step of the way, animosity between pro-pipeline and pro-Wet'suwet'en factions intensified. With the arrest of twenty-four demonstrators in early February 2020, protests in support of the Wet'suwet'en spread rapidly across the nation.

The Wet'suwet'en are a matrilineal Dene society organized into five exogamous clans and thirteen kin-based (extended family) groups, or houses. Each house—the primary unit of production sustaining Wet'suwet'en subsistence and cultural needs—retains jurisdiction over its traditional territory under the leadership of a hereditary chief. Having never surrendered their lands or abandoned their traditional style of governance, the Wet'suwet'en hereditary chiefs exercise authority over 22,000 square kilometres of unceded land. The hereditary chiefs assert that they, not *Indian Act* chiefs and councils who are accountable only to the federal government, speak for the Wet'suwet'en. As confirmed by the Supreme Court of Canada in *Delgamuukw*, the Wet'suwet'en never surrendered the inherent right to govern themselves according to their own laws, customs, and traditions.

The hereditary chiefs received a mandate three years ago to reject the pipeline based on an examination of its adverse environmental, ecological, social, and cultural effects. Even so, five of six Wet'suwet'en band councils decided to support the pipeline—a decision former BC treaty negotiator Brian Domney found unsurprising: *"When you are a First Nation politician responsible for taking care of your people, trapped on a reserve in abject poverty under the Indian Act after generations of oppression, and underfunded for statutory obligations by the federal government, when a corporation waves money under your nose, it's a big temptation."*[109] For UBC professor and Yellowknives Dene Glen Coulthard, pitting Indigenous rights against job creation is an *"incredibly unfair tactic* [that] *draws on a very latent kind of deep-seated, anti-Native racism in the country,* [and] . . . *positions Indigenous peoples as entitled spoiled folks who are acting as a member of the minority against the majority of Canadians."*[110] The *good Indians* are those band chiefs and councils that signed agreements with the proponent. As creatures of the *Indian Act*, however, their jurisdiction is limited to federal reserve lands. Thus, band council agreements do not amount to Wet'suwet'en consent to the project. Oops.

Domney blames the Wet'suwet'en crisis squarely on the province, "[BC] *acknowledged long ago that the hereditary chiefs are the appropriate people to negotiate with on matters of rights and title,*" and accused it of *"shopping around the First Nations world"* to find individuals and groups supporting its agenda. *"Because the chiefs with the sacred responsibility to steward their house territories for their people* [were] *not prepared to permit infringement of those rights and title, the corporation and government found their Indians in the elected band system."*

The passing of the *Income Tax Assessment Act* in April 2019 further stoked the flames of the conflict. As stated by former interim leader of BC's Green party, Adam Olsen:

> *Every member of* [the legislature], *with the exception of the BC Greens and our independent colleague, Andrew Weaver, voted to ignite the tragic situation that we face. . . . Honestly, what did you all expect? Did you really think that after decades of fighting for recognition, the Wet'suwet'en hereditary chiefs would just*

---

109   C. Bellrichard (2020). Former Treaty Negotiator Accuses B.C. Government of 'Picking their Indians' in Wet'suwet'en Conflict. February 20, cbc.ca

110   C. Pablo (2020). Blockades, a Genius Assertion of Indigenous Power: UBC-based First Nations thinker Glen Coulthard. February 19, thenarwhal.ca

step aside and let you do whatever you want in their territory?... Every vote to prematurely proceed with this project backed the Wet'suwet'en hereditary chiefs into a corner.... I will not let [my colleagues] *rewrite history to pretend that they are anything but responsible for the painful situation we are seeing playing right now in our landscape, leveraging Indigenous people against each other.*[111]

Both government and industry are culpable for creating deep divisions within the Wet'suwet'en communities, from which they have yet to heal.

The Wet'suwet'en chiefs take full responsibility to steward their lands on behalf of present and future generations. Even so, they are not opposed to economic development. Indeed, they have allowed GasLink to conduct preliminary work on their territories in the absence of consent to the project. More saliently, the chiefs recommended an alternative, less environmentally, less culturally destructive route through their traditional territories. But it was dismissed outright by the company. Not only would it add $800 million to the project, it was *"too risky environmentally"* the company claimed, even as other pipeline companies denounced GasLink's route over environmental concerns.[112] Better to deal with the *Indian Act* chiefs, rebuff the hereditary chiefs, ignore Supreme Court of Canada rulings, and forge ahead. After all, the *rule of law* was on the government's side. Right? Wrong!

The Rule of Law

Prime Minister Trudeau and BC Premier Horgan could not stop smiling. Ten thousand jobs for British Columbians—950 of them permanent—and $23 billion in direct government revenues were just around the corner. Within months of project approval, however, the smiles disappeared. Both politicians responded to the accelerating protests, blockades, skirmishes, and arrests by asserting that Canada must remain a country under the *rule of law*. Unbeknownst to most Canadians—and politicians apparently—the rule of law includes Indigenous forms of governance. As reaffirmed in a recent federal court decision, "*Indigenous legal traditions are among Canada's legal traditions ... [and] form part of the law of the land.*"[113] As per earlier SCC rulings in *Delgamuukw* and *Tsilhqot'in*, Indigenous law does not exist in opposition to Canadian law, it is part of it.

Rarely, however, are the constitutionally protected rights and title of Indigenous Canadians given a fair shake in the courts when governments authorize major natural resource developments. Consequently, Indigenous communities are forced into fighting

---

111 S. Wood (2020). How the Wet'suwet'en Crisis Could Have Played Out Differently. February 20, thenarwhal.ca

112 A. Kurjata (2020). Why Coastal GasLink Says it Rejected a Pipeline Route Endorsed by Wet'suwet'en Hereditary Chiefs. February 16, cbcnews.ca

113 *Pastion v. Dene Tha' First Nation*, 2018 FC 648, T-1808-17.

expensive and protracted court battles. While the *Delgamuukw* decision ruled that economic development can override Indigenous rights providing the infringements are justified through the courts, this has not happened in the GasLink project. Yet the Wet'suwet'en crisis could have been avoided had the BC government followed the *rule of law* in the first place and adapted its processes to accommodate Wet'suwet'en laws and legal customs. "*It's not something you can negotiate . . . it's something that* [we] *need to make space for,*" Molly Wickham of the Gidimt'en Clan, told Stephanie Wood of *The Narwhal* magazine.

In the same article, Jack Woodward believes that the Wet'suwet'en crisis could have been avoided had the subsequent trial that the *Delgamuukw* decision called for taken place. While the Wet'suwet'en and Gitxsan demonstrated ownership over their lands in the eyes of the Supreme Court, they did not prove "*governance and control*"—the *sine qua non* of Aboriginal title. The Wet'suwet'en have yet to bring this case forward leaving unanswered questions how the provincial and federal governments might revamp their policies to accommodate Indigenous forms of governance. Maybe thirteen years and the millions spent fighting for recognition of their rights and title in the courts had taken its toll? Or was the quarter century it took for the Tsilhqot'in to prove Aboriginal title to their lands the deterrent? In both cases, BC and Ottawa, as begrudging fiduciaries of the first order, fought the appellants tooth and nail.

Both levels of public government face a legal revolution in their desultory efforts to recognize and incorporate Indigenous governance into the *law of the land*. Neither appears willing to reach a just accommodation with its First Peoples. BC seems especially averse to addressing the land question in any honourable way. Until it does, and as more projects are approved, we can expect more and more nation-wide protests and other forms of civil disobedience in support of our Indigenous hosts. We can also anticipate greater division within Indigenous communities as they wrestle with the painful legacy of the *Indian Act* and unbridled resource development on unceded traditional territories. Meanwhile, work on the LNG pipeline continues.

Up next is the Trans Mountain Pipeline, a 1,000-kilometre pipeline that would triple the capacity of an existing line carrying Alberta tar sands oil through First Nations' territories to a terminal in Burnaby, BC. The expansion would push the capacity of the line to 890,000 barrels a day and result in a dramatic increase in tanker traffic through already congested waters. In February 2020, the Federal Court of Appeals upheld government approval of the expansion dismissing numerous First Nations' challenges. In one of the more irresolute and prejudicial decisions in recent memory, the court ruled that, "*If we accepted those submissions, as a practical matter there would be no end to consultation, the project would never be approved, and the applicants would have a de facto veto right over it.*" So, there you have it. Surprise should not be your first reaction. The Trudeau government had purchased the controversial project from Kinder Morgan two years earlier. With a sevenfold increase in oil tanker traffic, catastrophic oil spills are virtually a certainty and would guarantee the extinction of BC's seventy-three southern resident orcas, already endangered from pollution, ocean traffic, and a critical shortage of Chinook salmon. It is little wonder that Indigenous leaders and environmentalists have pledged to do *"whatever it takes"* to stop the pipeline.

So what about those much-ballyhooed job figures, government revenues, and other benefits of LNG's project to British Columbians? A closer look reveals the proponent's claims to be spurious. Two-thirds of all workers benefitting from the project will not reside in BC. Moreover, LNG will spend only $2.5 to $4.1 billion in BC during the first phase of the project, while up to $11.1 billion will go to foreign companies and workers. Finally, government revenues of approximately $500 million per year over forty years only amounts to about one percent of BC's annual budget.[114] Yet the project by 2050 will eat up 20 percent of BC's carbon budget, putting massive pressure on other sectors to meet the province's emission target of 40 percent below 2007 levels. All British Columbians had to do is hand over billions in subsidies to LNG Canada through cheaper electricity, lower corporate income tax rates, deferrals on provincial sales tax, and an exemption from carbon tax increases.

Rethinking Environmental Impact Assessment

Environmental assessment regulations in Canada have failed to embrace the space envisioned by the *Delgamuukw* and *Tsilhqot'in* decisions. Even after the controversial *Impact Assessment Act* of 2019 was passed, Indigenous knowledge effectively remains left out of environmental assessment and decision-making processes. Although the act mandates its inclusion, it does not offer any guidelines about how this might be accomplished. However, a new concept is emerging in the realm of environmental decision-making whereby it is no longer sufficient for governments to consider Indigenous knowledge as a way to loop its holders into environmental assessment processes. Rather, Indigenous peoples need to conduct their own assessments on their lands on an equal footing with those mandated by governments.[115]

According to a recent report by the Firelight Group, Indigenous-led assessments would *"rely on and protect Indigenous culture, language, and way of life in ways existing government-legislated systems have either never contemplated or are still not accommodating."* For Chief Nick Claxton of the Tsawout First Nation, Indigenous-led environmental assessments

---

114 C. Linnit (2019). 6 Awkward Realities Behind B.C.'s Big LNG Giveaway. April 6, thenarwhal.ca

115 J. Thomson (2018). How Indigenous-led Environmental Assessments Could Ease Resource, Pipeline Gridlock. 4 September, thenarwhal.ca

are a tangible way for *"the state to engage with Indigenous legal systems* [and]... *create space for Indigenous worldviews and respect for non-human relations, like salmon and southern resident killer whales."* While the Tsawout, Tsleil-Waututh, and a few other First Nations are leading the way in undertaking their own environmental assessments, the willingness to incorporate their results into government decision-making remains virtually non-existent. According to a study authored by Lauren Eckert, Chief Claxton, and others, *"this stuff is going to take a ton of political will and profound systemic change."*

For Glen Coulthard, blocking major transportation and shipping routes may be the most effective way currently to create the conditions for change. Specifically, *"negotiations have historically piggybacked-off direct actions, where Indigenous peoples have put their bodies on the line in order to protect their laws and lands for future generations, ... and resulted in the government having to negotiate on terms that it wouldn't have* [otherwise]." To wit: in late February 2020, Wet'suwet'en hereditary chiefs, the province, and the federal government began moving forward on a draft agreement to expedite the nation's rights and title process. By way of nurturing the political will of our politicians and governments to accommodate Indigenous rights, we need to explore ways to decolonize current environmental assessment policies and practices.

Valued Ecosystem Relationships and the Two-Row Wampum

Assessing the environmental impacts of individual natural resource extraction projects is the low-hanging fruit for Canada's governing and corporate elites. Backed by scientific methodologies, environmental impacts can be easily assessed, for the most part, on a case-by-case basis. But they are only the tip of the iceberg and a way to avoid the more proximate, adverse, complex, and interconnected ecological, cultural, and other negative impacts of natural resource development. By failing to consider the multiple and cumulative environmental and other impacts of each project, and then multiplying these by all projects within a region, a recipe for disaster is virtually guaranteed. Better to bury our heads in the sand and deal with the fallout later. Sound familiar?

The multiple and cumulative environmental impacts of resource extraction infringe Indigenous land-use rights—hunting, trapping, fishing, and gathering in the vernacular of Aboriginal jurisprudence—across their traditional territories. But they also create a snowball of other negative social, cultural, economic, health, and other impacts that wreak havoc on Indigenous communities. Unable to sustain traditional connections to their lands, community members see their health and well-being suffer. In addition, the ability to share traditional foods, cultural values, language, and ecological knowledge, and to fulfill social responsibilities and obligations instituted through traditional land-use, are compromised.

Yet this cascade of negative impacts has remained largely invisible, misunderstood, ignored, and/or downplayed by government and industry.

Our governments must be held directly responsible for their ongoing intransigence to institute any reasonable legislation to oversee the comprehensive assessment and mitigation of cumulative impacts created by their industrial authorizations. This is the stuff of a kleptocracy, not a democracy. If we do not hold our governing and corporate elites accountable, the cultural genocide of our founding peoples and the environmental degradation of their lands will accelerate beyond the point of no return and we will all suffer in, and be on the hook for, the aftermath.

The failure of Indigenous knowledge to make any inroads into *wildlife co-management* and environment impact assessment received top billing in the first half of this book. By subordinating and dismissing the knowledge of Indigenous peoples, we severely diminish their rights, connections, and responsibilities to their lands. We give currency only to those aspects of Indigenous knowledge that fit neatly with the scientific-colonial narrative. Liberally illustrated with personal anecdotes, this book has exposed how the knowledge, values, laws, and rights of Indigenous peoples are given short shrift in these colonial institutions. Thus, it is perhaps fitting that this tirade conclude with some suggestions about how we might create space for Indigenous peoples and their cultures in land-use management and environmental assessment. So, what other avenues might we consider to create a more ethical and level playing field for Indigenous peoples in decisions that directly and indirectly impact their lands, rights, and resources?

It was only in the last few years that the writings of Umeek, Bateson, and Deacon (among others) captured my attention—surely an unforgivable oversight for any anthropologist, especially one who has spent much of his career working with and for this country's Indigenous peoples. Nevertheless, over the previous three decades, I did not realize, at least consciously, that Inuit, Cree, Dene, and Métis elders and hunters with whom I had the great fortune to work with were guiding me in the same direction. Early in my journey I began to comprehend that it was not so much the animals or their habitats around which Indigenous peoples constructed their ecological knowledge, but their relationships to these parts, and the interrelationships among all parts of the whole. Subsequently, I felt compelled to write several academic papers that endeavoured to create the institutional elbow room for Indigenous peoples and their knowledge in the two areas of environmental resource management with which I was most familiar: *wildlife co-management* and environmental impact assessment.[116]

---

116 M. Stevenson (1996). Indigenous Knowledge in Environmental Assessment. *Arctic* 49(3):278-291. M. Stevenson (1999). What are we managing? Traditional Systems of Management and Knowledge in Cooperative and Joint Management, in *Science and Practice: Sustaining the Boreal Forest* (T. S. Veeman et al., eds.). Proceedings of the Sustainable Forest Management Network Conference, University of Alberta,

A few of these advanced the concept of *valued ecosystem relationship* (VER) as an equivalent to the commonly used *valued ecosystem component* (VEC) in environmental assessment. I had come to see that most Indigenous knowledge systems are concerned predominantly with—to put a label on it—maintaining VER's with their lands and resources. At a minimum, both VECs and VERs, and the knowledge systems and laws from which they derive—irrespective of their different histories, dissimilarities in focus, and perceived shortcomings by the other—warrant equal consideration in our attempts to develop sustainable relationships with our world.

I further argued that what is this if not the two-row wampum applied to environmental management? Given first to early European (Dutch) immigrants by the Iroquois (Haudenosaunee), the two-row wampum belt embodies the principle of mutual respect while acknowledging the autonomy and jurisdiction of each nation. The two rows symbolize separate tracks on life's river for each nation to navigate down, each with its own laws, customs, and traditions, neither taking charge of the others' vessel. While the concept of *valued ecosystem relationship* might be attractive in principle, operationalizing it will require us to cast aside our cultural blinders and expand significantly our perspectives and empathy toward the other.

The two-row wampum belt [117]

Indigenous knowledge systems may not have evolved to count all that there is to count in ecological systems. But they should be well-positioned to developing a host of indicators, thresholds, and ranges of variations for natural and culturally important phenomena (e.g., animal behaviours, health/physical conditions, reproduction rates, sustainable use practices, etc.). They may also lead to an especially nuanced understanding and awareness of the butterfly effect—the phenomenon whereby minute localized changes in a complex system of ecological relationships may cascade into significant irreversible impacts in other parts of the system.

---

pp. 161-169. M. Stevenson (2004). Decolonizing Co-management in Northern Canada. *Cultural Survival Quarterly* 28(1):68-71. M. Stevenson (2006). The Possibility of Difference: Rethinking Co-management. *Human Organization* 65(2):167-180. M. Stevenson (2013). Aboriginal Peoples and Traditional Knowledge: A Course Correction for Sustainable Forest Management, in *Aboriginal Peoples and Forest Lands in Canada* (D. B. Tindall, et al., eds.). UBC Press, pp.114-128.

117 Source: peopleshistoryarchive.org, Haudenosaunee artist unknown.

Nora Bateson reminds us that: *"Adjusting our lens in order to see what might be holding systems together is a radical step towards threading the world back together from the inside."* It was my hope that individuals with minds much sharper than my mine would have by now taken the concept of VER and run with it to develop what Nora Bateson calls *"thresholds of flexibility to maintain our relationships."* But as with other of my efforts to affect change in the status quo, it did and has not caused a ripple. Perhaps unravelling the tangle of connections that Gregory Bateson speaks about is more challenging and elusive than we ever thought? Perhaps the hills we have to climb are much higher than we imagined? But this does not mean we should not walk with our Indigenous hosts down unknown paths to get us where we all know we must go.

POSTSCRIPT:
I Thought I Look-in-ized You![118]

A HANDFUL OF SPORTS-MINDED READERS WHO HAVE MADE IT THIS FAR MAY REMAIN BESET by a question that has nagged them since the second chapter: What position did I play during my mercifully brief gridiron career? There is little disagreement among sports psychologists and football coaches that certain personality types are better suited to some positions in football than others. For example, desirable characteristics of an offensive lineman—besides being big, tough, and mean—include being:

> *"reliable, humble, loyal, generous, a team player, and really smart, because of all the adjustments they have to make. Defensive linemen on the other hand, don't need a whole lot of self-control. . . . They are a little crazy and rebellious . . . the toughest group to coach because they are stubborn and short-fused. . . . But that's the stuff you've got to have on the field to take on O-linemen and double-teams. . . . You have to have that attitude that you can't be denied. [But they're] . . . going to score lower on things like independent thinking.*[119]

As a former nose-tackle I take only minor exception to the latter assertion. Nevertheless, I would hope that by sharing my experiences and the wisdom of Indigenous elders, hunters, leaders, and scholars, others will be inspired to challenge the systemic biases and racial prejudices of those who find comfort in the status quo. We need to redress the many injustices perpetrated on our Indigenous hosts, and actively support their resistance and resurgence. We need to be particularly adept in calling out and transforming the mindsets of *"colonial agents in sheep's clothing."* But more than anything, we need to work together to reconfigure our institutions that keep our founding peoples on the sidelines at a time when we need them the most as we confront some of greatest social, political, cultural, economic, and environmental challenges in human history. We must be allies that *can't be denied.*

---

118   Thanks to Richard David, Mohawk Council of Akwesasne, for sharing this expression.

119   L. Nickel (2011). Personality Traits Matter in NFL, But How Much? April 19, archive.jsonline.com/sports/packers/120251309.html

MARC G. STEVENSON

My chief believes in assimilation.
But he says that there's so damn many of us non-Indigenous people,
it is going to take a very long time.
(Jim Webb)

EPILOGUE

One Hundred and Fifty Three Years plus Twenty-One Seconds of Silence

JUST DAYS BEFORE THE WORLD CHANGED—LIKELY FOREVER—I COMPLETED THE FIRST DRAFT of this critique exposing how Indigenous Canadians are given short shrift in *wildlife co-management*, environmental impact assessment, historic treaty interpretation, comprehensive land claims, provincial land-use planning, and cultural resource management. As countries across the globe attempt to recover from the COVID-19 pandemic of 2020-21, humanity is experiencing a watershed moment. Savage capitalism, neoliberalism, global climate catastrophe, environmental degradation, ecological collapse, massive social inequality, cultural genocide, the proliferation of right wing populism and authoritarian states, etc.—for too long we ignored the signs and buried our heads in the sand. We can no longer accept things as they were, hope for the best, and continue to place our trust in those who put us here. Reconstructing our world on the disintegrating foundation of the old is a recipe for global disaster and ultimately the fall of humanity. This is the essential and existential truth of our times. We are the virus.

The real challenge we face is not in vanquishing this coronavirus, or those to follow. If this pandemic has taught us anything, it is that we must re-structure our relationship with this planet and with each other. Our resurgence must embrace the concepts of responsibility, accountability, reciprocity, respect, humility, courage, empathy, compassion, cooperation, inclusion, and other values that most Indigenous peoples worldwide have aspired to *since time immemorial*. Indeed, our revival may be directly tied to theirs.

Amid the world's uneven and desultory attempt to manage this pandemic, our neighbour to the south imploded. Triggered by the brutal murder of George Floyd by a Minneapolis police officer in late May, and with unemployment rates not seen since the Great Depression, millions took to the streets to protest police brutality of black Americans and other peoples of colour. This was no random act of violence by a racist cop. It was a performance—a show of savagery intended to terrorize Black onlookers.[120] As maintained by Dalhousie professor Ingrid Waldron he was saying, *"this . . . can happen to you, . . . this is what I want you to see. . . . He was not just harming George Floyd, he was harming those who were watching."* The rioting and protests continued for months.

On June 2, 2020, in response to a reporter's question about ongoing civil unrest in the United States, Prime Minister Trudeau struggled for twenty-one uncomfortable seconds of silence to find some words that made sense. When they finally came, he acknowledged that systemic racism is not just America's problem, it's Canada's too. But nary a word was spoken about Indigenous racism. Rather, Indigenous Canadians were lumped into a newly minted category, *"Black and Racialized Canadians."* Was Trudeau's gaffe intentional? Surely, he must have been aware that Winnipeg police had shot and killed three First Nations' people, including a 16 year-old girl, in unrelated incidents over a 10 day period in early April.

So where was his outrage? Where was our outrage? Did Canadians across the country take to the streets in protest? Hardly, though a few hundred protestors assembled at the Manitoba legislative grounds one late June evening demanding justice for Indigenous lives and police reform in Manitoba. Canadian media apparently did not consider the Winnipeg murders worthy of much notice, and neither did the prime minister. The subtext of Trudeau's response was quintessentially Canadian: *"Even though we may have systemic racism in this country, when it comes to Indigenous peoples, it is not serious enough to warrant specific acknowledgment, attention, or reparation."*

Blatant denials of racism are baked into the Canadian psyche. And the silence it perpetuates serves only those who benefit from it.[121] As Pam Palmater, Mi'kmaq lawyer, professor, and political activist, asserts:

> *Silence is a form of violence. . . . So, yes Canada, we have a racism crisis in this country and it is killing Black and Indigenous peoples. Let's stop pointing fingers at the US and take steps to end the loss of life here in Canada. . . . White people need to lay down their weapons, and the worst weapon they have is denial.*

Indigenous racism in Canada is not the same as discrimination against Black, Asian, or other peoples of colour. Sure, most Canadians are suspicious of those who don't look, talk, or act like the majority. But our animus is compounded when we turn our attention to Indigenous peoples. Unlike our colonial ancestors and other immigrants to follow, Canada's First Peoples had something we did not: *land and resources*. And these we wanted

---

120   C. Linnit (2020). "This is About Vulnerability: Ingrid Waldron on the Links between Environmental Racism and Police Brutality." June 3, thenarwhal.ca

121   P. Palmater (2020). Yes, Canada Has a Racism Crisis and It's Killing Black and Indigenous Peoples. June 3, canadiandimension.com

more than anything, more than Indigenous survival skills, more than the fruits of their labour, more than their babies. But they were an impediment to our advancement, dreams, and desires. So we swindled them, turned our backs on them, and then tried to erase them from our minds by remaking them in our image and sweeping them off our streets.

Days after Trudeau's comments, Athabasca Chipewyan First Nation chief, Allan Adam, publicly revealed that he had been savagely beaten (and his wife manhandled) by several RCMP officers outside a Fort McMurray casino two months earlier.[122] Images of Chief Adam's bloodied and swollen face spread like wildfire across the internet and Canada's news outlets. Canadians were shocked. Meanwhile, in the midst of the furor over Chief Adam's assault, New Brunswick RCMP officers shot and killed another two First Nations' people in separate incidents. Yet Alberta's RCMP commander and some provincial premiers continued to deny that systemic racism exists in this country—a declaration the former was later forced to retract when substantial evidence to the contrary came to light.

Indeed, racial profiling and brutality of Indigenous peoples by police in this country are endemic. Recent analyses and reporting indicate that whereas Indigenous Canadians account for only four percent of the population nationwide, 15 percent of those killed by police are Indigenous. In Manitoba and Saskatchewan the number is 60 percent. Even so, police in Canada are rarely charged for killing Indigenous people, let alone convicted. But racial injustice does not begin or end with the police. Dr. Palmater continues:

> *Numerous justice inquiries and commissions have found that racism is pervasive in Canada's entire justice system; from police to prosecutors to judges. ... The National Inquiry into 'Murdered and Missing Indigenous Women and Girls' found Canada guilty, as a matter of fact and law, of both historic and ongoing genocide. Canada's complex web of discriminatory laws, policies, practices, actions and omissions targeted Indigenous women and girls for an insidious form of racialized and sexualized violence that is the direct cause of their high rates of abuse, exploitation, disappearances and murders.*

On any given day, Indigenous women and men make up 35 percent and 25 percent, respectively, of Canada's prison population. The Indigenous incarceration rate is ten times higher than that of non-Indigenous Canadians, and if you are Indigenous in Saskatchewan, you're thirty-three times more likely to be incarcerated. Little wonder that criminologists refer to Canada's prisons as the *"new residential schools."*[123] At every step of the way, from the moment an Indigenous person is detained by police to sentencing to parole board

---

[122] Investigation Launched after Northern Alberta Chief Accuses RCMP of Assault (2020). June 6, www.cbc.ca/news/canada/edmonton/athabasca-chipewyan-first-nation-chief-accuses-rcmp ... .

[123] J. Chan, L. Chuen, and M. McLeod (2017). Everything You were Never Taught about Canada's Prison Systems: A Primer on Canada's Urgent Human Rights Crisis. July 20, intersectionalanalyst.ca

hearings, a discriminatory legal system sets them up for failure. Indigenous offenders serve much harder time, are more likely to be placed in isolation, and to die in prison than non-Indigenous inmates. An investigative report by *Macleans* magazine leaves little doubt that, *"instead of reforming our policing and correctional systems, Ottawa* [remains] *content with incarcerating as many Indigenous people as possible, for as long as legally possible, with far-reaching consequences for Indigenous families."*[124] More often than not, Indigenous offenders return to their communities *"more hardened, hopeless, violent and angry"* than before. In the opinion of Toronto criminal lawyer, John Struthers, we are *"using our criminal justice system to defend ourselves from the consequences of our own racism."*

Antipathy towards Indigenous Canadians permeates all levels of government as well as many segments of Canadian society. Indigenous racism, and the denial and silence that surrounds it, constitutes a form of institutionalized violence and terrorism that has gripped Canada since its founding. And it is particularly ubiquitous and pernicious in efforts by Canada's governing and corporate elites to expropriate Indigenous lands and resources.

A growing cohort of scholars and Indigenous activists claim that Indigenous Canadians are disproportionately impacted by what it labels as *"environmental racism."* A toxic brew of government sanctioned resource development policies and practices, environmental racism allows heavily polluting industries to disproportionately impact rural Indigenous communities already disadvantaged by income and food insecurity, lack of access to public services, *broken promises*, climate change, etc.[125] To this I would add those colonial institutions and practices that have been the subjects of previous chapters. If anyone doubts whether environmental racism is really a thing, they need only look at the Sayisi Dene, Dene Tha', Mikisew Cree, Pikangikum, and other Indigenous groups discussed in this book to grasp its egregious social, cultural, economic, environmental, ecological, psychological, and health impacts. The fact that Indigenous Canadians continue to fight for their rights, lands, and resources under such circumstances is remarkable, and a legacy worthy of celebration.

When my literary agent, Robert Mackwood of Seventh Avenue Literary Agents, was shopping my manuscript around to Canadian publishers, the responses he received perplexed us both. The manuscript was *"entertaining," "well written,"* and had *"important things to say."* But it just *"wasn't a good fit for them."* What some asked, and what they really wanted to know, was: *"Is Stevenson Indigenous"*? Apparently, ever since the Joseph Boyden debacle,[126] you don't get to talk about Indigenous issues, culture, or history in this country

---

124 N. Macdonald (2016) Canada's Prisons Are the 'New Residential Schools', A Months-long Investigation Reveals that at Every Step, Canada's Justice System is Set Against Indigenous People. February 18, macleans.ca

125 C. Linnit (op,cit).

126 Indigenous leaders grounded in their cultures and communities questioned Boyden's dubious claim to an Indigenous heritage and his exploitation of it for personal gain.

unless you are Indigenous, regardless of what you have to say. In my case, you don't get to write about the systemic barriers inherent in little known and poorly understood colonial institutions that divest Indigenous Canadians of their lands, rights, and cultures. In other words, for the sake of political correctness and expedience, be silent, stay silent.

Readers will have to determine for themselves whether *Do You Eat the Red Ones Last?...* represents a furtive and calculated attempt to expropriate Indigenous knowledge and experience for personal gain or a heartfelt, if somewhat acerbic, effort to facilitate understanding, reconciliation, and co-existence. However, until we acknowledge through our actions, not just our words, that we are all in this together—that *"we are all here to stay"* as Chief Justice Lamar concluded in the *Delgamuukw* decision—our feelings and opinions matter little. The time has come to stop the denial, end the silence, recognize and relinquish our privilege, walk in the other's shoes, and to find the courage and wherewithal to figure it all out.

***Indigenous Lives Matter, Indigenous Cultures Matter
Now More Than Ever!***

ACKNOWLEDGEMENTS

NO ONE'S JOURNEY IS REALLY EVER OVER OR ACCOMPLISHED ALONE. THERE HAVE BEEN many people who have positively impacted my career and thinking as an anthropologist, archaeologist, and a person. While a short list follows, I would like to thank Cliff Hickey and Ben Stevenson for constructive comments on earlier drafts of this book. Meeka Mike, Tim Trottier, Rosemary Kuptana, Jean-Paul Gladu, Brian Spurling, Dave Burley, Tom Mexis Happynook, Rebecca Mike, and Gregory Kwiecien provided much needed feedback on various chapters. I am especially grateful to Friesen Press publishing specialist Brianne MacKinnon and Robert Mackwood of Seventh Avenue Literary Agents for their assistance. For this I owe them all a debt of gratitude, even if I did not incorporate all their advice and suggestions. In no particular order, I would like to thank the following people for walking with me down my path. Apologies to those I have absentmindedly left off this list.

Joavee Alivaktuk, Kaneea Etuangat, Meeka Kilabuk, Meeka Mike, Koni Alivatuk, July Papatsie, Henry Janzen, Amie Papatsie, Sara Tautuajuk, Etuangat Aksayuk, Qatsu Evic, Levi Evic, Simionie Akpalialuk, Andrew Dialla, Moe Keenainak, Jonah Kilabuk, Nowyook Nickitimoosie, Elaine Maloney, Cindy Mason, Cliff Hickey, Jack Nance, Milton Freeman, Michael Asch, Gurston Dacks, Doug Cole, Kendall Morris, Regna Darnell, Roy Carlson, Nelson Graburn, Michael Schiffer, Myrel Traverse, Pauloosie Angmarlik, Malaya Akalujuk, Kudloo Pitseolak, Peter Usher, Tim Dialla, Lucy Dialla, Pauloosie Veevee, Adamee Veevee, Elija Keenianak, Jamasie Mike, Fred LeMouel. Mary Batte, Michael Kisa, Jaco Koonooloosie, Towkee Maniapik, Evee Anaaniliak, Peter Anaaniliak, Jaco Evic, Simon Shamiyuk, Annie Alivaktuk, Joavee Alivaktuk, Pauloosie Nowyook, Charlie Akpalialuk, Tashugaq Nakashuk, Margaret Karpik, Steve Overguard, Koodloo Pitsualuk, Pauloosie Angmarlik, Herb Alexander, Dave Burley, Brian Spurling, Jean Williams, Tom Happynook, Kathy Happynook, Stan Copp, Ingrid Bell, Steve Sharp, Heather Nicol, Steve Zoltai, Grezgory Kwiecien, Kathryn Graham-Stevenson, Gary Adams, Doug Proch, John Brandon, Bob Janes, Chuck Arnold, Jack Ives, Bernie Lieff, Bob Redhead, Marty Magne, Al Gibbs, Jim Johnston, Chris Hanks, Jack Nance, Doug Stenton, John Combes, Linda

Sears, Liz Todd, Ken Hughes, Chuck Hume, Ronny Chambers, Brent Liddle, Larry Tremblay, Jack Nance, Jeff Hunston, Jack Brink, Gabriela Prager, Heinz Pyszczyk, Milt Wright, Tiger Burch, David Damas, Dave Monteith, Gary Magee, Katherine Trumper, Glen Williams, Gordon Hambre, Tony Green, Aime Ahegoona, Adrian Tanner, Fikret Berkes, Peggy Smith, Pamela Perreault, Harry Bombay, Jean-Paul Gladu, Iain Davidson-Hunt, Lillian Trapper, John Turner, Janet Pronovost, Mattew Strang, Paddy Peters, Charlie Peters, Hugo Asselin, Jim Webb, Conroy Sewepagaham, Johnsen Sewepagaham, Celestan Nanooche, Josie Papatasie, Linda Sears, David Natcher, Monique Ross, Dale Bischoff, Vic Adamovicz, Terry Veeman, Don Sharp, John Turner, Peter Usher, Bruce McNab, Shirley Devries, Bruce MacLock, Lucille Partington, Jim McGrath, John Jules, Warren Fortier, Robert Charlie, Barry Waito, Don Sharp, Sam Shirt, Debra McGregor, Tony Mercredi, Trisha Merrithew-Mercredi, Alex Peters, Morris Monias, Eugene Monias, Algina Monias, Shasi Kant, Jim Frideres, Sarah Allen, Cindy Mason, Elaine Maloney, Gary Lipinski, Jim Fyles, Betty Kennedy, Heather Kennedy, John Stager, Marv Abugov, Dave Scott, (Dwayne Sonny) Nest, Deb Lawrence, Regna Darnell, Matt Munson, Baptiste Metchooyeah, Noah Maniapik, Floyd Apannah, Josh Kolay, Peter Chonkolay, Johnny Beaulieu Jr., Willie Chambaud, Albert Seniantha and Fabian Chonkolay, James Metchooyeah, Gabriel Ahkminachie, Robert Metchooyeah, Lorney Metchooyeah, Joseph Martel, Albert Seniantha, James Ahnassay, Charlie Chisaakay, Stephen Chonkolay, Harry Chonkolay Jr., Jimmy Seniantha, Roger Tecomba, Roger Sutha, Adrian Tecomba, Stephen Tsonchoke, Jean Baptiste Talley, Eric Kolay, Curtis Talley, Gabriel Didzena, Ralph Makokis, Fabian Chonkolay, Nora Bassa, Ronnie Semansha, Wilfred Chonkolay, William Yatchotay, Garret Talley, Warren Danais, Jack Danais, Alec Waspcolin, Adrian Tecomba, Theresa Kipling, Erik Kolay, Jane Kolay, Shane Providence , David Martel Sr., Francis Ahkimnachie, Peter Boxall, Dilbert Salopree, Roy Salopree, Isadore Gallant, Stanley Salopree, Alfred Chalifoux, Jerry Pastion, Tommy Seniantha, Norman Chonkolay, Johnny Ahnassay Sr., David Providence, Ricky Seniantha, Floyd Apannah, Debbie Overguard, John Innes, Stephen Ahnassay, Connie Martel, Edward Akazay, Willie Martel, Harry Metacat, James Danais, Roy Salopree, Isadore Gallant, Wilfred Hookanooza, Irena Creed, Peter Duinker, Ricky Seniantha, Joe Beaulieu, Sylvester Seniantha, David Sutha, Abraham Talley, Curtis Talley, Keith Beaulieu, Harvey Denechoan, Marcel Metchooyeah, Albert Seniantha, Tommy Seniantha, Andrew Talley, Jeanne Chonkolay, Angus Chonkolay, Edwin Gallant, James Martel Jr., Colin Chambuad, Peter Sabourin, Fred Tambour, Robert Lamalice, Pat Martel, Pat Buggins, Daniell Sonfrere, Eric Buggins, Martin Pelletier, Raymond Sonfrere, Fred Dedza, Margaret Donnelly, Alfred Chalifoux, Alphonse Scha-Sees, Ron Trosper, Rodney Metacat, Joan Damkjar, Jeff Chonkolay, Joachim Bonnetrouge, Albert Lafferty, Alec Sunrise, Berna Landry, Pat Martel, Val Bonness, Ernest Aquinnah, Eddie Martel, Luc

Bouthillier, Leonard Hookanooza, Roger Akinneah, Alfred Hookanooza, Jean-Marie Hookanooza, Modeste Pierre, Raymond Martel, Daniel Squirrel, Frank Bonnetrouge, Jack Brink, Emily Squirrel, Angelic Nadli, Margaret Donnelly, Bernard Bonnetrouge, Dolphous Matto, Ted Landry, James Elleze, Sam Elleze, John Spence, Archie Minoza, James Thomas, Marie Thomas, William Michel, Edie Martel, Delphine (Yatchotay) Kover, Leonard Hookanooza, Eric Damkjar, Jean-Marie Hookanooza, Naomi Krogman, Raymond Martel, Jimmy Seniantha, Lucy (Mercredi), Marcel Seniantha, David Ahkimnachie, George Tecumba, Jean Pastion, Joseph Seniantha, Gabriel Ahkminachie, Keith Pastion, George Chisaakay, Madeline Chonkolay, Albert Bonnetrouge, Adrian Tecomba, Clem Paul, Bob Turner, Alice Lafferty, Floyd Kuptana, Rosemarie Kuptana, Aqqaluk Lynge, Gordon Hamre, Judy Cozzetto, Doug Harvey, Bob Gamble, Carolyn Bonnetrouge, Jim Wolkie, Ray LeBlanc, Bill Taylor, Mary Green, Mabel Rueben, Nelson Green, Nora Ruben, James Ruben, Adam Gruben, Sam Green, Mary Ruben, Peter Green, Elizabeth Green, Garret Gruben, Roy Illusiak, Jonah Nakimyuk, Moses Krengneatok, Hank Wolkie, Fred Thrasher, Norman Kudluk, John-Max Kudluk, Ellen MacDonald, David Ruben, Markus Rueben, Ruben Green, Eddie Green, Lynita Langley, Frank Green, Jim Wolkie, Albert Ruben, Colin Adjun, Joe Milooksook, David Tiktalik, Noel Auadluk, David Bernard, Bister Kailik, Peter Komminguak, Walter Tupilak, Bennet Hikomak, Stanley Klengenburg, Gerry Attatakok, John Kapakatoak, Jimmy Onik, Bob Klengenberg, Allan Kiptanatiak, Hans Jurgen Muller-Beck, Chris Johnson, Kathy Arden, Carolyn MacKay, Jennifer Bellman, Adrian D'hont, Trevor Teed, Ernie Camsell, Archie Loutit, Ellen Bielawski, Paulosie Veevee, Adamee Veevee, Davidee Veevee, Rick Hamburg, Lucy (Dialla) Magee, Katherine Trumper, Andy Theriault, Dona Leedham, Eric Butterworth, Glen Semenchuck, Clarence Makowecki, Mellisa Blake, Barb Dillion, Susie Nakashook, Sharon Wilcox, Jim Kilabuk, Tim Trottier, Jim Tanner, Barry Hochstein, Minnie Stewart, Becky Mike, Meeka MIke, Johnny Mike, Rita Mike, Leanna Mike, Agnes Gruben, Roland Felix, Oleepeeka Kisa, Joanasie Maniapik, Sakiassie Sowdlooapik, Curtis MacKay, Leelee Kakee, Tommy Nowdluk, Lucasie Nowdluk, Michael Karpik, Tommy Papatsie, Anne Keenlyside, Roel Teunissen, Martha Shooapik, Diana Kiliabuk, Leah Nutagra, Mikijuq Koala, Gordon Koshinski, Joannie Ikkidluaq, Stuart Innes, Josie Papatsie, Palamonee Etooangat, Wally Wolfe, Sue Cross, Peggy Monroe, Birgid Thompson, Mary Akpalialuk, Angie Norris, Bill Erasmus, Michael Vandell, Stephen Vandell, Priscilla Canadien, Victoria St. Jean-Fabian, Berna Matto, Minnie Aodla Freeman, Ingmar Egede, Lucasie Araqutyna, Marge Jackson, Stella Spak, Ila Bussidor, Stan Boutin, Bruce Turner, Livee Kulllualik, Jake Keesic, Charlie Peters, Oliver Hill, Reggie Peters, Matthew Strang, Mary Thomas, Sakej Henderson-Youngblood, Russel Diabo, Henry Lickers, Peter Kelly, Brian Slattery, Jack Woodward, Stephen Wyatt, Ovide Mercredi, Jean-Guy Goulet, Perry Moulton, Al Lameman, Billy

Etooangat, Snowbird Marten, Archie Antoine, Lawrence Courtoreille, Annie Alivaktuk, John O'Connor, Carolyn Buffalo, Ken Staroszik, Bill Wilson, Bjorn Simonsen, Manny Jules, Simon O'Byrne, Roy Vermillion, Greg Nyuli, Steve Courtoreille, Allan Adam, Melody Lepine, Robert Antoine, Jocelyn Marten, Grezgorz Kwiecien, Inukie Adamie, Naulaq Adamie, Les Carpenter, Phil Fontaine, Terry Teegee, Tom (Mexis) Happynook, Charlie Watt, Bill Wilson, Tony Mercredi, Rosemary Kuptana, Andrew Weaver, Kim Darwin, Terry Marten, Steve Courtoreille, Paul Quassa, Paul Okalik, Gert Albrecht, Clem Paul, Jack Anawak, Bill Erasmus, Bernie Meneen, Frank Meneen, Mike Stern, Carolyn Whitaker, Sally Whiteknife, Chris Hopkins, Dave Flanders, Russel Collier, Julia Gibot, Alice Martin, Eddie Courtoreille, Ronnie Campbell, Billy Joe Tuccaro, George Poitras, Peter Cizek, Jackson Whiteknife, Archie Simpson, Margo Vermillion, Joe Tuccaro, Billy Whiteknife, George Martin, Larry Marten, Matthew Lepine, Mary Simpson, Charlie Simpson, Gerry Oetelaar, Valarie Courtoreille, George Vermillion, Helena Welsh, Cookie Simpson, Leona Lepine, Joseph Dickie Tourangeau, Shirley Courtoreille, Ted Marten, Lori Montour, Dave Mannix, Lloyd Waquan, Hans Jurgen Muller-Beck.

Printed in Canada